NEIGHBOURHOOD POLICING

CLARENDON STUDIES IN CRIMINOLOGY

Published under the auspices of the Institute of Criminology, University of Cambridge; the Mannheim Centre, London School of Economics; and the Centre for Criminology, University of Oxford.

General Editors: Loraine Gelsthorpe and Kyle Treiber
(*University of Cambridge*)

Editors: Alison Liebling
(*University of Cambridge*)

Tim Newburn, Jill Peay, Coretta Phillips, and Robert Reiner
(*London School of Economics*)

Mary Bosworth, Carolyn Hoyle, Ian Loader, and Lucia Zedner
(*University of Oxford*)

RECENT TITLES IN THIS SERIES:

Neighbourhood Policing

The Rise and Fall of a Policing Model

MARTIN INNES
COLIN ROBERTS
TRUDY LOWE
HELEN INNES
of
Universities' Police Science Institute & Crime and
Security Research Institute, Cardiff University

OXFORD
UNIVERSITY PRESS

OXFORD
UNIVERSITY PRESS

Great Clarendon Street, Oxford, OX2 6DP,
United Kingdom

Oxford University Press is a department of the University of Oxford.
It furthers the University's objective of excellence in research, scholarship,
and education by publishing worldwide. Oxford is a registered trade mark of
Oxford University Press in the UK and in certain other countries

First Edition published in 2020
Impression: 2

Published in the United States of America by Oxford University Press
198 Madison Avenue, New York, NY 10016, United States of America

British Library Cataloguing in Publication Data
Data available

Library of Congress Control Number: 2019957836

ISBN 978-0-19-878321-3

Printed and bound by
CPI Group (UK) Ltd, Croydon, CR0 4YY

General Editors' Introduction

The *Clarendon Studies in Criminology series* aims to provide a forum for outstanding theoretical and empirical work in all aspects of criminology and criminal justice, broadly understood. The Editors welcome submissions from established scholars, as well as excellent PhD work. The Series was inaugurated in 1994, with Roger Hood as its first General Editor, following discussions between Oxford University Press and Oxford's Centre for Criminological Research. It is edited under the auspices of three centres: the Institute of Criminology at the University of Cambridge, the Mannheim Centre for Criminology at the London School of Economics, and the Centre for Criminological Research at the University of Oxford. Each supplies members of the Editorial Board and, in turn, the Series General Editor or Editors.

Neighbourhood Policing: The Story of the Rise and Fall of a Policing Model is perhaps unusual in that it reflects a ten year programme of research rather than a single empirical study on community or, as it is more commonly described, neighbourhood policing, but this adds to the importance of the book in its story of the development of neighbourhood policing. Publication of the book is timely both in the context of concerns about knife-crime, and in regard to calls for a return to neighbourhood policing following its more recent decline, notwithstanding an earlier success story. The book draws on new empirical material as well as different writings already published by the authors. Pulling a book together which includes multiple sources of information and which records the politics of policing as well as the empirical realities and the impact of new technologies on neighbourhood policing is not an easy task, but Martin Innes and colleagues have achieved this very effectively.

To elaborate, the book blends a substantive criminological analysis of neighbourhood policing and its aims, methods and achievements, with an element of social history that seeks to situate this approach to policing in a particular social, economic and political context. This social historical and criminological approach is reflected in the organisation of the chapters. They are informed by empirical data collected across several different projects, but they are connected together and integrated by virtue of attending to the principal components and processes associated with the neighbourhood policing model. The main chapters of the book attend to the key issues of criminological and sociological interest, seeking to distil the key insights about the policy development and delivery of this particular inflection of community policing. They are framed by the opening and concluding materials, which seek to locate these themes and issues within the overall trajectory of development of UK policing. By engaging with neighbourhood policing in this way, the book speaks to the significant place that this approach has achieved within the contemporary policing landscape, providing a rigorously evidenced assessment of both achievements and weaknesses. In so doing, it responds to a significant gap in the contemporary scholarly literature.

This book will be of particular interest to policing and community development scholars. As the authors indicate, viewed as a value proposition rather than as a set of practices, efforts to foster and sustain police–community connectivity over the years have been deeply influential in shaping visions and conceptions of what democratic policing should be and how it is to be delivered.

As General Editors, we warmly recommend this book; it makes significant contribution to the field of policing studies. We have no doubt that this will become an indispensable reference for research scholars and policing teachers and academics, and we hope that managers in various criminal justice contexts will read it too. The book also deserves wide readership amongst policy-makers. We are very pleased indeed to welcome **Neighbourhood Policing: The Story of the Rise and Fall of a Policing Model** into the *Clarendon Studies in Criminology series*.

Loraine Gelsthorpe and Kyle Treiber
Institute of Criminology,
University of Cambridge
March, 2020

Preface and Acknowledgements

This book tells the story of the design and delivery of Neighbourhood Policing, and how it has been edited and adapted in response to a range of influences. Framed in this way, the analysis ranges across its origins in managing rises in fear of crime, through the boom and bust years of the UK economy, its partial reconfiguration as part of a wider response to the emergence of new national security threats, and on to the present day.

When we first decided that we wanted to write a book about Neighbourhood Policing bringing together the large amounts of evidence we had collated, a key motivation was that the outlook for its future survival looked poor. Somewhat pessimistically, we were compelled to try and capture the deep learning that has been acquired, in case at some later time, or in some different place, others were tempted to revisit this mode of community policing. After all, public sector austerity measures had hit policing and the community safety sector hard, with all police forces reducing officer numbers and a general pattern of redirecting resources towards response and investigation functions. Accompanying this economic disinvestment was a perceived normative disinvestment also, with a number of politicians and some senior police leaders questioning the 'public value' of an intensive, preventative, and citizen-focused style of policing. The focus on the value of community intelligence and how to obtain it seemed to have been lost after only a relatively short period of time. But during the process of writing, some signs of a revitalization have begun to become apparent, such that after the rise and fall in popularity of this way of doing policing, it is potentially on the cusp of 'rising again'. If this is so, then we hope the publication of this volume will be timely and will serve to provide a strong evidence base on which to re-establish and maybe redefine how to better police communities.

A research programme lasting fifteen years inevitably incurs a large number of debts. We have been fortunate to have had the support of a significant number of policymakers and police officers, who have enabled and facilitated aspects of the research at different moments and across a variety of locations. Our journey started with the National Reassurance Policing Programme (NRPP), led by Sir Denis O'Connor. Denis had the remarkable vision to invest considerable resources in academic research to build an evidence-based approach to policy and practice development, long before anyone else in the police service was really thinking about what has come to be known as 'evidence-based policing'. Denis has a particular skill for asking the question that defines the essence of a problem, and not being willing to settle for an imprecise or inadequate answer. In the years following the NRPP, he has continued to take a keen interest in Neighbourhood Policing and in research associated with it. Both we, and the UK police service, owe him much.

During the NRPP years we also benefitted greatly from interactions with other senior members of the programme management team, Tim Godwin, Carl Crathern, and Gavin Stephens. At the time, we were a relatively inexperienced research team, who were given levels of support, guidance, and access that looking back, were truly remarkable. We gained immeasurably from the opportunities that you provided us.

As well as the central project team members, the local teams in the eight pilot forces provided significant amounts of help and hospitality, and we would like to record our thanks to the many staff who assisted us from: the Metropolitan Police Service; Surrey Police; Thames Valley Police; Leicestershire Police; West Midlands Police; Greater Manchester Police; Merseyside Police; and Lancashire Constabulary. From the latter force, we reserve particular thanks for Mike Alexander and Dave Aston who provided invaluable operational insights throughout their rigorous implementation of Reassurance Policing and beyond. Alongside our policing partners, Rachel Tuffin and Paul Quinton at the UK Home Office oversaw the official evaluation of the programme that ran alongside our fundamental research, and were a pleasure to work with.

As well as the practical support and guidance we received from UK policing, an intellectual debt is owed to Professor Nigel Fielding of the University of Surrey. Indeed, drawing upon his own extensive research into community policing, many of the initial concepts and instruments underpinning the NRPP approach originated in collaborative research between Nigel and Martin Innes. But as interest in the work picked up nationally, with typical generosity, he allowed the research team to take the project on and run with it. From then on, in the quintessential model of a good academic mentor, he unfailingly offered insightful advice or input when asked, but never sought to impose his views. The contents of Chapter 4 were originally presented at a conference to celebrate Nigel's considerable scholarly achievements across the fields of policing and social research methodology, upon his retirement from the University of Surrey in 2018.

Not long after completion of the NRPP, the authors left Surrey and headed West. Our research in this field may well have concluded had it not been for the foresight and innovative practice of the then Chief Constable of South Wales, Barbara Wilding. She was another senior police leader who recognized the transformational potential of rigorous and robust research. The work she funded forms the basis of Chapter 6. Since arriving in Wales, we have enjoyed a special relationship with South Wales Police that has enabled our work to continue to explore many aspects of the Neighbourhood Policing function. Officers and staff for whose help along the way we are particularly grateful include Bob McAllister, Huw Cogbill, Andy Davies, Umar Hussain, Gareth Madge, Richard Mence, Richard Watkins, and subsequent Chief Constables Peter Vaughan and Matt Jukes. In respect of our work on Community Support Officers we are also indebted to Mike Harmer at the Welsh Government, who funded the original study and provided significant help and support throughout it. Similarly, we would also like to thank the staff of the Wales Extremism and Counter-Terrorism Unit, with whom we have enjoyed a close working relationship.

Beyond Wales, our various studies have been made possible by the enthusiastic involvement of many police forces and community safety teams around the United Kingdom. One long-running relationship of note has been with the Safer Sutton Partnership, who have provided remarkable assistance enabling the conduct of a unique longitudinal study of Neighbourhood Policing in action over an extended period. This work is reported in Chapter 7 and an earlier iteration of aspects of it appeared in Lowe and Innes (2012) published in the journal *Policing and Society*. We are indebted to the Sutton team, particularly Warren Shadbolt, Glenn Phillips, Dave Gare, Ian Kershaw, Chris Lyons, and Preeti Sidhar, as well as the numerous neighbourhood officers and PCSOs from the Metropolitan Police Service who have withstood the rigours of conducting SENSOR fieldwork on top of their already demanding day-jobs. Similarly, our sincere thanks to Richard Horton of West Midlands Police, whose help with our work on the impact of Neighbourhood Policing on matters of national security was invaluable.

During our time at Cardiff University we have had the opportunity to talk about issues of Neighbourhood Policing and community safety with a number of excellent colleagues and students, including Patrick Carr, Trevor Jones, Mike Levi, Simon Moore, Alun Preece, Amanda Robinson, Jonathan Shepherd, and Marnix Eysinck Smeets. We would also like to thank our Editor at Oxford University Press, Peter Daniell for his support and forbearance as we missed multiple deadlines, owing to other commitments and pressures.

Much of the empirical data collection and its subsequent analysis would not have been possible without the help of a remarkable cast of dedicated researchers and fieldworkers with whom we worked on numerous project teams over the years. Our thanks go to Laurence Abbott, Bethan Davies, Kieran Evans, Sophie Garr, Daniel Grinnell, Sinead Hayden, Charlotte Leigh, Helen MacKenzie, Phil Murray, Lisa Twyman, and Nicola Weston.

And finally, our appreciation and thanks to all the community groups and passionate individuals who helped us conduct our fieldwork 'on the ground', as well as the hundreds of members of the British public who welcomed us into their homes, opened their hearts, and plied us with tea.

In writing Chapter 7, we were grateful to Taylor Francis Group for granting permission to draw upon and expand data previously published by them as: Lowe, T. and Innes, M. (2012) 'Can We Speak in Confidence? Community Intelligence and Neighbourhood Policing v2.0'. *Policing and Society*, 22(3), 295–316.

Whilst the work reported in what follows has benefitted from the contributions made by all of those listed above, any errors or omissions remain the responsibility of the authors.

November 2019

Contents

List of Figures

List of Tables

List of Abbreviations

ACPO	Association of Chief Police Officers
ASB	antisocial behaviour
BCS	British Crime Survey
CAPS	Chicago Alternative Policing Strategy
CPCG	Community Police Consultative Group
CSO	Community Support Officer
CSP	Community Safety Partnership
DAC	Deputy Assistant Commissioner
EBP	evidence-based policing
HMIC	Her Majesty's Inspectorate of Constabulary
ILP	intelligence-led policing
IMD	Indices of Multiple Deprivation
LSOA	Lower Super Output Area
MFJ	Movement For Justice by Any Means Necessary
MPS	Metropolitan Police Service
NIM	National Intelligence Model
NMA	Neighbourhood Management Area
NRPP	National Reassurance Policing Programme
OA	Output Area
PACT	Police and Communities Together
PCSO	Police Community Support Officer
POP	problem-oriented policing
SNT	Safer Neighbourhoods Team
TPO	Test Purchase Officer

1

The Public Understanding of Crime and Policing

It is 2003, on a housing estate in the North of England. 'Has there been another murder?' Stepping out of the lift on the ground floor of the high-rise block of flats in the Queen's Park estate,[1] to be confronted by a phalanx of uniformed police officers, the woman posing the question simply assumed that the presence of several police officers meant what it always did in this part of Blackpool— that yet another homicide investigation was underway. 'You know,' she continued, 'some poor bastard was found lying outside the door of the block over the way there last month. People just stepped round him all day. It was twelve hours before anybody thought to check if he was alright, and it turns out he was dead. He was pushed or jumped out of the tenth floor or something. Twelve hours though he was lying there. Twelve hours!'

As we entered the lift, the pungent stench of urine was all too evident, and on the dulled metallic sheen of the walls of the lift were brown crusted arcs of some form of liquid. 'Oh, that's blood from where the druggies shoot up in here,' said one of the police officers casually as he pressed the lift button to close the door, 'the bloody CCTV has been knackered for months' he added, gesturing to a discrete camera lens in the uppermost corner of the small cabin. One of the female researchers was later told by a resident that, when using the lifts in the block, she was safest 'pressing the buttons with a pencil,' as 'some of the druggies stick their used "sharps" [needles] in the lift buttons and break them off'.

---

[1] The Queens Park estate has now been completely redeveloped as part of an area regeneration scheme by Blackpool Council: <https://www.blackpool.gov.uk/Residents/Housing/New-housing-developments/Queens-Park-development.aspx>.

Neighbourhood Policing. Martin Innes, Colin Roberts, Trudy Lowe, and Helen Innes, Oxford University Press (2020). © Martin Innes, Colin Roberts, Trudy Lowe, and Helen Innes.
DOI: 10.1093/oso/9780198783213.003.0001

The Queen's Park estate, located at that time in the Brunswick ward of Blackpool, Lancashire, had suffered from a range of overlapping and interconnected social problems that had been consistently evidenced by prominent levels of deprivation on the Indices of Multiple Deprivation (IMD) for England. As a composite empirical measure of the proportion of people living in a small area (the Lower Super Output Area or LSOA) who experience a lack of material resources relative to other LSOAs, the IMD continues to show that Blackpool has a sizeable proportion of its residents living in deprived neighbourhoods and is the most deprived larger seaside town in England (Humby, 2013).

Brunswick, home to around 7,000 people, has been in the top 10 per cent of most deprived wards in England in successive indices published by the Department for Community and Local Government every three years since it began in 2004. Census statistics show unemployment higher than the national average and 11 per cent of residents economically inactive due to permanent ill-health or disability. The number of lone parent families is nearly twice the national average at 23 per cent (ONS, 2012).

In the early 2000s, policing the Queens Park estate was challenging. As our researchers got to know the area and its residents better, a number of stories were forthcoming that illuminated the issues from different perspectives. For example, the local police explained how a significant number of the problems they were called upon to deal with could be traced back to the local council's policy to use the area to house increasing numbers of Blackpool's drug addicts. They also reported how they mounted repeated drug raids in the area, but with little success. Sometime later, one of the residents living in the tower blocks explained why the police found it so hard.

He told how there was one individual living in a flat in one of the grey tower blocks who was well known to be the main drug supplier in the area. The window of his flat gave him a clear view of the main road into and out of the estate. As a consequence, he was able to see the police cars and vans approach whenever a raid was imminent. His solution to this was to have his partner sitting in a car below another window. The respondent described an almost comedic scene of the police entering the main door of the block of flats, very shortly after which a package was lowered out of the window to the car below, which would then drive off.

Consequently, by the time the police actually made it up the stairs to the flat there were no drugs on the premises.

Fear of crime and insecurity on the estate was high, as were levels of physical disorder. In part this related to architectural design, as in November, when the research team first arrived, a bitterly cold wind came in from the sea, capturing rubbish in the corners and passages of the estate. But there were other forms of disorder too, in the form of pervasive graffiti and vandalism. The aesthetic of the large swathes of concrete used to build the estate was not improved by the frequent material traces of criminal conduct evident in many areas. Police crime figures for the ward in 2002/3 and 2003/4 show dramatically worsening levels of recorded crime and disorder, particularly for violent crime (+300 per cent) and criminal damage (+116 per cent).[2]

When researchers talked to residents, they referenced a range of crime and disorder issues.[3] For instance, one interviewee talked about how:

> ... there is a lot of problems with drugs and crime, someone got their head beat in a few days ago, and it's going on all the time, but I can't say in the main it might be local people I don't know but there is a lot of druggies that hang around round here. (Brun_P1_085)

Another focused upon the unsettling and insecurity inducing anti-social behaviour of some young people:

> It's a nervous place to be honest. For example, this Saturday afternoon there's about 5 or 6 boys ranging from 10 up to 13 or 14 and they were on the car park out here just running across people's cars, just running and jumping on them! This went on for an hour and we went out saying 'get down!' and you get a load of abuse and then it starts getting more than abuse and you tend to pull back and go in then. (Brun_p1_92)

The activities of these young people included significant criminal acts leaving material traces that contributed to an overall

---

[2] Number of ward-level police recorded incidents 2002/3 to 2003/4: Violence against the Person: 94 to 385: Criminal damage 181 to 391. Data courtesy of Lancashire Constabulary.

[3] Throughout this volume, we draw upon raw qualitative data extracts from respondents involved in a number of studies conducted during a fifteen-year long research programme. Each study employed different conventions for identifying individual respondents, so where verbatim quotations are utilized, the respondent identifier cited directly after the quotation is that used for the original study and no attempt has been made to standardize.

impression of a disordered environment. For example, two teenage boys had recently been convicted of arson on the local school which had been severely damaged in the resulting fire. Visible from the windows of most of the flats on the estate, the burnt-out hulk of the school building was a potent symbol of the problems in the area. A second visual symbol was ongoing vandalism of the only local phone box, sited near the main entrance to the estate. For residents, the ongoing cycle of vandalism and repair was a potent signifier signalling the impotence of the authorities in providing basic security on the estate. The insecurity felt and routinely reported by residents was a product of a combination of crime, social disorder, and physical disorder.

Responding to, and tackling, these kinds of issues is the principal focus of the community policing tradition. At the time when these interviews were being conducted, the police in the area, along with officers in seven other forces, were preparing to participate in a programme of work designed to test the extent to which a particular formulation of community policing could impact upon these kinds of challenges.

This book tells the story of what happened next. In doing so, it has three principal aims. First, it seeks to provide a documentary record of how Neighbourhood Policing, as a particular formulation of the community policing tradition, can be and has been delivered to date. It focuses in particular on highlighting some of the more innovative aspects that have been brought forward under this model. Second, the book seeks to make some broader theoretical points about the careers of policing models more generally, including the significance of situating them in their historical and social contexts. Third, it attends to the 'craft' of policing neighbourhoods, based on the assertion that how policing is performed is as important as what it does. In respect of Neighbourhood Policing, the way police perform their interactions and encounters with citizens, each other, and partner organizations shapes both objective and subjective perceptions of crime and disorder.

Community policing: theme and variations

Community policing has been described and understood in different ways. Some commentators have sought to identify a set of core practices that define how policing activities and services are delivered (Fielding, 1995). Others have preferred to cast it more as a philosophy, constituted by a particular set of ideas and values (see Ferreira, 1996), that can be situationally operationalized according to the requirements of the setting. Its origins in the United Kingdom and United States were, in part, a counterpoint to modes of reactive policing dominant in the latter parts of the twentieth century. Whilst prioritizing a swift police response to emergency calls and the apprehension of criminals, reactive policing isolated the police from public as local patrols shifted from foot to motor vehicles and police stations closed. Evidence also suggested that this approach did not have a significant reductive impact on crime levels, whilst high profile incidents of public order policing during the miners' strikes of the Thatcher-era did huge reputational damage to the police and public confidence in them (Waddington, 1991).

A broader formulation of the goals of policing, one that sought to widen its community base and input to help tackle and prevent crime, began to gather momentum. Police could not be expected to shoulder sole responsibility for preventing crime, so beginning with the Ditching circular (211/78) and culminating in the 1998 Crime and Disorder Act, crime prevention became a duty shared by chief police officers and the local authority (Newburn, 2008), and discourse shifted to talk of 'community safety' and multi-agency cooperation at a local level (Crawford, 1998). Significantly, it was communities who demanded more visible police action against a range of regular, but not necessarily criminal, 'incivilities' occurring in their local areas. The New Labour government brought to the fore the management of low-level environmental, physical, and social disorders under the banner 'antisocial behaviour' (ASB) and made it a central part of their five-year crime reduction plan between 2004 and 2008 (Home Office, 2004). This widening of the range of local problems and solutions to be policed and enforced at a local level coincided with the extension of the 'police family' to include a new tranche of unwarranted, uniformed officers called Police Community Support Officers (PCSOs). These officers, formally introduced under the 1992 Police Reform Act (Home Office, 2001), first appeared on the streets of London in 2002 and thereafter were rapidly recruited across England and Wales to engage in visible foot patrol and focus on antisocial behaviour.

Cutting across different perspectives on the relationship between policing and communities are a series of themes and defining traits that can be identified with all those policing approaches that have been labelled under the rubric of 'community policing'. These include: strategic and tactical attempts to reduce the distance between police and 'policed'; a recognition that community views should be afforded an influence in delineating police priorities; and a sense that the fundamental police mission is not purely 'crime control' or law enforcement. As surmised by John Alderson, a senior police officer and early champion of the community policing movement, it encompasses 'social as opposed to legal action' (1979: 239).

Iterations of community policing theory and practice, although shaded in subtly different hues, have all tended to share a fundamental premise—that there are significant benefits to be accrued by connecting police with communities (Wycoff, 1988; Trojanowicz and Bucqueroux, 1990). Engaging with local communities is, amongst other things, suggested as a mechanism for increasing confidence and trust in the police with the added potential of enhancing a community intelligence 'feed' (Fielding, 1995). In the UK context, the publication of the Scarman report following street riots in Brixton in 1981 was particularly influential, highlighting fundamental failures in policing associated with the use of oppressive powers over and above communication and responsiveness to local communities, notably those of colour (Scarman, 1982). Fundamental issues of police competence were revisited just over a decade later in the formal inquiry into the death of Stephen Lawrence, and coexisted alongside charges of institutional racism and leadership failure within the force (MacPherson, 1999).

Viewed as a value proposition rather than a set of practices, efforts to foster police–community connectivity also resonate deeply with the so called 'Peelian Principles' (Cox and Fitzgerald, 1992). These nine normative statements of 'good policing' that are, at least in the popular and police imaginations, attributed to Sir Robert Peel when founding the Metropolitan Police around 1829, set out a series of doctrinal statements including that 'the police are the public and the public are the police'. Notwithstanding that it is now widely agreed that these 'principles' are simply part of the 'foundation myth' of the institution of policing, they have nevertheless been influential in shaping visions and conceptions of what democratic policing should be and how it is to be delivered. Community policing, in terms of its underpinning concepts and orientation, has a deep affinity with these key 'philosophical' tenets of the UK policing tradition. Trojanowicz and Bucqueroux (1990: 2–3), for example, defined community policing as '9 Ps': 'a philosophy of full service personalized policing, where the same officer patrols and works in the same area on a permanent basis, from a decentralized place, working in a proactive partnership with citizens to identify and solve problems'.

Definitions notwithstanding, it is equally important not to overstate the significance of these defining traits. It is precisely because community policing has remained relatively loosely defined that it has 'travelled' so well. Not being overly directive at a conceptual level allows people to read into it different interpretations. Similarly, but in a more practical register, a certain degree of pragmatic flexibility and adaptability has helped community policing move across different situations and contexts.

This conceptual looseness has, however, also provided opportunities for critique of community policing as little more than a public relations gimmick. For example, Weatheritt (1988) asserted that much of what was cast as community policing was little more than rhetorical 'window dressing' as opposed to constituting 'real' change to what police do. Redolent concerns have also been made more recently by Manning (2003) who argues that community policing in the United Kingdom and United States is little more than an add-on to the core function of response policing.

An alternative way of identifying the essential qualities and boundaries of something that is relatively loosely configured is to define it in terms of what it is not. Adopting such an approach is especially insightful in respect of community policing, given how its initial formation was in reaction to the failings and limitations attributed to what, in the American context, Sparrow, Moore, and Kennedy (1990) dubbed 'the professional model' of policing. New directives for police officers were introduced to enhance their reputation as an independent, competent, and law-abiding workforce. Amongst these were rules restricting officers from living in the places where they policed and the edict that 'police officers shall not make any unnecessary conversation with the public' which remained on record in some parts of the United Kingdom until well into the 1980s. With their actions rooted in law, the core of the police mission was understood as being about responding to crime and emergency calls from the public.

Intriguingly, whilst the directives given to officers at that time seem wide of the mark today, the latter vision of what Reiner (2012) dubbed 'fire-brigade policing' continues to exhibit a recurrent powerful allure over the police imagination. This is evidenced by how community policing has been subject to serial reinventions and reintroductions, where it is presented as an innovative 'solution' to issues inhering in crime control focused policing strategies (Sparrow, 2016).

In the United Kingdom, a position statement on community policing was first articulated by John Alderson in 1979. In particular, he lamented how the still relatively recent shift from police foot patrols to patrolling in cars, in conjunction with a much-increased reliance upon telephone reporting of crime through the new 999 system, was distancing police from routine co-present interactions with members of the public. Alderson's statement was important because, whilst these kinds of concern had been circulating prior to this time, he was an 'insider'. To have a Chief Constable acknowledge and validate elements of the critique of the dominant policing approach was transformative for the fortunes of the nascent community policing model. As we shall see this is part of a recurrent pattern, whereby 'auto-critique' mounted by senior leaders from within policing plays an important role in terms of why, over time, certain ideas and models come into the ascendant (and also experience decline).

Since Alderson's time of course, more sophisticated and nuanced conceptualizations of community policing have been brought forward, oftentimes reflecting how its fortunes have waxed and waned. In this respect, there is a subtle but important distinction between those studies and accounts that have proposed establishing a particular configuration, and those where the accent is more upon assessing and evaluating the impacts and consequences of established models. Indeed, one of the principal reasons why support for community policing has fluctuated over time is attributable to the struggle to establish reliable evidence about what it delivers.

In an important contribution based upon fieldwork in Seattle, Herbert (2006) concludes that a principal reason community policing programmes fail to realize their benefits is that typically the 'weight of expectation' it places upon communities to engage with police and participate in social control work is simply too 'heavy' for most communities to bear given the constraints upon their capacities and capabilities. As he describes it, in the areas where it is most needed, people are primarily focused upon getting by and supporting their families, and lack the social, political, and economic resources needed to engage meaningfully with police in an ongoing way.

A more supportive picture emerges from Skogan's (1996) decade-long evaluation of the Chicago Alternative Policing Strategy (CAPS). Skogan's work is important because of the scale at which it was conducted—looking at implementation of a significantly resourced effort across a city—but also because his detailed data analysis tracked what happened across Chicago's neighbourhoods over a decade. This is significant insomuch as it gives a sense of what happened as the reform programme matured, whereas most evaluations focus upon relatively small timeframes.

Established in April 1993, CAPS was based upon a quasi-experimental research design, with implementation and measurement activities initially focused upon five prototype districts, each of which had a matched comparison site. Following early successes across a range of indicators in the prototype districts (Skogan, 1996; Skogan and Hartnett, 1997), CAPS was expanded to all Chicago's police patrol divisions in 1995. The original aims of the programme included crime reduction, increasing public trust and confidence in the police and improving the general quality of life for citizens in Chicago.

Informed by previous community policing experiments and programmes, the Chicago version sought to systematically implement community policing principles in order to focus the police department's resources on the city's chronic crime and disorder 'problems'. To resource this shift, nearly 1,000 extra police officers were hired, and all the city's uniformed officers were trained in problem-solving techniques (Skogan, 1996). CAPS encouraged public involvement in policing, sought to engage problem-solving by police officers, and to foster new and better partnerships with other agencies. Police officers were given relatively long-term assignments to a beat, and were encouraged to spend as much time as possible 'on the ground' responding to calls, interacting with members of the public, and engaging with preventative projects.

Of particular consequence for our present concerns is the fact that, alongside a systematic implementation effort, CAPS was subject to a well-designed measurement and evaluation regimen. Over a ten-year period, a large number of cross-sectional and longitudinal surveys have been employed by the programme evaluators to document and track a variety of change processes associated with the policing reforms. As part of this more general evaluation approach, surveys were used to monitor changes in Chicagoans' fear of crime and to infer the role of policing in inducing these changes.

Data reported by Skogan and Hartnett (1997) drawn from the wave-one 'baseline' (April–May 1993) and wave two (June–September 1994) surveys give a sense of the early impact that CAPS had upon public opinions and attitudes in the five prototype areas. Controlling for a variety of factors, they identified positive effects from raising the visibility of police activities and by engaging problem-solving techniques against the public's priority problems. Focusing upon fear and concern in particular, they noted that the activities of the police have played an important 're-assurance' function, which contributed to changes in people's perceptions (Skogan and Hartnett, 1997; Skogan and Steiner, 2004).

A vital finding from the work conducted is that these kinds of benefit were not consistently sustained over time, nor were they equally distributed across Chicago's neighbourhoods. In his book summarizing the learning and findings from Chicago's decade-long experiment with community policing, Skogan (2006) concluded that the impacts of the deep and far-reaching reforms enacted by the Chicago Police Department were stratified across the city's ethnic communities. Overall, the groups who gained most from the changes tended to be African American neighbourhoods. White communities typically gained less, but as Skogan notes, on average they started in a better position. Least benefit was felt in Hispanic communities afflicted by entrenched multiple deprivations. Variations such as these raise interesting questions about how processes of police reform interact with broader processes of social and economic change.

However, whilst the story told about CAPS is broadly positive, subsequent revelations about what else was happening in the Chicago Police Department at this time have tarnished it somewhat. An independent investigation by the UK *Guardian* newspaper found that more than 7,000 Chicago citizens were covertly detained by police in the 'off-the-books' interrogation centre, Homan Square, between August 2004 and June 2015 (Ackerman, 2015). Analysis of arrest records obtained from a Freedom of Information request showed that of this total, 6,000 were black

Americans, a racial disparity in detentions vastly disproportionate to the demographic of the city of Chicago (Ackerman
and Stafford, 2015). Reports from detainees at Homan House, a
number of whom were arrested for low-level drug crimes or other
misdemeanours, tell of vulnerable people being held and shackled
for up to days at a time without access to legal counsel or public
notification of their whereabouts.

It would be wrong, however, to suggest that the fluctuating fortunes of community policing across different places and jurisdictions, and across different points in times, are solely attributable
to matters of evidence. For it is equally important to acknowledge that community policing exists alongside several other policing models, which have greater and lesser affinities with the
core principles and practices that propel community policing approaches. For some students of policing, these alternative conceptualizations have been defined as distinct from community police
traditions, whereas for others they are mere permutations of the
'master-type'.

Problem-oriented policing

One policing model that has often been interpreted as especially
closely aligned with, albeit distinct from, community policing is
problem-oriented policing or 'POP' (see Cordner, 1988; Sparrow,
2016). In his original formulation of POP, Goldstein (1979) cast
it as a way of resolving a tendency amongst police officers and
the organizations to which they belong to focus upon individual
cases or incidents. This is not altogether surprising given that
'cases' and 'incidents' are the basic working unit of much police
activity. However, from Goldstein's point of view this is inefficient
insomuch as it neglects the extent to which individual incidents
tend to cluster in space and time, and frequently have common
causes. As such, if police could design and deliver interventions
tackling these causal factors, then it should be possible to have a
powerful effect in terms of preventing future similar occurrences,
thus inducing reductions in crime and disorder rates.

According to Sparrow (2016), POP is important on the grounds
that, unlike most policing models, it is less concerned with a substantive domain of police work (such as community relations and
intelligence) than with embedding particular patterns of thinking
and acting. That is, at least in theory if not always in practice

(see below), it adopts a relatively systematic, logical approach to the tasks of 'problem-finding' and 'problem-solving' (Longstaff et al., 2015).

Elaborating this initial position in his book, Goldstein (1990: 66) defined three principal problem types:

1. A cluster or 'hotspot' of similar, related, or recurring incidents rather than a single incident;
2. A substantive community concern;
3. A unit of police business.

In practice, it is the first of these that has been the pre-eminent concern of police organizations seeking to implement POP.

Finding and solving problems are organized around the four key stages of the so-called 'SARA model'. This is initiated by 'scanning' activity, involving a relatively systematic look across the environment being policed and also wide-ranging available data to identify potential incident clusters or series that might be configured as 'problems'. The problem is then subject to 'analysis'. This component has been nicely described by Sparrow (2016) as analogous to how we treat the task of untangling a knotted piece of string. As he puts it, the kinds of problem that police deal with that warrant application of POP techniques are typically complex tangles of multiple issues and causes. Thus, the 'problem knot' needs considering from a variety of angles before it is possible to know where to start from in engaging with it. Effectively, this is what the analysis phase performs.

The third component of the SARA methodology involves crafting a 'response', in the form of interventions shaped by the insights of the analysis. These may involve fairly orthodox law enforcement tactics, but Sparrow (2016) advocates that if done properly the design and delivery of problem-solving responses should unlock more creative and innovative opportunities for doing things that include multiple agencies working together. This might involve thinking both about 'upstream' prevention, but also post-event harm mitigation options. Having delivered its interventions, the process concludes by 'assessing' the impacts achieved. Depending upon the results, the process may need to be repeated if the presenting problem has persisted.

This vision of police systematically, proactively, and creatively solving problems by identifying and tackling the underlying causes of key social problems has attracted a lot of support for POP. For much of the 1990s in the United Kingdom, it was strongly championed by the Home Office. However, echoing the situation of community policing outlined above, it appears that translating the theory into operational practice is hard. For instance, a Home Office evaluation of POP in three forces in the United Kingdom concluded that:

What has emerged, however, is that implementing a problem-oriented approach is more difficult than might appear at first sight. (Leigh et al., 1998: vii)

Such pessimistic conclusions resonate with the international research literature that describes how, although successes have been achieved through this approach when used as a motor for police reform (Eck, 2006), the general consensus is that it has been less successful than might have been anticipated in triggering a radical step-change in the conduct of policing (Braga and Weisburd, 2006).

There is now extensive evidence on this point. For example, Gary Cordner and Elizabeth Biebel's (2005) assessment of POP in San Diego set out to evaluate just what capacity the methods that underpin POP have for transforming the delivery of policing over the longer term. Although the POP approach has received a generally positive reception among both policing practitioners and scholars, as representing an innovative and systematic response to several challenges that bedevil contemporary policing organizations, the evidential supports for its efficacy are comparatively limited. Numerous individual case studies record the purported successes of POP techniques on a defined problem; however, many of the evaluations have been underpinned by comparatively weak research designs (Weisburd and Eck, 2004). As a result, a question remains about whether the implementation of POP is transforming practice, or as Cordner and Biebel (2005) note:

… responses rely primarily on enforcement, and it seems that the POP terminology and process are merely used to 'dress up' or legitimize a much more traditional approach to policing.

This is clearly redolent of the 'rhetoric vs reality' equivocations identified in relation to community policing. But a second area of concern more 'tailored' to POP is, who gets to define what counts as a 'problem' and what data evidences that decision-making process? Consistent with the tenor of Cordner and Biebel's scepticism, there is a tendency for police to just rely upon the kinds of re-ported and recorded crime data they always use to denote prob-lems rather than take their lead from communities experiencing issues first-hand. This persists despite police awareness that what gets reported and recorded as a crime provides only a partial pic-ture of the totality of incidents that take place. However, rather than enriching their view and perspective by blending informa-tion from a range of different sources, under time pressure and as a form of 'easing behaviour' they revert to the materials they are most familiar with—recorded crime administrative data gen-erated by their organizations.

One way in which any such limitations can be overcome and systemic gaps in police data plugged is to survey people about their local neighbourhoods. The idea of using community surveys as part of a POP approach is not new. Indeed, in his earlier in-volvement in the COPE project in Baltimore, Cordner (1988: 15) identified how:

The key to community-oriented policing is getting the community's views on problems and their solutions … The COPE experience has demon-strated the fallacy of assuming that a police department's sense of a community's problems matches community resident's actual concerns.

Despite such advocacy, the importance of obtaining community input in defining problems has not been sufficiently appreciated. What police departments define as problems for communities and what the people they are policing self-define as their problems are often very different (see Innes, 2014). Numerous community surveys demonstrate that when asked about what the problems are that affect their quality of life and cause insecurity in their neighbourhoods, people attribute significant salience to forms of physical and social disorder (Taylor, 2001). These are precisely the kinds of low-level problems that the police have traditionally tended to dismiss as unimportant and where their data capture is weakest. Consequently, in the absence of community input, POP is likely to continue to focus its efforts on police-defined criminal problems, thereby in all likelihood failing to address at least some of the 'social harm' associated with antisocial behaviour that the law recognizes can cause people to feel 'harassment, alarm or dis-tress' (Home Office, 2014).

In summary then, it seems that although POP is sometimes used in the fashion originally imagined by Herman Goldstein (1979) and can, under certain circumstances, have a significant and radical impact on crime and disorder problems (Weisburd et al., 2010), this may be the exception rather than the rule.

Broken windows

The potential for neglect of non-criminal or at least borderline criminal problems is a position that is 'corrected' by policing underpinned by 'broken windows' logics. Taylor (2001) identifies five variants of what he labels the 'incivilities' thesis, of which the 'longitudinal' broken windows theory is by far the most high profile. Indeed, reflecting this status, policing approaches underpinned by broken windows logics have arguably been the most hotly debated and contested of all those reviewed in this chapter.

Importantly, from the point of this book, in its original formulation—as presented in the *Atlantic Monthly* article published by Wilson and Kelling (1982)—broken windows was manifestly situated in the community policing tradition. Based around the apocryphal Officer Kelly, the article describes how, by maintaining order and robustly tackling a range of incivilities and physical disorders, Kelly's local interventions disrupt a causal chain of events with the potential to induce a low crime neighbourhood to 'tip' into a trajectory of development leading to it becoming a high crime environment. Stripped to its core, this pattern of causation posits that untreated disorder in an area induces fear of crime that leads law-abiding citizens to retreat from use of public spaces. As a consequence, the weakened state of local informal social control makes it a more attractive environment for potential offenders to predate in because opportunities for crime increase, leading to more offences being committed.

Reflecting the political and popular attention that this theoretical proposition at the heart of broken windows-based policing has garnered, it has subsequently been subject to extensive empirical testing. It gained early support from Skogan's (1990) survey-based analysis which found some evidence for the key claims expounded. More recently, an observational experiment conducted by Keizer et al. (2008) provided additional evidence to validate the pivotal claim that the occurrence of untreated disorder is criminogenic.

However, several recent studies have been more sceptical. Facilitated by the growing availability of small-area data, there has been a shift in research focus towards micro-units of analysis within neighbourhoods such as street segments, to show variation in disorder and the clustering of crime within neighbourhoods (Welsh et al., 2015). Taylor (2015) points out that the nature of any association between spatial indicators and crime often remains indecipherable owing to difficulties inherent in establishing the theoretical meaning of ecological indictors and of matching geographical and temporal measures to the conceptual framework. Taylor also reminds us of nonrandom selection effects at the neighbourhood level (e.g. outward migration) that have a bearing on crime and disorder.

However, it is the practical 'real world' consequences of police trying to operationalize such concepts that has garnered most trenchant criticism and concern. Associated with broken windows, aggressive order maintenance extended to even the most minor of law infringements was controversially cited as the cause of the crime drop in New York city during the 1990s and 2000s (Zimring, 2011). A number of concerns have gravitated around the harms that arise when 'broken people' are treated in the same way as 'broken windows'. As Stuart (2016) amongst several other studies identifies, the ethos of 'broken windows' is seemingly quite susceptible to 'tipping over' into forms of 'zero tolerance'. Developing the concept of 'therapeutic policing', Stuart's account (2016) is rather more subtle than some of those that preceded him (cf. Choongh, 1997). What he attends to is how police interactions with the destitute inhabitants of 'skid row' in Los Angeles are inflected with a paternalistic sense of discipline that is itself part of a reconfigured logic for conducting the conduct of the poor.

Moreover, Bowling (1999) has suggested that the reductions in crime in New York can be traced back more to changes in the dynamics of the city's drug markets, rather than any assertive policing strategies targeted at incivilities and antisocial behaviour. Sampson and Raudenbush (1999) conclude, on the basis of their systematic observation of Chicago neighbourhoods, that both disorder and more serious crime possess similar structural roots. As such, rather than looking at disorder as a cause of crime, both disorder *and* crime should be interpreted as products of particular 'neighbourhood effects'. This is a theme picked up and discussed in more detail in Chapter 3.

It is not that broken windows is fundamentally wrong in terms of the causal sequence it advocates, as in certain circumstances and under particular conditions, disorder is criminogenic in the ways described. There is, however, a generalizability issue, in that the occurrence of disorder and incivilities does not intrinsically generate more crime. There are other pathways and possibilities that need to be accounted for. Taylor's (2001) detailed work in Baltimore, for instance, noted that the areas experiencing higher rates of crime and disorder at the point in time he was assessing them were those that had historically seen higher levels. There is also a 'control creep' issue, inasmuch as more and more disorder can be interpreted as falling within the broken windows purview, as opposed to retaining a clear focus upon those problems that absolutely require police interventions.

There are, then, important limitations and concerns with the broken windows approach and its links to intensive police enforcement activity that can be detrimental to police–community relations (Longstaff et al., 2015). However, what it does do is connect issues of perception and reaction to the occurrence of actual incidents, rather than seeing them as independent matters. In this sense, it affords a greater sense of the complexity and challenge for analysts seeking to study and understand the impacts and consequences of crime and disorder across different physical and social environments. It is not sufficient, as some have been wont to do, to either study incident rates or perceptual and attitudinal variables in isolation from each other. Rather, a comprehensive theory of the impacts of crime and disorder needs to encompass both the actual incidence of events, and the shape and form of public reactions to these. Sometimes actual levels of crime will track perceptions quite closely, but at other times they will display divergent patterns.

Such considerations are vitally important, both in configuring a community policing-type approach, and in evaluating the performance of any such model. What they attest to is how there can be different routes into generating the kinds of benefits and outcomes that proponents of community policing are routinely seeking. Aggregate crime reduction may not be accomplished just by targeting crime; there may be other intervention points that can be leveraged.

Intelligence-led policing

Albeit not as inherently aligned with the community policing tradition as the previous two formulations outlined above, intelligence-led policing (ILP) is important to the origins story of Neighbourhood Policing in two distinct ways. First, as discussed in more detail in Chapter 2, at the time when the experimental work that laid the foundations for Neighbourhood Policing was being formulated, ILP was arguably the most influential policing strategy in the United Kingdom. In this sense, discussions of the significance of police attending to issues of public reassurance were partly a process of 'reaction formation' against ILP and the delivery outcomes it sought to privilege. Second, and more positively, the accent that ILP placed on establishing a disciplined approach to information and intelligence management, especially through harnessing the National Intelligence Model (NIM), was something that the National Reassurance Policing Programme integrated within its core processes and systems.

In the United Kingdom, much of the development work associated with ILP was undertaken by Kent Police under the leadership of Sir David Phillips. As an approach, it was promoted and propelled to a national level by Her Majesty's Inspectorate of Constabulary (HMIC) and especially the Audit Commission's (1993) Tackling Crime Effectively report. Maguire's (2000) insightful appraisal of ILP's implementation during this period ascertained that it gravitated around a perceived need to establish rational mechanisms for prioritizing what issues would be the focus for policing interventions, less so any overarching policing philosophy (Tilley, 2008). According to Maguire's analysis, this was performed through the use of risk assessment instruments, together with clearly defined crime reduction targets.

ILP and the establishment of its widely endorsed delivery mechanism, the NIM, have shared emphasis upon 'smart' and targeted policing focused upon risky people, places, and events, coheres with wider social discourses (Maguire, 2000). Most evident in this respect is the influence of the Audit Commission's (1993) suggestions of how to make policing more effective and efficient—a vision informed by Neo-Liberal managerialist sensibilities concerning public service provision.

Variants of these kinds of principles can be detected in the US context in relation to discussions of COMPSTAT and hotspots models of policing. COMPSTAT (short for COMPARE STATistics) is intriguing given how it interweaves with the discussions of broken windows rehearsed previously. As Silverman (1999) and several other authors have testified, the initial implementation of broken windows-type logics co-occurred with this introduction of a new strategic management system directed towards holding police managers accountable for the performance of their staff. Silverman (1999) concludes that the latter was probably more influential than the former in inducing the New York crime drop from the early 1990s onwards. Employing computer technologies to produce up-to-date pictures of crime prevalence and distribution, and using these to focus the attention of local district police commanders, proved to be a powerful way of improving the effectiveness of an underperforming police department.

Not dissimilar logics underpin 'hotspots policing' (Braga and Weisburd, 2006)—a further iteration of ILP. But where orthodox formulations of ILP tend to focus upon problematic people, hotspots policing is predicated upon identifying where crime and disorder tends to cluster in space, targeting resources and situational interventions to those locations to reduce opportunities for crime (Sherman, 1992; Weisburd, 2015). Consistent with ILP, the basis of this approach is the systematic collection and analysis of data to facilitate targeted interventions directed towards those micro locations that drive up police demand.

Framed in this way, there are clear parallels between ILP and POP. Both advocate a more structured, systematic, and targeted approach to collating and analysing information in order to steer and direct policing activities (Tilley, 2008). They also share a recognition of the importance of a certain organizational reflexivity in policing, in order that the efficacy of any such police actions can be routinely assessed.

There is undoubtedly much to commend such approaches. It would be perverse after all to suggest that police powers and assets should not be directed to those people, places, and problems where they are most needed. However, perceived through a community policing lens, the problem with ILP (and one it shares with POP) is the lack of direct democratic input into who decides what the priority risks and targets are to be. In effect, these decisions become internal police ones, with senior officers selecting the priority issues that will be worked upon, to the neglect of non-reported criminality and crime that transcends physical borders.

It has been well evidenced by numerous studies of policing that police awareness of the prevalence and distribution of crime and disorder is an artefact of their deployment decisions. That is, because of crime reporting effects and levels of hidden victimization, the more police focus their attention on a particular area (whether geographically or substantively defined) the more incidents they will 'discover'. This is a phenomenon captured by Ditton (1979) in his notion of crime waves as 'control waves' whereby variations in the volume of criminal convictions can be explained by varying amounts of social control.

Relatedly, if one is seeking to make judgements about what are the most pressing crime risks that warrant attending to, then 'scale' matters. Processing information at a police force level may lead one to attend to different issues from those that would come to the fore when viewed at a neighbourhood level. Indeed, it is entirely plausible that the issues and needs in a small number of acutely deprived, high crime localities will be very different from those of a larger number of more average neighbourhoods in any given force.

When the clear focus becomes tackling crime, this can lead to the adoption of intervention strategies that appear relatively 'invisible' to local publics and a community context where methods other than enforcement can pay dividends. If your pre-eminent concern is with tackling a serious crime issue, then it is tempting to routinize the use of covert police intelligence, on the grounds that these are often most effective. However, such an approach risks neglecting issues of public confidence and legitimacy. From a community policing perspective, these are vital considerations and lead to a recognition that the ways policing is undertaken matters just as much the 'successes' it achieves. That issue frames our theoretical approach to analysing Neighbourhood Policing as a particular inflection of the community policing canon.

Police drama

Tracing in outline some of the key priorities associated with the most prominent policing models from the past half century has been intended to accomplish two things. First, it highlights how these approaches differ from each other, valuing and accenting particular aspects of the police mission. Second, rehearsing these models and their principal components is important for illuminating how, in its early design and development, Neighbourhood Policing appropriated aspects from each, blending them together in a particular way. This is a theme that will be picked up in more detail in Chapter 2.

In their review of the empirical supports for several of the main contemporary policing styles, Weisburd and Eck (2004) examine their respective impacts on levels of crime, disorder, and fear. They conclude that orthodox 'law enforcement' policing styles show little impact on levels of crime, disorder, or fear. More recent innovative approaches are more promising however, with:

1. Community policing strategies encouraging increased and enhanced citizen–police contacts, reduced levels of fear of crime, but not actual levels of crime and/or disorder.
2. Targeting police resources at crime hotspots is most likely to reduce overall recorded crime levels.
3. Problem-solving strategies are effective at preventing, and thus reducing, levels of crime and disorder.

Further empirical support for the general tenor of these findings can be gleaned from Zhao et al.'s (2002) review of twenty-six evaluations of community policing undertaken between 1974 and 1999. They conclude that, of sites solely with additional police presence, 59 per cent saw a decrease in fear (with 38 per cent no change and 3 per cent an increase). In sites with some additional proactive policing component, 75 per cent saw a decrease in fear (with 36 per cent no change and none an increase).

Implicit within these findings and the fact that different policing models can be oriented to generate such different outcomes, is a recognition that there is a breadth to the police function in liberal democratic societies and disagreements about what the proper focus of police work is. Some explicitly prioritize crime control and law enforcement, whereas others define the police function as involving a broader and more amorphous security management remit that encompasses public perceptions and disorder issues. This has proven to be a fundamental and defining tension at the heart of the Anglo-American police institution. It is reflected in the different models outlined above, some of which are self-evidently more crime focused than others that prioritize the management of disorder and security. Adopting a long view of police reform, it is possible to see how reform innovations and initiatives have oscillated between these 'broader' and 'narrower' articulations of the police. Community policing, and the perspectives that possess a family resemblance to it, clearly align with the more expansive conception of the police mission. Commensurate with this is a need to take seriously the question of '*how* police are understood to influence public perceptions of crime disorder and neighbourhoods?'

Certainly, when compared with most other jurisdictions, what the public thinks of the police matters more in the British policing tradition. Revisiting aspects of the preceding discussion, this is a further way in which a connection to the so-called 'Peelian principles' can be established. Peel's apocryphal vision of the police institution clearly foresaw them undertaking a wide range of interventions in support of improving the security of neighbourhoods and their communities.

What this does steer us towards however, is a recognition that how policing is performed is as important as what it does. Specifically, in respect of Neighbourhood Policing and its progenitors, we need to situate it in a framework that is sensitive both to how it is intended to, and how it actually does, shape the objective levels of crime and disorder as well as the public's subjective interpretation of these.

In this regard, a profitable line of enquiry was initially worked out by Manning (1977). He talked about policing as a series of 'dramatic' engagements in the world, wherein policing actions express collective societal values as well as tackling 'real world' harms. For Manning, these symbolic aspects of the police function and how they are interpreted by those who experience them, are of equal significance and salience, as the physical manifestations of police actions.

In composing this influential perspective on policing, Manning drew significantly on Erving Goffman's dramaturgical sociology. Specifically, there are two dimensions of Goffman's scholarship that are especially germane to analysing policing. The first derives from his work on the presentation of self and the extent to which individuals, groups, and institutions are continually engaged in actively managing the public appearances that they project into the world. In this sense, Goffman develops the analogy of the theatre to articulate how what happens 'on stage' in the view of significant others may be distinct from what is occurring behind the scenes, away from any public gaze. It is this aspect of Goffman's work that is most self-evidently brought through by Manning and others such as Loader (1997) who have attended to the symbolic role of policing in social life.

There is, however, a second feature of Goffman's work that has been far less influential upon policing studies, and that we think possesses considerable potential. This is micro-sociological analyses of the rituals, rules, and rhythms that are invoked by people when they are in each other's presence to mutually co-ordinate their respective actions and behaviours. Across a number of studies focused upon different forms of encounter and engagement, Goffman showed how there were definable interactional techniques, strategies, and tactics used by participants to steer, repair, and influence the trajectory of the interaction. These included: displays and suppression of thoughts and emotion; attempts to mislead the other about one's real motives or intent; as well deliberately overlooking infelicities and breaches of social conventions that might otherwise disrupt the flow of the encounter. Towards the end of his life, Goffman came to think of this field of study as constituting a defined 'interaction order' with its own specific modes of regulation and performance (Goffman, 1959; 1983).

This latter strand has featured far less prominently in studies of policing. This is surprising given how so many studies of the police and their work, especially in the ethnographic tradition, have attended to the conduct of street encounters between police and citizens cast in a variety of roles such as victim, suspect, and witness. One would think that there would be considerable value attached to harnessing some conceptual resources that could 'tune' analytic attention into the question of 'how' officers involved in such interactions seek to deploy particular interactional strategies aligned with their aims. In their day-to-day work, police are cast as figures of authority who, in responding to calls for service from members of the public, are ever alert to the potential for risk and danger to arise.[4] This subtly infuses how they engage in, and navigate, such interactions and transactions.

---

[4] The potential for danger is a long-standing theme within sociological analyses of police work (see Rubinstein, 1973), and has been identified as a key structuring quality upon the working personality of police officers (Reiner, 2010; Loftus, 2009).

Furthermore, over the past ten years there has been significant interest in the notion of procedural justice and its role in building public confidence in policing (Loader and Mulcahy, 2003; Tyler, 2006). Stated simply, this holds that how police interact with citizens especially in terms of treating them fairly and with respect, is at least as important in shaping their opinions, attitudes, and perception of the police as any outcome that results. However, the vast majority of studies have been predicated upon quantitative research designs and secondary analysis of large-scale public surveys (Jackson and Bradford, 2012). As such, one might anticipate that there is much to be gained for such accounts by attending to detailed and high-resolution analyses of the interactional dynamics of how police manage their encounters with victims, suspects, and witnesses. Accordingly, one particular aim of this book is to work through this logic, providing some highly detailed analyses of interactions between Neighbourhood Police officers and members of the public.

Set against this backdrop, the intent behind this book is that it should provide an empirically rich and nuanced account of Neighbourhood Policing and its origins, the ways in which it was implemented, as well as how and why it has entered a process of relative decline. In pursuing these aims, we are also keen to derive, at a conceptual and more theoretical level, a sophisticated account of the various means by which this style of policing influences perceptions, disorder, and crime. Specifically, where Manning's work has teased out how institutional performances are freighted with symbols and rituals of meaning, we want to counterweight this by attending more to how police perform their interactions and encounters with citizens, each other, and partner organizations. It is an approach that is concerned with the 'craft' of Neighbourhood Policing, conceiving of it as a series of performances for public consumption.

Overview

In what follows, we tell the story of Neighbourhood Policing. As well as conveying what Neighbourhood Policing is, the analysis seeks to develop a detailed account of how and why it is performed by officers in particular ways. As well as capturing the policy development trajectory, it also seeks to articulate and interpret issues about what officers do when interacting with members of the public cast in a variety of roles.

One of these issues concerns the development of a new construction of evidence-based policing (EBP). EBP, inspired by the scientific rigour applied in the field of medicine, is an approach that has gained considerable traction over the last couple of years in terms of advocating the use of research to steer the delivery and evaluation of policing practice (Sherman, 1998). However, what has not been recognized by such approaches is that they have focused upon studying policing 'treatments'. Herein, we develop the idea that rigorous research can also be harnessed in terms of its 'diagnostic' potential—that is in identifying the issues and problems that police should treat as priorities, and which ultimately could support the goals of a Neighbourhood Policing approach.

The next chapter focuses upon the National Reassurance Policing Programme (NRPP) funded by the Home Office in 2003 to empirically test the concept of reassurance policing. Reassurance policing was the direct precursor of Neighbourhood Policing and pivoted around the 'reassurance gap' between falling rates of recorded crime and growing public perceptions of crime prevalence as captured in the British Crime Survey (Jansson, 2006). The NRPP was a quasi-experimental undertaking, through which a number of the predicate principles and processes taken up by Neighbourhood Policing were originally worked out and tested. The two-year NRPP was important, both for setting out a far more structured and systematic approach to community policing delivery (certainly when compared with previous iterations), and for rigorously testing these against a range of outcome measures. This work and its findings are discussed in some detail.

The analysis of public reassurance and what policing can do to influence it frames the focus of Chapter 2. The shift from reassurance to Neighbourhood Policing embodied a number of considerations. But one issue that it raises concerns what precisely is a neighbourhood and how should it be formatted as a unit for the delivery of policing. This is a key theme for Chapter 3 alongside a consideration of the developing policy framework that supported Neighbourhood Policing.

Chapter 4 moves on to analyse the nature of police–citizen encounters themselves, developing a theoretical position on the conduct of community policing, whilst in Chapter 5, the focus shifts to concern itself with establishing an account of the work of PCSOs.

Chapters 6 and 7 adopt a more grounded approach to track Neighbourhood Policing practices. This starts with a detailed treatment of practices associated with police presence and what it means to do visible policing. The key insight developed through this discussion is to conceptualize the idea of police performance. And finally, Chapter 8 explores the value and importance of Neighbourhood Policing assets in addressing national security risks and threats.

Collectively then, the sum of the contents of these chapters is designed to build a detailed account of how Neighbourhood Policing delivered a range of innovations, and thus became a crucible for reforming the police institution more generally. This is important because, as Sparrow (2016) contends, past iterations of community and problem-solving policing have frequently been constrained in terms of what they have accomplished by being implemented in a 'reduced' form. What is required is a broader view of 'the core mission' and of 'the dimensions of performance', allied with a richer information environment and more sophisticated users.

The research programme

The book draws upon a fifteen-year long research programme that has investigated Neighbourhood Policing from a variety of angles and perspectives. The various studies that collectively comprise this overarching programme of research have adopted different research designs and data collection and analysis methods, shaped by their particular focus and interests. It has included extensive amounts of ethnographic field observations and in-depth interviews with members of the public about their perceptions and experiences of policing. It has also encompassed secondary analysis of large-scale public attitude surveys, as well as evaluative quasi-experimental research designs based on the real-world implementation of new policing structures and practices.

In what follows, where a chapter relies especially upon data and materials from a particular project, then its methodology is described at that point, but in general the reader is directed to a more in-depth methods appendix at the end of the volume. However, in terms of orienting the reader more broadly, in terms of how Neighbourhood Policing has been studied, it is appropriate to provide a few precursory remarks here.

Broadly speaking the materials informing this book can be distinguished into two categories. First, there is data and analysis conducted as part of the development and design of Neighbourhood Policing. Of particular note in this respect are the significant amounts of data generated as part of the National Reassurance Policing Programme (2003–2005). There is also, however, data covering Neighbourhood Policing in a more mature stage of its implementation in England and Wales. For instance, the data covering the work of PCSOs in Wales and the discussion tracking how Neighbourhood Policing evolved over a ten-year period in the London Borough of Sutton. Thus, at the level of the book, the different methods can be understood as engaged in a form of complementary triangulation, insomuch as they do not all converge on the same issue. Rather, reflecting their respective strengths and empirical affordances, they provide perspectives on different facets of Neighbourhood Policing in terms of its organization, conduct, and social impacts. Blended together, they provide a more rounded and comprehensive picture of Neighbourhood Policing than could be established on the basis of one method or standalone study.

That said, we cannot claim that the account we develop is necessarily representative of Neighbourhood Policing as a whole. As is discussed in some detail in the next chapter, and alluded to above, one of the defining characteristics of Neighbourhood Policing is that it should be able to flex in order that it can be 'fitted' to local situational requirements. There are then varieties of Neighbourhood Policing, as opposed to one tightly defined, highly prescriptive, model about what must be delivered. However, because we have drawn our empirical material from across a range of forces and contexts, we are fairly confident that what we describe provides a reasonable facsimile of what Neighbourhood Policing looked like in the majority of areas where it was undertaken.

The use of the past tense in the last sentence was deliberate. Theoretically, one aspect that we are interested in teasing out is how Neighbourhood Policing has changed and adapted over time. This is an important and under-appreciated issue within the study of policing (and perhaps many other areas of public policy). Due to a combination of pressures, much of the social research conducted into policy and practice is undertaken quite intensively over a comparatively condensed time period yet treated as representative of what that policy and/or practice is.

However, studies such as those undertaken by Skogan (2006) highlight the perils of this. The original trials of the CAPS approach were quite tightly regulated and the early benefits sufficient to support a decision to roll-out the programme city-wide. Similar impacts were not, however, achieved in other areas of the city. In some localities, these took time to happen, in other areas they never materialized at all. Moreover, as his careful evaluation makes clear, the 'mature' CAPS programme running after several years was not the same as the innovations introduced at its start.

One of the advantages we have in the UK context is that we were directly involved in its inception and have carried on researching and studying it, albeit in different guises and from varied vantage points, continuously since it was first introduced. As such, we think there is merit in trying to develop a 'lifecycle' approach to innovations in policing models. Tracking them over time, from their birth, as they mature and then start to decline. Such an approach has the potential to develop a more nuanced account of particular policing styles that is more appreciative of how they are configured to particular moments in time and place. Furthermore, it will better key us into how and why different policing models rise and fall.

2

The Story of Reassurance Policing and How it Became Neighbourhood Policing

After having been eclipsed for a number of years by competing frameworks, in part because of some of the practical limitations and conceptual frailties rehearsed in the preceding chapter, a revival in the fortunes of community policing in the United Kingdom took hold in the early 2000s. That this resurgence occurred at this particular moment is attributable to a blend of factors.

At a macro-level, there was increasing consternation amongst a small number of senior police officers and policy makers, that although according to police data and the British Crime Survey (BCS), recorded crime had been falling since the mid-1990s, levels of fear of crime did not appear to be tracking these reductions.[1] This was resonating with the local experiences of people like Denis O'Connor, the then Chief Constable of Surrey. As he described it, when attending community meetings in Surrey, he would often start by reporting the good news to those attending that recorded crime was down, only to be met with a derisive and dismissive reaction of disbelief. When he talked about this with other senior officers, such as Assistant Commissioner Tim Godwin responsible for 'Territorial Policing' in London, they recognized this pattern. These senior officers began referring to a 'reassurance gap' in policing—a distance between peoples' objective safety, at least as gauged by recorded crime rates, and their subjective perceptions of security.

---

[1] For example, a Home Office published study found that levels of public concern about levels of anti-social behaviour and physical disorder had increased over this period (Wood, 2004).

Neighbourhood Policing. Martin Innes, Colin Roberts, Trudy Lowe, and Helen Innes, Oxford University Press (2020). © Martin Innes, Colin Roberts, Trudy Lowe, and Helen Innes.
DOI: 10.1093/oso/9780198783213.003.0001

Layered onto this mix was a creeping sense of disenchantment with some of the public outcomes of intelligence-led policing (ILP). Especially through instruments such as the National Intelligence Model, being 'intelligence-led' was being valorized by a number of policy entrepreneur Chief Constables, as the pre-eminent organizing framework for policing. Specifically, in areas such as Kent, where a 'strong' programme of ILP was being implemented, it was becoming apparent that whilst some benefits in terms of crime suppression were resulting, this was at the expense of levels of fear of crime, public confidence, and low-level crime and disorder.

Challenged by this seeming paradox that crime was reducing, but fear of crime and several other perceptual measures were proving stubbornly resistant to change, Denis O'Connor approached academics at the University of Surrey to see if they might be able to offer any insights into the situation. This chapter tells the story of what happened next.

In order to contextualize this story, the next section outlines the 'policy arc' in terms of how Neighbourhood Policing was designed and delivered. Conceptualizing it as an arc captures a process of emergence, a peaking of interest and attention, followed by relative decline and diffusion. Having traced out its genesis and implementation, and how this unfolded over time at this broad level, the following sections provide more detailed and thorough accounts of its key components. In particular, the chapter examines the work of the National Reassurance Policing Programme (NRPP). This was the quasi-experimental precursor of Neighbourhood Policing, where a lot of the 'design work' in terms of key principles, processes, and systems happened. Following on from which, the discussion considers how the findings from the NRPP were translated into the 'scaling up' involved in establishing a nationwide police reform programme.

The policy arc

The idea that reassuring the public is a core function of policing was first formally articulated by Charles Bahn in an article published in 1974. Albeit somewhat idiosyncratically expressed in terms of its policy implications—he discussed the value of having officers stand on raised podiums and of recruiting tall red-haired officers—Bahn's fundamental concept was nevertheless significant. He drew attention to the role of police visibility in shaping public perceptions, something that many other commentators had either willingly or unintentionally negated or overlooked. Relatedly, he provided an explicit recognition of how influencing peoples' subjective perceptions through policing activities may be causally enmeshed in shaping the sense of security they feel and experience. It is worth remembering that his argument was being published around the same time that the findings of the Kansas City Preventative Policing Experiment were capturing attention (Kelling et al., 1974). These findings were interpreted as suggesting that visible police patrols had no discernible impact upon crime rates. To which, Bahn's repost was that police presence can be important in other ways than simply having a direct impact upon crime.

Coherent with this position, but formulated in a way avowedly more intent upon influencing policy trajectory, the concept of reassurance was subsequently picked up and highlighted in a report by Her Majesty's Inspectorate of Constabulary (HMIC) (2001). Ruminating upon the increasing consternation about levels of fear of crime at the time, David Povey, Her Majesty's Chief Inspector, asserted that policing could help to assuage such public concerns, when it was 'visible, accessible and familiar'. This was an important intervention on two fronts. First, because it represented a check on the general direction of government policy, which was becoming increasingly fixated upon crime reduction outcomes, defined specifically in terms of recorded volume acquisitive crimes. Second, because prior to this point there had been several decades of research indicating that, when surveyed, citizens repeatedly attached public value to visible policing and complained that they rarely ever saw uniformed officers on patrol. However, senior officers had consistently denied the salience of such complaints, on the grounds that, as evidenced by findings from the Kansas City Preventive Patrol Experiment and other allied Home Office studies, levels of foot patrol had little or no impact upon crime prevalence. But what the HMIC report recognized is that such forms of policing presence may be freighted with other benefits. In talking about 'a reassurance gap', O'Connor and Godwin were starting to articulate what these might be.

The initial conversations with the researchers at the University of Surrey significantly expanded the thinking about such issues. Almost a full decade before anyone had started working on 'crime harm indices' and the idea that not all crimes are equal in terms of their impacts upon the public, nascent work was underway to explore the idea that there were certain 'signal crimes' that were especially potent in communicating messages to people about the distribution of safety and security across social space (Innes, 2001; Innes and Fielding, 2002). Inspired by these ideas, a small exploratory study was commissioned in areas of Surrey and South London to investigate how the signal crime concept might be applied to the practice of community policing. Based upon in-depth interviews with residents in the areas concerned about their experiences and perceptions of crime, disorder, and policing, a picture began to emerge of a divergence between what the local police were identifying as priority issues, and the kinds of problems that the residents invoked as shaping their views. In effect, the police were focusing their resources on key volume acquisitive crimes, where the local public were talking a lot more about various forms of social and physical disorder, some of which was 'criminal', but not all was. Framed by the signal crimes perspective, the problems communicating messages to locally situated publics about levels of security were not necessarily police priorities.

Armed with this local evidence base, together with increasing political consternation about the implications of 'the reassurance gap', O'Connor and Godwin were able to secure Home Office funding to support a more systematic investigation of the emergent ideas and how they might be rendered operationally relevant as part of a defined policing model. The NRPP, as it was dubbed, was introduced within sixteen research sites, distributed across eight police force areas. The idea was to systematically test what a policing process modelled on these kinds of precepts might look like and to establish what it could deliver. We will return to the NRPP below to provide a more detailed account of its component parts, for now it is sufficient to know that a considerable research effort was bound into the programme both in terms of component 'design' and evaluating outcomes.

Running in parallel with these rapid developments, the concept of reassurance was integrated into the National Policing Plan 2003/6. Alongside improved police performance, provisioning greater public reassurance was delineated as 'the primary objective for the police service for the Plan's three-year duration'. Reflecting this enhanced status, Statutory Performance Indicators for reassurance were established as part of the Policing Performance Assessment Framework (Dalgleish and Myhill, 2004).

The outcome evaluation for the NRPP was undertaken by a team from the Home Office. Measuring progress achieved across the sixteen sites between 2003 and 2005, based upon a range of subjective and more 'objective' indicators, using a multi-method design, the evaluation concluded that the approach employed did appear to deliver a range of benefits. Importantly, the evaluation documented that not all of the research trial sites benefitted equally, and that there was some form of association between those that implanted the theoretical model with the greatest fidelity, and those experiencing the larger gains.

Informed by these results, and other materials (discussed later), a decision was taken to scale the NRPP to implement it nationally. As part of these manoeuvres, several significant changes in terminology were made. 'Reassurance' was perceived as a somewhat 'arch' and clunky concept, and so it was replaced with the term 'Neighbourhood Policing'. This was a formulation that had been attached to a trial conducted in London some years previously (see Irving et al., 1989), and was seen as being more politically 'sellable'.

This was not just conceptual rebranding, however. Whilst clear family resemblances were retained, there were several subtle, but important, shifts in the configuration of the Neighbourhood Policing approach that was rolled out nationally. Namely, a greater accent upon using a defined geographical territory as the key operational unit of delivery, and the assignment of dedicated police resources to this. Arguably, this was accompanied by an increased emphasis upon crime reduction outcomes than was the case with the NRPP model. This was at the expense of diagnosing and treating signal crimes and signal disorders through a carefully calibrated methodology (on which more later).

The national implementation programme for Neighbourhood Policing commenced in 2005/6, lasting for three years. Individual forces had considerable latitude in terms of what precisely Neighbourhood Policing looked like in their area. Indeed, this ability to flex to local circumstances was adjudged important both philosophically, given the precepts of adopting a neighbourhood-based approach, and practically. However, the bounding parameters were that all neighbourhoods were to have a dedicated policing team.

It is important to recognize that key elements of this approach were coherent with a broader localization agenda at this time

(Bullock and Sindall, 2014), the apotheosis of which was the introduction of Police and Crime Commissioners as a fulcrum for establishing a far greater sense of local public accountability. Equally however, the model selected for implementation was a 'resource hungry' one. Consequently, the election of a new government in 2010, with a clear austerity agenda to reduce public spending, impacted upon the ability of forces to sustain the numbers of officers associated with the systems and processes they established in the mid-2000s (Lowe et al., 2015). These resourcing issues were amplified by a growing recognition that having dedicated resources for tackling neighbourhood problems and conflicts was not doing much in terms of targeting and tackling some emerging crime types.

Most prominently, there were increasing concerns being expressed about how issues of child sexual exploitation and online crime were going to be tackled by forces working through significant workforce reductions as they strained to cope with reductions in central government funding. Reflecting which, a number of forces started to talk in terms of 'local policing' as opposed to Neighbourhood Policing, signalling how their officers were expected to take responsibility for response tasks, as well as prevention and problem-solving. It is perhaps unsurprising therefore, that in their 2017 inspection on police effectiveness, HMIC expressed concerns that Neighbourhood Policing had been eroded, having seen the greatest decline as officers were being abstracted for other duties as forces decided to try and preserve their reactive policing functions (HMIC, 2017). They concluded that the police service in England and Wales was no longer consistently implementing Neighbourhood Policing techniques and methods that are known to be effective in preventing crime and problem-solving. To understand what these effective practices are we need to return to the evidence base established by the NRPP. However, before doing so, the organization of the programme will first be described.

Programming reassurance

The eight forces participating in the NRPP were drawn from a larger group who had been invited to apply. They were selected on the grounds that, in terms of their policing make-up and the areas policed, they should provide a diversity of contexts across which to test the innovations in policing methods. Within each force, only small geographic areas were selected for implementation, again on the basis that the sixteen 'trial sites' should encompass a variety of situations and contexts. The intent being to ensure that any policing model developed through the work should not be 'over-fitted' to a particular set of circumstances, given the ultimate ambition was to establish something that could be 'scaled up' nationally. Figure 2.1 below depicts the eight forces and sixteen 'trial sites'.

Readers familiar with these areas will recognize that they range from some highly deprived urban areas, through to semi-rurality. In addition to the trial sites six areas were selected as 'control sites', subject to similar forms of data monitoring as undertaken in the trial sites, but with no interventions being delivered. This quasi-experimental design was established in an effort to ascertain whether, over the two-year intervention timeframe, the trial sites saw changes over and above those experienced more generally.

As part of their involvement, each of the eight forces supplied a small team of officers to help oversee implementation in their areas. Although they could bid for specific funds for innovation,

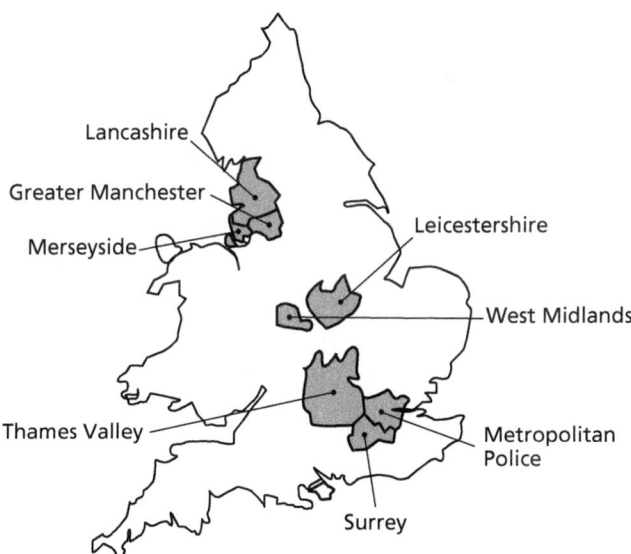

Figure 2.1 Eight NRPP Trial Sites

the idea was that the local policing assets were funded by the forces and were part of their commitment to the project. Each of the local teams reported into the national programme team who were fairly diligent in their monitoring of what was happening 'on the ground'.

There is a growing literature, especially in healthcare, around what is referred to as 'implementation science' (Damschroder et al., 2009). This reflects a growing recognition of how complex policy interventions frequently struggle, in the face of the messy and contingent nature of real life, to sustain fidelity to the original design model, and as a consequence succumb to what is referred to as 'implementation failure'—the results never materialize as anticipated, because what gets done departs from the original concept. With this in mind, the national team performed an important compliance function for the NRPP, repeatedly checking that local innovations were in accord with the programme's precepts.

Working closely with the policing teams were two sets of researchers. A team from the Home Office were responsible for evaluating the programme in terms of its implementation and outcomes. The University of Surrey researchers were co-located with the national police team, and were engaged in design and development of the policing interventions trialled across the sites. This involved intensive diagnostic work undertaken to generate insights into what crime and disorder incidents were driving insecurity at a local level in each of the selected areas.

Reassurance policing theory and practice

The model of reassurance policing originally implemented and tested as part of the NRPP was built around three principal components:

1. A visible, accessible, and familiar policing presence;
2. Targeting signal crimes and signal disorders through systematic collection and analysis of community intelligence. Accompanying which, was an attempt to foster 'control signals';
3. Co-producing local social control with community safety partners and the public.

The idea of blending these three elements was to establish a systematic and structured delivery methodology. In particular, there was a specific intent to learn from the evidence and insights emanating from the Chicago Alternative Policing Strategy experiments, as well as responding to the failings that had been identified across a number of earlier evaluations of community policing programmes, as rehearsed in the preceding chapter.

Each of the three components was integrated into the operating model on the grounds that it would perform a specific function to help secure the range of outcomes being aimed for. Moreover, the expectation was that these components would interact in shaping the outcomes delivered. This was because it was hoped that a reassurance policing model would generate a range of measurable changes, including:

- The promotion of public reassurance by improving levels of confidence in the police, and reductions in levels of fear of crime.
- In so doing, the hypothesis was that this would in turn bolster levels of collective efficacy and informal social control, which would induce crime and disorder suppressing conditions.
- There was also a more direct focus upon reducing signal crimes and disorders, as a route to reassuring local audiences, and crime reduction per se.

Providing a uniformed police presence is a common feature of most formulations of community policing. But integrated within the processes of this approach, it was understood as performing a particular set of functions and sending messages to the public audience. In signalling the presence of an active formal social control capacity, the idea was that police presence should have a deterrent effect upon potential miscreants, but also reassure local communities that resources are available to buttress their own informal social control efforts, should support be required.

This was not uncontentious. For example, in an evaluation of a scheme based upon HMIC's initial formulation of reassurance, Crawford et al. (2003) identified that, given the varied and diffuse demands upon police organizations, the delivery of visible, accessible, and familiar officers can prove problematic. They concluded:

The New Earswick experience suggests that small-scale changes to the level of patrol presence may well go unnoticed by residents, even in a relatively confined and geographically bounded village. In order to reassure residents and 'make a difference' in terms of visibility, accessibility and familiarity, relatively substantial increases in patrol presence may be needed. (p.41)

This concern with the 'dosage' of police patrol may though be indicative of a more profound problem with how reassurance has been constructed. A limitation of the HMIC formulation of reassurance is an assumption that the presence of visible signifiers of police presence will work by overriding any sources of insecurity arising from the presence of crime and disorder in an area. Furthermore, it adopts a police-centric view of security production, not really acknowledging that security is unlikely to result from institutional actions undertaken in isolation. Rather, security is more likely to be tractable and sustainable when it is co-produced, with publics playing their part in enacting informal modes of social control that interlock with the more formal actions of the police and partner agencies (see Innes, 2003), even when this public participation just involves myriad small acts of social ordering and behavioural regulation.

The empirical data from the fieldwork undertaken as part of the NRPP though suggests police visibility and its effects are more nuanced. This was most clearly evidenced by what amounted to a natural experiment that took place when the research teams were conducting fieldwork in two sites. Two murders happened. Following their standard operating procedures, police presence was surged in the area with the intent that it should reassure communities. In one of the sites this increased police presence was explained to the community via a public communications campaign, setting out that it was part of the policing response to a criminal homicide. Broadly speaking, public opinion was accepting and supportive of this increased police visibility as a reasonable response to a particular set of circumstances. The second site did not see any such strategic explanatory communications though, and during interviews with members of the public, considerable consternation was detected, with several expressions of concern about what was signalled by the extra policing.

In terms of 'accessibility', the NRPP innovated by establishing that public engagement activities can and should be undertaken proactively by police, rather than left as a reactive task. This reflected how many past community policing schemes had set up mechanisms for engaging communities—often based around community meetings. Fundamentally however, these still relied upon members of the public making the effort to come to the police meeting. The efficacy of this approach was self-undermining, inasmuch as it tended to elicit participation from what officers refer to derisively as 'the usual suspects'. Instead, the NRPP approach promoted the idea that officers dedicated to locally delivered policing should see it as part of their role to go out and make enquiries to research what people's local concerns and needs were. The methodology derived to support this far more systematic approach is described in much more detail in Chapters 5 and 6 herein.

Turning to the issue of 'familiarity'—the final component in 'the reassurance triptych'—the practical solution was to try and limit officer 'abstractions' from their assigned neighbourhoods and to give them quite lengthy assignments. A key piece of learning from previous attempts to implement community policing was that there was an understandable tendency for police organizations, when an emergency happened or resources got 'squeezed', to see community officers as redeployable. Moreover, because the kinds of work involved in community policing were not typically valorized by the action-oriented mores of police occupational culture, officers were quite amenable to having their attention redirected in this way.

Signal crimes and diagnostic community intelligence

The idea of enhancing police presence and visibility is not new. It is a common feature of most community policing-oriented reform programmes. Albeit, the NRPP's construction of police visibility and its effects was more sophisticated and nuanced than is typical, as reflected in the commentary about the public reactions to the two murders that were described. Framing the process of public interpreting of the murders and the police responses to them in this way is certainly consistent with the precepts of the signal crimes perspective and its accent upon the value of control signals.

Positioned in this way, the NRPP, although it had affinities with the 'problem-solving' focus emphasized by advocates of Goldstein's (1990) model, was not merely replicating it. Far greater import was being ascribed to assiduous 'problem-finding'. The idea being that, by tuning police interventions to those incidents that are disproportionately harmful to the condition of local social order, it is possible to leverage multiple positive outcomes.

To a significant degree, the signal crimes perspective functioned as the 'theoretical engine' for the NRPP model. Originally developed as a general framework for capturing the communicative properties of incidences of crime and disorder, and social control responses to such occurrences, its primary interest is in how defined actions and events influence people's perceptions and experiences of security. For instance, Innes (2014) describes how the perspective and its precepts can be applied to systematically analyse the ways people individually and collectively ascribe meaning to a range of problem types. This includes understanding the salience of and reactions to specific instances of antisocial behaviour, through to tracking and tracing how the impacts of homicides and terrorist attacks 'travel' across different segments of the public, measuring the variety of cognitive, behavioural, and affective reactions induced.

Goffman (1972: 247) defined a signal as:

a conventional sign, which, by prearrangement, has been arbitrarily established for this purpose—the purpose of announcing that there is something about which to be alarmed.

Distilled into a simpler formulation, a signal is 'a sign that has an effect' (Innes, 2004). Applied to the task of understanding and interrogating how people individually and collectively interpret and make sense of crime, disorder, and social control, focusing upon signalling processes enables a conceptual accent upon how they function as forms of communicative action that send messages to a wider audience. Typically, but not exclusively, such messages speak to the distribution of risks and threats across social space and the kinds of people, places, and events in the environment that are potentially dangerous and troublesome.

In terms of translating this conceptual frame into a practically usable methodology, Innes (2004; 2014) argues all signal events comprise three elements—an expression, content, and effect. The expression is a descriptor for the issue or problem responsible for causing some kind of defined effect. Devoid of any effect on perception, emotion, or behaviour, the crime or disorder event is simply part of the background 'noise' to everyday life. The remaining element of this conceptual triptych is the 'content' which is used to capture the bearer of risk. That is, whether the risk is directed towards the perceiver, someone with whom the perceiver has some form of connection, or to a group of people in general. The relationship between these three elements is exemplified in the following quotation from someone talking about a crime in their neighbourhood:

There had been a burglary, either it was that night or the night before … I was very anxious then … and it was the first time in eight years I actually did not feel one hundred per cent safe. (Ash214)

In this extract, 'burglary' is the expression and the effect is one of 'fear'. Because the interviewee locates this effect as impacting upon her, we can say that the content is one of 'personal risk'.

The important point here though is that this woman was not the victim of the crime, but even so it affected her. It is these more diffuse communicative properties that the signal crimes perspective is particularly attuned to. Through an extensive empirical research effort (summarized in Innes, 2004; 2014) it has been demonstrated that this capacity to send messages can be detected in relation to all kinds of signal events: signal crimes; physical and social disorders; as well as the formal and informal control signal responses to these.

Critically, the capacity of an event to signal risk and threat is not wholly dependent on how it is categorized in law. Forms of disorder and antisocial behaviour, when located in particular settings and situations, can have equally profound consequences for perceived insecurity as crimes. The implication being that where police attention has displayed a tendency to gravitate towards those matters legally classified as crimes, following a signal crimes logic, officers need to be open to a greater diversity of problems shaping how local citizens think, feel, and behave. This is captured in the following fieldwork extract from a lady talking about her experiences in her neighbourhood:

Graffiti is the thing that sort of bothers me more because it is in my face every day. I mean obviously rape and murder are more horrendous crimes, but it is graffiti that I see.

Here the respondent conveys how repeated, local exposure to physical disorder sent a signal about the type of neighbourhood in which they were residing. Even more significantly, this quotation articulates how the level of social harm associated with different acts may not automatically map onto their relative levels of harmfulness as it is conceptualized in law.

Wrapped into the practical processes of reassurance policing, the signal crimes perspective afforded a 'problem-finding' double-movement. First, it 'widened the police radar' to be sensitive to the fact that a diverse range of problems and events could shape the prevalence and distribution of insecurity, both subjective and objective, at a local neighbourhood level. Second, it also sought to focus in more precisely upon the specific incidents that were proving harmful to people's feelings of safety and security. So rather than thinking that graffiti or knife crime is a problem across a whole town or city, the idea was to locate, with considerable accuracy and precision, exactly where and when such issues were presenting, informed by insights and evidence generated by engaging with local communities. As an approach, it took the idea of context and situation seriously, understanding that the crime and disorder events that impact upon the public's perceptions will vary across space and time. In effect then, the signal crimes-based logic was providing a demand management function, by explicitly steering police attention and activities to those events having a disproportionate impact upon neighbourhood security.

As part of the NRPP, these precepts and principles were used to develop a community intelligence picture for each of the trial sites based upon setting out the key signal crimes and disorders detected in each area. This was based upon in-depth interviews with a sample of local residents and workers, asking them a series of questions about local crime, disorder, and policing issues, and the relative impacts they had upon them (a more detailed account of the methodology can be found in Chapters 6 and 7). Analyses of these data to identify the presence of signal crimes and disorders, and combining the materials from individual respondents to provide a collective view of the area, was designed to give the local policing team a clear sense of focus for targeting their intervention activities.

Figure 2.2 below provides a summary of the key signal crimes and disorders identified through this process, ranked according to the relative reach and significance of the impacts each issue was found to be having. Obviously, behind this summary there is considerable contextual detail and insight. But even just these headlines are sufficient to convey several important attributes of the NRPP work.

Remembering that these data were originally collected in the early 2000s, although highly localized and focused, they display similar patterns to analyses of national survey data from around this time (Wood, 2004). Taking the sixteen NRPP sites together, youth disorder and antisocial behaviour, together with drugs related issues, dominated in terms of the kinds of locally presenting

Site	1	2	3	4	5	6	7	8	9	10
St Helier	Youths	Graffiti	Litter	Damage	Mugging	Violence	Drugs	Burglary	Murder	Credit card theft
Colville	Drugs	Youths	Mugging	Robbery	Theft	Murder	Violence	Guns	Litter	Assault
Upper Edmonton	Drugs	Burglary	Mugging	Theft	Assault	Youths	Begging	Litter	Damage	Murder
Falcon-wood & welling	Youths	Damage	Violence	Burglary	Verbal	Assault	Speeding	Theft	Rape	
St Marys	Drugs	Youths	Damage	Litter	Mugging	Assault	Drinking	Rape	Burglary	
North Walton	Youths	Litter	Damage	Drinking	Violence	Speeding	Verbal	Arson	Skateboards	Mugging
St Helens Town Centre	Drugs	Youths	Burglary	Drinking	Violence	Mugging	Damage	Arson	Litter	Lighting at night
Aston	Drugs	Guns	Litter	Youths	Mugging	Speeding	Murder	Parking	Burglary	Damage
New Parks	Youths	Drugs	Damage	Burglary	Verbal	Litter	Violence	Parking	Speeding	Arson
Brunswick	Drugs	Youths	Assault	Burglary	Mugging	Drinking	Arson	Verbal	Urination	Noise
Ingol	Drugs	Youths	Drinking	Anti-social neighbour	Damage	Violence	Gangs	Verbal	Assault	Dark areas
Greenham	Youths	Drugs	Damage	Graffiti	Arson	Theft	Violence	Rape	Dark areas	
Burgfield	Youths	Drugs	Assault	Damage	Speeding	Theft	Violence	Drinking	Litter	
West Park	Youths	Drinking	Assault	Graffiti	Violence	Rape	Verbal	Alleys	Drugs	
Ash	Youths	Damage	Drugs	Verbal	Speeding	Burglary	Violence	Drinking	Rape	Assault
Failsworth	Youths	Drugs	Mugging	Violence	Damage	Drinking	Burglary	Litter	Sus-Persons	Verbal

Figure 2.2   Rank Order of Top Signal Crimes by Site

problems that members of the public saw as causing insecurity. Indeed, it is striking just how prevalent forms of social and physical disorder are in terms of this approach to diagnosing neighbourhood security priorities. It is not that crime problems do not feature in the lists of public concerns, but they are mixed in with other forms of disorderly and troublesome conduct and the physical detritus of these. This is clearly consistent with the theoretical precepts of the signal crimes perspective and its understanding that levels of perceptual harm associated with an issue do not depend upon how it is formally defined in law.

Further practical insights can be gleaned from these data by comparing across sites. For what can be observed in this respect is how, although the profile of problems identified for individual sites displays some commonalities, in terms of the details there are important differences also. The mix of priority problems varies across the areas. It is indicative of how policing interventions and problem-solving efforts need to be precisely calibrated to local conditions and circumstances.

The theoretical innovation associated with adopting such an approach, in terms of connecting specific effects to defined incidents and actions, as opposed to the more aggregated type of analysis typical of fear of crime studies, should not be under-estimated. It resolves a long-standing limitation that Jacobs (1996) identified some time ago now, with extant frameworks for studying social reactions to crime. This concerns how the dominant approaches for understanding reactions to crime and disorder in the social sciences, such as fear of crime and moral panic-based studies, have been focused upon delineating reaction patterns in the aggregate, as opposed to being able to separate out the objective and subjective consequences directly attributable to specific events. To put it another way, there is an analytic gap between 'normal crimes' that elicit little discernible public reaction, and those that seed a widespread condition of 'moral panic'. It is to those crimes that are more than ordinary, but less than the triggers for moral panics, to which the signal crimes construct orients itself (Innes, 2014).

At this juncture, it is sufficient to highlight that what this applied version of the signal crimes perspective was doing was providing a diagnostic lens through which to ascertain the crime and disorder issues that warrant being the focus for Neighbourhood Policing interventions owing to the effects they generate. It was understood that not all crimes and disorders are equal in terms of the harm they induce, and that those functioning as signals to people, sending messages about levels of local security, are different from those that are little more than part of the background 'noise' of urban living.

Co-producing social control

Of the principal components for delivering reassurance policing, it was the idea of co-producing outcomes with partners and the public that police struggled with most. As was intimated in Chapter 1, a defining attribute of all community policing programmes has been an intent to reduce the sense of distance between police and 'policed'. A vast array of partnering, consultation, and collaborative mechanisms have been proposed over the years for accomplishing this, with varying degrees of success (and failure). In seeking to integrate the principles of co-production, the NRPP model was adopting quite a radical approach. For when compared with less intensive modes of partnership and collaborative working, what marks co-production out is its 'end-to-end' quality and attempt to equalize power relations between those engaged in the process. As Innes (2014) describes it, 'true' co-production only occurs when individuals or groups from different backgrounds share the work of: co-defining a problem; co-designing a solution; and, co-delivering this response.

Although it has subsequently been exported to and incorporated into thinking about many public service domains, the notion of 'co-production' was actually first coined by Elinor Ostrom in relation to her work on community policing in the 1970s. Echoing concerns articulated by several other studies of the police from this period, Ostrom and her team found that when police officers spent time in patrol cars and were not so closely involved with the public as occurred when they patrolled on foot, something was missing. They inferred that it was actually the contributions made by the public when interacting directly with police that effectively determined the efficacy of policing services (Boyle and Harris, 2009). Ostrom defined the nature of this relationship as co-production, or:

The process through which inputs used to produce a good or service are contributed by individuals who are not 'in' the same organisation. (Ostrom, 1996)

The NRPP integrated this kind of thinking into its base operating model. This was on the grounds that the nature and range of the problems that were anticipated to be highlighted through the neighbourhood community intelligence collection process outlined above would require engagement with many issues where policing was only part of the 'solution'. Specifically, the intent was that structures would be put in place to enable co-productive working arrangements both with other public service agencies, but also directly with local communities themselves.

This latter aspect is important and has been under-appreciated in much of the commentary on both the NRPP and Neighbourhood Policing. Especially within the NRPP, there was an explicit interest in the interactions between formal and informal social control. Part of the rationale for seeking to reassure communities was that if people are sufficiently confident about their safety, then they are more likely to take responsibility for managing some of the minor infractions of social order (that when they get brought to police attention come to be labelled as antisocial behaviour). The function of policing here is that if the scale or intensity of threat should escalate to a level where informal community regulations and resolutions are insufficient, then there are additional resources to respond. Indeed, this is in part why police presence and visibility is accorded such importance; it provides a symbolic reminder that, should it be needed, formal social control is available to intervene where more informal mechanisms are inadequate.

There are clear analogies here with the literature on collective efficacy. In their much admired and commented upon studies in Chicago, Sampson and Raudenbusch (1999) concluded that, in terms of area level variations in visible crime and disorder incidents, it was the shared willingness and perceived ability of local residents to intervene—what they labelled collective efficacy—that was the key explanatory factor. In terms of the NRPP then, this established two key pathways. How could policing be configured in such a way that formal social control interventions seed and propagate enhanced informal social control capacity? And second, under what conditions and circumstances will communities connect directly with police to co-produce solutions to neighbourhood-level problems and the harms that they are triggering?

However, and as hinted at previously, across the majority of the NRPP sites, police struggled with this concept and its operationalization. The exception to this general pattern were the two sites in Lancashire, where far more progress with this element of the NRPP model was made. This difference partly reflected Lancashire Constabulary's long-standing commitment to and investment in problem-solving during this period.

Uniquely amongst the sixteen NRPP forces, when engaging with local residents, Lancashire gave far more control over to community representatives. For example, in terms of the regular Police and Communities Together (PACT) meetings that they instigated, it was agreed that this would be chaired by an elected community representative rather than a police officer. They also worked hard to involve their local authority partners, so that their problem-solving efforts could be holistic and well-rounded, attacking key issues along multiple vectors. A related and intriguing further innovation was that in the minutes of the meeting, care was taken to ensure that all those at the meeting were assigned actions. Depending upon the nature of the issue or problem selected for attention at a meeting, the responsibilities placed on the community attendees were not necessarily onerous, but they were detailed nonetheless.

Compared with similar meetings observed elsewhere, this more genuinely co-productive approach created a different interaction and dynamic between police and public. There was not the sense that the community representatives were bringing their problems to the meeting, and the police were taking them away to do something about them. Rather, there was an effort to work collaboratively to both 'problem-find' and 'problem-solve'.

There are important implications for the research literature in these findings. Namely, the quality of police–public transactions matter in terms of what, if any, material outcomes transpire from them. The majority of studies (often based upon quantitative data sources) have been sceptical (Herbert, 2006), or at best equivocal (Bullock and Sindall, 2014) about the value and power of community engagement. Viewed from the perspective of the NRPP's qualitative evidence of how such engagement attempts were transacted across a variety of contexts and circumstances, this is not that surprising, given that most struggled or failed. However, not all of them followed this path. A few examples of such efforts were highly productive. These demonstrate that although police organizations may find close engagement and co-production relations with the public difficult, they are possible.

But there is a 'dark-side' to co-production also. One of the reasons that the communities in Lancashire mobilized so well was because of the anger many people felt about the disorder and crime issues they were encountering routinely in the areas where they lived. As a result, a small group of men on one of the estates banded together and started engaging in community safety patrols. Dressed in yellow fluorescent jackets carrying large metal torches, these men were quite assertive and aggressive in their contacts with young people in the area in particular. This is an intriguing example because of how engagement in vigilante-type activities such as this has tended to be attributed to a deficit in police presence. In this instance however, this behaviour formed purportedly 'in support' of the police. It was almost as though the men involved perceived a degree of 'permission' for their patrols from the PACT meeting process, even though, this was never a formally minuted action.

A question remains, however. Why did the integration of co-productive modes of working prove so difficult for most of the forces? Perhaps part of the answer, can be found in Herbert's (2006) study of community policing in Seattle. For he concludes rather pessimistically that the reason why so many community policing programmes have been subject to implementation failures is that the 'weight of expectation' they have for community involvement and participation is simply too much. Given the other demands and commitments on their time, especially in harder pressed neighbourhoods where people are struggling to just get by, community policing just needs more attention and investment than the majority of people can give it.

What happened?

The Home Office-led evaluation of the processes described above was designed to examine the implementation of the programme, capturing data on the enablers and blockers across the sites in terms of adopting the innovative processes. In addition, the evaluation sought to measure the impacts of these new approaches across a range of outcomes that were thought potentially amenable to being influenced. This evaluative effort was structured around comparing results from six of the trial sites with similar data collected from 'matched' control sites elsewhere. For example, after the first twelve months, based upon a telephone survey of local residents it was found that public confidence had increased by 15 per cent in the trial wards and 3 per cent in the control sites.

The additional ten research sites were tracked in terms of their performance across the range of outcome indicators, but were not compared. Table 2.1 below summarizes the key outcome measures identified for the evaluation and the numbers of sites where changes attributable to the programme were detected. In the table a separation is made between areas where statistically measurable changes were identified, and those where any change was non-significant, on the grounds that the former provides stronger evidence of programme effects.

The top four rows in Table 2.1 focus upon indicators associated with crime and perceptions. The next three rows address public attitudes to policing, and the last two, indicators of collective efficacy. Summarizing the data in this way captures how the overarching movements in the data were broadly positive, especially in terms of fear of crime reducing and public confidence in the police rising. That said, there was considerable

Table 2.1 Summary of NRPP Outcome Data

Indicator	Experimental Sites Significant Change (6)	Experimental Sites Not Significant Change (6)	Other Research Sites Positive Change (10)
Recorded Crime	3	3	1
Perceptions of Crime	0	3	7
Perceptions Anti-social Behaviour	1	3	7
Fear of Crime	2	3	10
Public Confidence in Policing	4	1	7
Police Visibility	3	2	9
Perceptions of Police Engagement	2	4	8
Perceived Community Cohesion	1	1	0
Trust in Neighbours	1	3	1

inter-site variation in terms of what effects the reassurance model induced.

In terms of explaining these results, we can infer that the implementation of the reassurance policing processes and systems worked in different ways in different sites. In some of the high crime and high disorder communities, it was assertively targeting signal crimes and signal disorders that was most impactive. By dealing with these problems, improvements in neighbourhood security were manufactured. Whereas in other less troubled areas, it appears that the process of engaging community members and taking their concerns seriously was sufficient to improve perceptions of the area and confidence in the police. Cutting across these variations, the Home Office evaluation data certainly suggested an association between the quality of implementation achieved and the kinds of outcomes delivered across the sites.

As well as considering the aggregate patterns, it is also worth briefly highlighting some of the more intriguing results achieved, as these illuminate important facets of both the community situations and policing processes. For example, in Brunswick ward in Lancashire, a comparatively deprived area with high levels of drug dependency amongst the resident population, over the two years of NRPP, the police recorded crime rate rose by 28 per cent, but the majority of those surveyed thought it had actually declined (Morris, 2006). This seems to reflect how enhanced police engagement with residents resulted in more crime being reported to police than previously, whilst simultaneously, by focusing their efforts explicitly upon the signal crimes and disorders, the police created an impression of improving security.

Ultimately, the Home Office evaluation concluded that:

Taken together, the evidence presented ... provides a consistent picture which shows that positive change in key outcome indicators in the trial sites, such as crime, perceptions of anti-social behaviour, feelings after dark and public confidence in the police, was attributable to the National Reassurance Policing Programme. (Tuffin et al., 2006: 93)

Because it was based upon a relatively robust research design, the findings and this conclusion gave confidence to those shaping national policy that it would be worth investing in scaling this approach to a national level.

From reassurance to Neighbourhood Policing

The move from Reassurance to Neighbourhood Policing that started in 2005/6 involved several subtle but important shifts. The nature of these are partially captured by the change of terminology. As noted previously, Neighbourhood Policing was felt to have a greater 'common-sense' resonance than the notion of 'reassurance', by officials in the Home Office and Cabinet Office. But beneath the surface this also signalled other alterations. Notably, reassurance was an outcome that was being sought, whereas 'neighbourhood' was the principal unit of delivery. Perhaps more significantly, Neighbourhood Policing integrated a more explicit interest in crime reduction. As noted previously, with the NRPP, crime reduction was deliberately not set as a primary outcome—albeit there was an expectation that crime would fall if the other outcomes were correctly aligned. A further difference between reassurance and Neighbourhood Policing models was a drift away from the more structured and systematic processes used in the former to diagnose the presence of signal crimes and disorders that had been at the core of the NRPP.

This greater conceptual and methodological looseness is conveyed in how Neighbourhood Policing was being described in a Home Office report from this time:

Neighbourhood policing is an approach that seeks to increase contact between the police and the public in defined local geographic areas in order to make the work of the police more responsive to the needs of local people. (Quinton and Morris, 2008)

Compared with the level of prescription associated with the three interlocking principal elements of the NRPP, the lack of definition here is striking. But equally important is how the Association of Chief Police Officers (2006) was working with a concept that was even broader, involving:

• The provision of a consistent presence of dedicated neighbourhood teams that are visible, accessible, skilled, knowledgeable, and familiar to the community.
• Feeding back intelligence-led identification of community concerns.

- Encouraging joint action and problem solving with the community and other local partners, improving the local environment and quality of life within the community.

It is perhaps unsurprising that different forces ended up implementing very different mechanisms under the auspices of Neighbourhood Policing.

Given the diversity of areas and communities involved, any model had to allow sufficient flex for situational variation. However, in some ways this was problematic. For instance, what was meant by 'neighbourhood' was never defined. Forces were able to develop their own definitions of what, for their purposes, constituted a neighbourhood and many of them differed quite substantively. They also departed significantly from what many ordinary members of the public would understand as neighbourhoods, covering much larger geographic territories. We will return to the issue of what is a neighbourhood in more detail in Chapter 3. It is indicative however of the ways in which, although the Neighbourhood Policing Programme was based upon a core set of 'ingredients', the 'recipe' followed in terms of actually blending them together was decided on a largely force-by-force basis.

In London, they continued with the NRPP approach of using electoral wards as surrogates for neighbourhoods. Underpinned by a significant uplift in funding, the Metropolitan Police Service implemented what became known as the '1,2,3' model. This referred to how every ward across London was assigned a Safer Neighbourhoods policing team comprising 1 sergeant, 2 police constables, and 3 Police Community Support Officers (PCSOs). They were largely removed from response policing tasks and were explicitly focused upon community engagement, problem-solving local crime and disorder problems, and providing a visible policing presence. It is important to emphasize that this was not a universally applied approach. In many other parts of the country, the police-defined neighbourhoods were far larger, and the dedicated Neighbourhood Policing assets smaller. Indeed, it was not a system that lasted that long in London. This reflected how, from a relatively early stage, questions were being asked about the differences in workload and demand between different policing teams, depending upon the nature of their area. It was therefore suggested that it might be more appropriate for areas with high crime to retain an increased quantity of dedicated neighbourhood policing officers when compared with other more stable and less stressed localities. Unsurprisingly, as public spending austerity began to be felt across the public sector from 2011 onwards, there was a rapid shift to the latter approach.

As intimated in the discussion of London above, the 'on the ground' delivery of the services most likely to 'touch' citizens were typically undertaken by a mixed team of uniformed police officers and PCSOs. Indeed, the ability of the police service across England and Wales to supply dedicated Neighbourhood Policing services was fundamentally enabled by the significant uplift in the number of PCSOs within forces that occurred between 2003 and 2007. By 2007/8 an additional 16,000 PCSOs had been recruited in England and Wales, supported by a central fund made available by the Home Office. These officers assumed a central role in the public-facing aspects of how Neighbourhood Policing was configured and delivered.

In terms of the roles and duties performed by these PCSOs and their supervision by police constables and sergeants within 'Neighbourhood Teams', important guidance was issued in 2006 by the National Centre for Policing Excellence. With clear trace echoes of the NRPP, this document reasserted the importance of foot patrol, community engagement, and problem-solving as the key delivery mechanisms for effective policing at a neighbourhood level. It elaborated these themes in terms of 'ten key principles of Neighbourhood Policing'. Quinton and Morris (2008) summarized some of the more significant of these principles as follows:

- Neighbourhood policing is an organisational strategy for police, partners and the public to work together to solve problems, enhance neighbourhood conditions and increase feelings of security;
- It should be integrated with other policing functions (such as response, protective services and investigations);
- It uses the National Intelligence Model as the basis of deployment decisions;
- It requires rigorous performance management of teams and individuals.

In the remaining chapters we will develop far more detailed accounts of these themes and what they involved.

Conclusion: Neighbourhood Policing as a 'dirty concept'

In telling the story of how reassurance policing was translated into Neighbourhood Policing, and how the latter was in some ways an 'edited and revised' version of the former, this discussion touches upon a deeper theme about policy development and the relationship between theoretical policing models and what gets implemented in practice. For the history of policing research is replete with evaluative critiques and commentaries that suggest that because practice has departed from the theoretical precepts of an orienting position, then this implies some form of implementation or theory failure. It would certainly be possible to adopt such a narrative for telling the story of Neighbourhood Policing, especially given the struggles to adduce robust evidence of its outcome effects.

An alternative framing, however, might be to suggest that the fact similar issues are replicated across different programmes implies something about the complexities and challenges of doing things in the real world. Maybe expectations about what theoretical and research-driven models look like when implemented need to be adjusted. Cast in this light, both reassurance policing and Neighbourhood Policing can be construed as 'dirty concepts', in that when they were put into practice, they departed in particular ways from the 'pure' theory that stimulated them in the first place. But rather than understanding such muddying and tarnishing of the 'pure' theoretical constructs as an unalloyed problem, it may be that this 'dirtying up' of the concepts is part of the price that has to be paid for research informing practice. Pragmatic compromises and the 'bending and stretching' of key tenets to accommodate the contingencies of real life are necessary conditions for engaging with, what are after all, often complex social problems. Positioning both reassurance policing and Neighbourhood Policing as 'dirty concepts' in this way certainly affords unique insights into how they were designed and delivered, and how they evolved and adapted.

As an experimental field trial, the NRPP was subject to fairly high levels of intellectual and practical support, with robust compliance mechanisms seeking to regulate how it was implemented. But even with such support wrapped around it, the evaluation

data clearly articulate how not all of the participating police forces were able to integrate all of the components equally
well, nor were similar outcomes achieved. There are a number
of reasons for this. In some of the trial site areas this had to do
with the particular history, culture, and structures of the police
force concerned. For example, generally those organizations
with a longer history of commitment to community policing and
problem-solving performed better in implementing the principal
elements of the NRPP model. In other localities, the struggles to
fully implement could be attributed to the socio-economic and/or
cultural make-up of the neighbourhoods and communities where
the new policing processes were being embedded.

With the decision to scale up and roll out nationally,
Neighbourhood Policing was an even more 'loosely' formulated
construct than its immediate predecessor. This was in order to
allow for adoption by different forces so that they could integrate it within their wider structures and processes. In this sense,
Neighbourhood Policing was the archetypal 'dirty concept', in
that any notion of defining a 'purist' model was sacrificed to enable adoption and implementation. As such, whilst it has become
commonplace amongst senior police officers and policy makers to
talk about 'Neighbourhood Policing' as if it were a clearly demarcated and stable entity, this is misleading.

Certainly from a citizens' perspective, depending where you
were in the country, your experiences of Neighbourhood Policing
will have been very different. As such, it is probably more accurate
to talk about there being varieties of Neighbourhood Policing,
as opposed to conceiving of it as a tightly defined model. It is
better understood as constituting a 'theme and variations' type ar-
rangement. This is the approach we adopt in the remaining chapters where we interrogate specific aspects of how Neighbourhood
Policing work has been performed by officers.

3

Neighbourhood as a Policing Delivery Unit

Although there are notable exceptions to the overarching pattern, the great majority of policing agencies define themselves territorially. Their identities and the boundaries for their responsibilities tend to be connected to particular spaces and places, whether these be national, regional, or more locally oriented. This is a tradition that Neighbourhood Policing self-evidently sustains, or perhaps more properly, 'reinvents'. As outlined in the preceding chapters, what Neighbourhood Policing effectively did was to blend together elements from several established models and locate them within a community policing ethos. Significantly however, rather than pivoting around the concept of community to orient its service delivery, it adopted a spatial unit of 'neighbourhood' as its base.

In this chapter we want to interrogate what is meant by 'neighbourhood' in the context of Neighbourhood Policing. That is, in 'mobilizing' neighbourhood as an adjective to define a particular approach to policing, what conceptual work is it intended to do? What benefits and disadvantages does organizing policing around such a unit afford? In contrast to all the other chapters in this book which focus upon policing, this one is more concerned with the connected concept of neighbourhood. After all, it is an idea that has a considerable heritage in social science. Specifically, our concern is with understanding how and why, when implementing Neighbourhood Policing, different police forces arrived at markedly different answers to the fundamental question of 'what is a neighbourhood?'

In pursuing this line of enquiry, empirical material is introduced to evidence that police definitions of a neighbourhood may bear little relation to how citizens perceive the boundaries, frontiers, and identities that distinguish the area in which they live. As is

Neighbourhood Policing. Martin Innes, Colin Roberts, Trudy Lowe, and Helen Innes, Oxford University Press (2020). © Martin Innes, Colin Roberts, Trudy Lowe, and Helen Innes.
DOI: 10.1093/oso/9780198783213.003.0001

elucidated, this disjuncture has the capacity to induce certain tensions between police and communities. Elaborating this approach, the chapter highlights a series of examples suggesting that patterns of crime, and in particular the occurrence of high-profile signal crimes, can themselves have material and long-lasting effects upon how people perceive and conceive of their neighbourhood. This finding may be of wider interest to the urban studies literature, where the 'neighbourhood effects' position has acquired considerable influence. For adherents of this perspective, socio-economic and demographic characteristics of local areas 'structure' the prevalence and distribution of social problems that present therein. By contrast, our data allows us to attend to how the occurrence of key problems and the 'collective memories' and reputations that form around a place, influence residents' perceptions of what, and who, is and is not, perceived to be a part of a defined neighbourhood.

The chapter commences by setting out some of the different ways in which neighbourhoods have been defined and how, as a concept, it has been used by different police forces to operationalize their Neighbourhood Policing approaches. We then describe the methodology that was designed for capturing citizen-defined neighbourhoods and introduce some empirical data on this. We conclude the chapter by bringing these empirically grounded findings into contact with the research literature on neighbourhoods to consider their respective implications.

The idea of neighbourhood

The idea of neighbourhood in social science is not new. Empirically its significance can be traced back to the Chicago school of urban sociology in the 1920s and in particular the seminal work 'The City' by Park and Burgess, published in 1925. The authors documented long-standing social forces at work in driving processes of urbanization, resulting in the structure and formation of US cities. In doing so, they considered how changes associated with transport, employment, and commerce impacted on smaller, traditional units of neighbourhood, both physically and socially, within and between people who traditionally lived in close and long-lasting proximity to each other.

Almost intuitively then, 'neighbourhood' is conceived as being a relatively small unit, smaller and more discrete in structure than its often-interchangeable partner term 'community'. Nonetheless, empirical studies of community life often incorporate measures of 'neighbourliness' within them to explore social and cultural aspects of local life, deploying them as a barometer of collective health and vitality. According to Burgess (1925), both community and neighbourhood result from the same three key social forces: ecological, cultural, and political. The principal difference between them being more a hierarchical one: neighbourhoods can be conceptualized as local districts within a community and community itself nests within zones of urban growth, namely the city. This hierarchical or 'nested' concept of neighbourhood is shared by others (Russell and Ward, 1982; Hunter, 1979) and its translation allows for residents of a neighbourhood to be part of multiple, overlapping communities (Guest and Lee, 1983).

The fluidity and vulnerability of both neighbourhoods and communities have been associated with urban change. The pessimistic sense of a 'loss of community' has become a widespread and recurring refrain that generations of social researchers interested in urban life have attended to. The deterioration of local ties and associational life has been linked to a variety of detrimental outcomes for citizens, including poorer health, well-being, and crime (Putnam, 2000). Albeit as a partial counterweight, the positive accent given to local ties and their causal role in determining a range of outcomes has been critiqued as being premised upon an overly romanticized view of the past. It is also evidenced that cities, towns, and neighbourhoods are not static units, but ones that are created, change, and evolve over time. Sectors of a city, for example, may take on the character and qualities of their inhabitants and come to be recognized as localities with sentiments, traditions, and histories of their own.

In essence, the characteristics ascribed to a neighbourhood vary according to whether the primary interest concerns a locality's (subjective) identity, its geographical and urban form, or its practical application as a unit of decision making. This means it is difficult, if not impossible, to give a single uniform definition of neighbourhood appropriate for all that it is held to concern and affect. To illustrate this, and to begin to tie the neighbourhood concept more closely with Neighbourhood Policing, the next section focuses on its recent export and translation into public policy and service delivery within England and Wales.

Neighbourhood public service delivery

In recent decades, 'neighbourhood' has become an increasingly important concept for public service delivery in the United Kingdom. It was given especial impetus by the New Labour government's agenda of 'new localism', which began in 1997 and continued throughout their terms of office. The strategy sought ways of devolving policy decision making to a more local level and, unlike traditional efforts to promote localism, retained a role for central government in driving forward local change. It also took a wider interpretation of 'local' than simply local authority, in part because it incorporated the notion of a 'community' and its local services, including the police.

As a consequence, area-based community initiatives helped define many facets of public-facing services funding and delivery arrangements around this time, from Neighbourhood Policing to Health Action Zones (Judge et al., 1999) and national programmes of neighbourhood management and renewal in areas of poverty and deprivation (Lupton et al., 2013). These nationally conceived, locally delivered programmes became a pivotal part of manufacturing enhanced forms of local governance, for which Lowndes and Sullivan (2008) identify four predominant rationales: the empowerment of citizens and communities (the civic rationale); partnership to take a holistic approach to an area (social); government through new forms of representation and participation (political); and management in terms of more effective local service delivery (economic).

Although the aforementioned policies and initiatives predated Neighbourhood Policing, the vision at the end of the 1990s and start of the 2000s was to tackle the adverse outcomes associated with worst-off neighbourhoods, providing more equitable local public services and thereby halting the cycle of deprivation and social exclusion. The stated intention was that 'all neighbourhoods should be free of fear' and to eliminate 'neighbourhoods where so many people's number one priority is to move out' (Social Exclusion Unit, 2001: 24).

Policing has not been exempted from these imperatives and trajectories of development towards more local governance and accountability. In addition to the establishment of a neighbourhood model of policing delivery, government formalized local leadership roles in policing through the establishment of elected Police and Crime Commissioners in 2001, and in some areas of England there exist directly elected mayors (Stoker, 2004). These 'catalytic leaders' (Sullivan and Skelcher, 2002) were positioned with the intent that they should provide critical oversight and accountability for operational leadership within existing institutional arrangements such as the Council Leader, the Chief Executive, or the Neighbourhood Manager (Goss, 2005), in order to drive forward the pursuit of improved outcomes at a neighbourhood level.

The traction acquired by these logics in public policy generally, and policing in particular, has been achieved despite a lack of definition and consensus about what precisely constitutes a neighbourhood, coupled with the absence of a coherent, agreed upon methodology for calculating the size and boundaries of individual neighbourhoods. In practice and entirely pragmatically, service deliverers in many areas have tended to operationalize 'administrative' neighbourhoods to guide and steer their work, grounded in a variety of administrative datasets and understandings, most typically the electoral ward (a local authority area used for electoral purposes). Other alternatives utilized for these purposes have included statistically derived spatial units, such as: Census Output Areas (OA) in England and Wales; Data Zones in Scotland; and in the United States, Census tracts. To understand the approximation of neighbourhood these different approaches provide, it is necessary to consider how they are derived from Census statistics.

Census OAs, published by the Office for National Statistics, represent small-area statistics from the UK Census (replacing more aggregated Enumeration Districts post 1991). OAs, constructed for comparative statistical purposes from eight postcode units, are purposively designed to have similar population sizes (the recommended size is 125 households) and in England and Wales to be as socially homogenous as possible based on tenure of household and dwelling type. OAs are themselves grouped to calculate Super Output Areas. This latter unit was introduced by the UK government as stable and consistent small area data became made widely accessible via the recently defunct Neighbourhood Statistics (NeSS) website. The Super OA is comprised of three hierarchical layers: 'lower', 'middle', and 'upper' that fit with an electoral ward boundary, and may ultimately supersede electoral wards as an official means of reporting statistics for local areas.

The Lower Super Output Area (LSOA) is a statistical geography commonly used to report on local area multiple deprivation in England and Wales. As an estimate of what this means in terms of defining a neighbourhood unit, there exist more than 32,000 LSOAs in England and 1,900 in Wales post the 2011 Census. Each contains between 400 and 1,200 households. The definition of a 'deprived neighbourhood' from these geographic criteria represents a focus for public policy intervention and action, giving rise to a variety of forms of neighbourhood governance to achieve a range of purposes. For example, from 2001 until very recently in Wales, Community First represented a national programme to tackle poverty and support vulnerable people in 'clusters' identified as being among the 10 per cent most deprived areas on the Welsh Index of Multiple Deprivation at LSOA level (National Assembly for Wales, 2017).

In the United States, the US Census Bureau area statistics equivalent to a neighbourhood are 'Census tracts' of populations between 2,500 and 8,000 residents. Whilst they follow visible, identifiable features (e.g. main roads, waterways, and streets), they do not always cohere with city boundaries and can be subject to change over time. Large-scale neighbourhood research in the United States has a well-established approach of combining tract-level data on crime with socio-demographic characteristics, most notably in the city of Chicago. The 2000 National Neighbourhood Crime Study (NNCS) brought together US tract-level data on crime and socio-demographic indicators such as race and social class for a representative sample of ninety-one large cities, with the stated purpose of investigating sources of crime within different communities (Peterson and Krivo, 2010).

From even this brief overview, it is possible to surmise that there is a lack of consensus about the best way to define and measure a geographic unit for public policy purposes. In England and Wales, for example, it is entirely possible for residents in an area to interact with *Neighbourhood* Policing Teams, *Community* Health Boards, and *Local* Education Boards. Moreover, such differences in the definition and application of statistical geography matter both materially and symbolically. Labelling an area 'deprived' for instance, might itself influence or shape the decisions and behaviours of both residents and outsiders alike in respect of it. They can also induce complexities and construct barriers in terms of how different local public service providers work together. For example, on multiple occasions during the research programme, the researchers observed situations where Neighbourhood Policing Team officers were having to attend several meetings with partner agencies about the same problem, purely because their organizational boundaries were not aligned, and as such police needed co-operation from more than one partner team.

Such considerations notwithstanding, what is absent from a primarily physical conceptualization of small areas or neighbourhoods is their subjective or perceptual attributes. A different approach to neighbourhood studies is to focus less on how they appear geographically from the outside, and more on how they are experienced from the inside (Brower, 1996). Put simply, adopting a more subjective perspective puts the meaning of neighbourhood to the people who live there at the forefront of inquiry, the area it covers for them, the boundaries they mark, and their perceptions of place and sense of security therein. This is based on an appreciation that, whilst we can group together small geographies based on statistical similarities in their measurable characteristics and proximity to each other, this approach does not necessarily cohere with how people think and behave where they live. To try and understand what this might add methodologically and empirically, the next section introduces the concept of a 'self-defined neighbourhood'.

Self-defined neighbourhoods

The previous section suggested that the kinds of 'administrative' constructs of neighbourhood devised and utilized by police and their public service partners may not cohere with the ideas of those residing in, or passing through, these areas on a day-to-day basis. Meaning matters and without it, there is a risk of lapsing into what is termed 'environmental determinism' or the 'ecological fallacy'. This involves the social and cultural aspects making up the social life of a neighbourhood being inferred by reference to physical attributes alone, with the consequence that individual action and behaviour are reduced to a product of, or response to, place (Golledge, 1987). If we accept the premise that neighbourhood is 'more than' geography, it only becomes place sensitive when imbued with information about its relative location; the patterns of its streets; and the social significance of buildings, perceptions, and understandings by people who live there, or attend to it in some way.

The centrality of geography in the constitution of neighbourhoods has been widely challenged as a necessary but not sufficient part of its definition. Blokland (2003) argues that neighbourhood is a geographically circumscribed, built environment, which people use practically, but its boundaries are also symbolic. Others assert that physical geography and place have a significance, both at an individual level and as a force of its own with detectable and independent effects on social life (Werlen, 1993).

A more fruitful line of enquiry then is to try and marry both perspectives and recognize the 'double construction' of neighbourhoods, encompassing both the physical and symbolic elements of a place (Soja, 1996). Large-scale surveys have attempted to do this by asking people to subjectively define their neighbourhood area based on a pre-set physical distance. For instance, Kearns and Parkinson (2001) created scales of neighbourhood, the smallest of which—the 'home area'—was proscribed as five to ten minutes' walk from home. Brower (1996) made an additional distinction between the home area (the residents' idea of home) and the neighbourhood area, the latter being identifiable from a group of home areas that share a commonly defined residential area.

Method

Our process of interrogating what can be considered 'natural' or 'self-defined neighborhoods' is based upon the kinds of in-depth interview methodologies described in more detail in Chapters 6 and 7. As a part of these interactions, a sample of members of the public in both South Wales and Sutton were asked to plot what they thought of as 'their neighbourhood', and any other areas that they perceived possessed distinct identities, on to digital maps. To do this, they drew on to the maps the boundaries of any such spaces, thus providing a record of the physical footprint of what neighbourhood(s) existed for them. They were also asked if the areas they identified had particular names, or if there were any additional neighbourhoods or areas that they would definitely not visit.

This method is not without precedent and builds on studies of neighbourhood that have used cognitive mapping techniques.

Environmental psychologists Downs and Stea (1977: 6) defined the process of cognitive mapping as: 'a mental process to come to grips with and comprehend the world around us'. In a research setting, it represents a directed, interactive process of translating spatial environmental information into mental representation in such a way that it foregrounds what is functionally important to people. For example, routes associated with peoples' regular or routine activities that reflect their immersion in, and movement around, their environment. The cartographic skeleton is therefore imbued with meaning, including meaning about safety and risk. Not only might it tell us about behaviours such as avoidance of certain areas, it can also help illustrate how people make distinctions between 'safe or dangerous' or 'ours or theirs' when thinking about their neighbourhood.

Findings

Following completion of the interviews, the resulting data from each individual account was layered on top of each other and an algorithm used to calculate where the boundaries depicted by different respondents were aligned with each other. From this process it was possible to establish that people's conceptions of neighbourhood frequently vary in size and shape, a finding shared with other studies that have used cognitive mapping (Ladd, 1970; Lee, 1964).

The concept of drawing 'neighbourhood' was salient and intuitive to people, however, and whilst no two mental maps were exactly the same (since no two people react to the environment in precisely the same manner), it is possible to discern statistically significant differences in neighbourhood between social groups, what Glaster (2001) terms 'generality', or the degree to which individuals' neighbourhoods vary by different attributes. Data from 693 people living in Cardiff, Wales showed that younger people (age twenty-one and under) had, on average, neighbourhoods larger in size and perimeter than older age groups up to the age of sixty-five years. Between sixty-six and seventy (a time that often coincides with retirement age in males), neighbourhood size increased and was comparable with the younger age group (Orford and Lee, 2014). Presumably this is associated with these older respondents having more time to spend in their neighbourhood, thereby acquiring enhanced familiarity with it.

Of additional significance was how the visualization techniques utilized in analysing these data made evident many areas where there were 'fuzzy boundaries' to neighbourhoods. Fuzzy boundaries are indicative of low 'accordance' between neighbourhoods for different individuals living or working in close proximity to each other (Glaster, 2001). In other words, there was not a great deal of consensus between people in respect of where one neighbourhood ended and another began.

However, whilst this was true, there were also some localities where 'bright line boundaries' were evident. In these cases, almost everyone interviewed agreed that 'this area was different from that area'. Oftentimes this would be attributable to the presence of a geographic, physical feature such as a river or an arterial road. Intriguingly however, this did not explain the presence of all such 'bright line boundaries'. Indeed, it was in areas with distinct crime problems that these kinds of neighbourhood distinctions were often evident.

To digest the significance of this finding, it is an appropriate juncture at which to briefly revisit reasons why undertaking an investigation of the nature of neighbourhoods from a citizen's point of view might occasion several advantages for policing policy and practice, including:

- Establishing a more meaningful unit for public services to report their activity on so that it 'makes sense' to local communities, thus increasing their engagement with providers.
- Providing a framework for positioning community engagement events in ways most likely to attract local citizen participation. This is hypothesized on the basis that people are most likely to attend neighbourhood engagement events if they are actually taking place in what they understand as 'their neighbourhood'.
- Being useful in helping to anticipate how 'fear' will travel in the aftermath of major and serious crime events, thus aiding community impact management efforts to minimize harm and distress.

The discovery of bright line boundaries with high degrees of consensus in areas with crime problems raises some more profound questions about what they connote and mean. It is this issue that we seek to take forward herein.

Figure 3.1 below provides a representation of the data collected through the neighbourhood mapping process for a small area of

Coincident Neighbourhood Boundaries

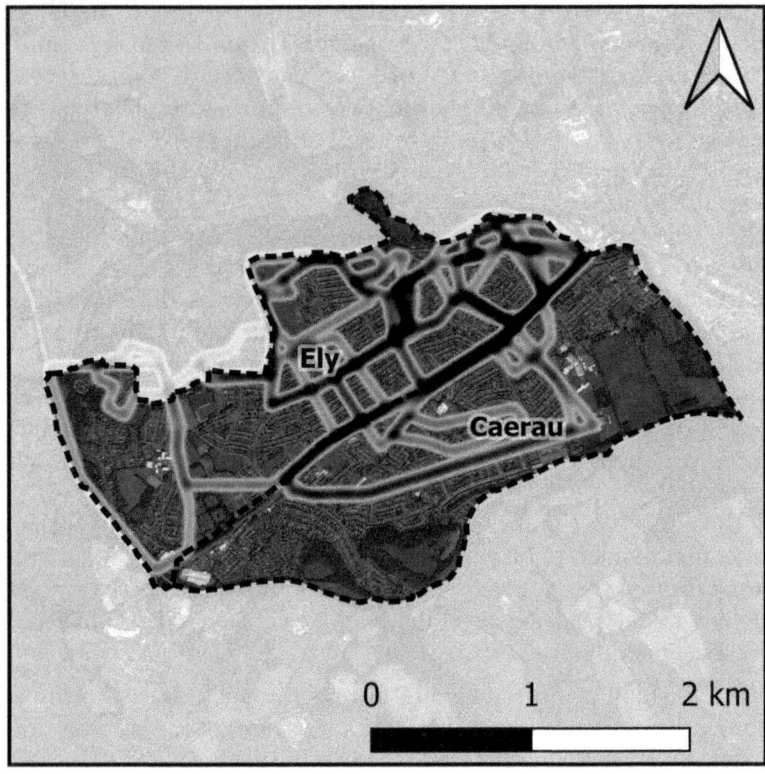

Legend

▬▬▬ Coincident Neighbourhood Boundaries

⌐▄⌐▄⌐ Ward Boundary

Figure 3.1 Self-defined Neighbourhoods Showing Bright Line Boundaries for Cardiff West Electoral Ward, South Wales

Map data: Google, Maxar Technologies; Image © 2019 Maxar Technologies.

Cardiff. The physical area in question is about 2 sq km and the results from the overlaid respondent maps perfectly depict what we mean by 'bright line' boundaries.

As can be seen in Figure 3.1, there were particular areas where nearly everyone interviewed was in agreement about the frontiers between different neighbourhoods within that one electoral ward. Visually, one can discern about eight separate neighbourhoods within the ward area. What such lines depict is how local people encode finely grained distinctions and identities between these areas and their residents. People define their senses of identity and belonging both in terms of who they are, but also 'who they are not', and it is these kinds of cognitive and affective processes of categorization that such lines help to shed light on and physically map out. Yet not all areas of Cardiff had such clearly demarcated neighbourhood boundaries resulting from the mapping exercise. This raises the question 'how can we explain why they occurred in some areas, but not others?'

To try and answer that question in respect of this particular area of Cardiff, it is relevant that during the 1980s it was the scene of some high-profile public disorder, and subsequently it has remained a relatively high crime area. One potential explanation is that this has become inscribed into both the collective memories that people have about the area, and how they think about their relations with each other. In effect, the fact that most residents identified multiple, strongly defined neighbourhoods in the area concerned may be an indicator of a lack of community cohesion, described as a kind of 'social glue' that binds people of different backgrounds together within an area, making them more tolerant and understanding of each other (OECD, 2011). Support for this explanation was certainly reflected in some of the qualitative commentary elicited from respondents as they were engaged in the mapping process.

This was not the only locality where these sorts of patterns were observed. In another area of Cardiff, the neighbourhood mapping process showed that there was an area where lots of people said they did not like to go or tended to avoid. It transpired, from interviews with a couple of long-term residents of the area, that about a decade earlier a quite brutal murder had taken place. As a result, it had acquired a reputation as a risky area where bad things happen. It appeared from the interviews that many younger people, and those who had more recently moved into the area, did not know precisely why this was a 'bad area' even though they perceived it poorly.

A similar process associated with an area picking up a 'sticky reputation' occurred in fieldwork conducted in Surrey. During the interviews with residents, a number mentioned a rape that was purported to have happened some time previously. For instance, one woman told how she,

… would never consider running along the towpath of the canal 'coz of rape or sexual assault. (Ash213)

This same area was repeatedly identified as a location actively avoided by locals. Some residents were able to articulate a reason for this avoidance behaviour, but for many others, their concerns were more nebulous and less well justified. For example, the following account was provided by someone who did not live in the immediate neighbourhood, but nearby, and it captures how the occurrence of this incident played into her perceptions of the area concerned:

See I've heard of rape, that was just in Ash Vale … I think that was down by Ash Wharf down near the canal. It's just the canal, everything happens on the canal, you get attacks on the canal. (Ash218)

What was especially striking about this particular example, was that the claim of a rape turned out not to be true. According to another resident interviewed, and validated by several others:

What happened was a young lady from one of the barracks, I'm not quite sure but I think it is Purbright, had been in Aldershot on a night out. She got a little bit amorous with somebody and then she basically cried rape and said it had happened in the village. Why she picked our village is beyond me, but there were police around for quite a while … At that point it was fear. I have no other way of putting it … I never felt intimidated, then that happened, and it was like it can happen and can happen in the village … You start thinking well it can happen. (Ash 214)

Despite this being a false allegation, it had seeped into how many local people were constructing the neighbourhood's identity as a troublesome location where 'bad things' were liable to happen.

Taken together what these examples suggest is *how* the occurrence of crime can have a powerful influence in terms of shaping collective perceptions of a neighbourhood and its reputation. The significance of this is that it effectively inverts the orthodox social science position on neighbourhood effects and how the condition of (objectively defined) local areas shapes the kinds of social problems that present in them (Sampson, 2012). The position of Sampson and others is based on well-established empirical observations that a number of crime (and other) detrimental environmental outcomes aggregate at the neighbourhood level, and can be predicted by neighbourhood level characteristics, such as the concentration of poverty, racial segregation, and residential stability. 'Neighbourhood effects' therefore symbolize that the neighbourhood construct is not just a summation of individual behaviour, but itself has features that statistically correlate with individual behaviour and outcomes in that place.

Our position, based not on statistical geography and survey data but on the coherence of subjectively defined neighbourhoods and qualitative interviews, suggests that both the immediate and long-lasting imprint crime can have on local public consciousness may itself discern how and why people construct their neighbourhoods in the way that they do. Just like neighbourhood effects, this can ultimately find expression in people's individual behaviours, and account for both stability and change in public perceptions of neighbourhood.

A number of environmental criminologists have applied the cognitive mapping technique to make inferences about the 'rationality' of people's crime and fear of crime. Brantingham et al. (1977) and Pelfrey and Pelfrey (1995) both observe that the symbolic meanings people ascribe to an area mean that they can, at times, act in a way that appears to depart from what might objectively appear 'normal', or rational, in that setting. It underscores that perceptions are a powerful force guiding behaviour.

Kaplan and Kaplan (1982) give three examples of public perceptions about areas which go some way to explaining why they often don't match up with the broader geographic distribution of crime. First, the less well known an area is to someone, the more likely negative connotations will be ascribed to it. Second, people have a tendency to rate their own cities or neighbourhoods as safer than others. Third, local environmental perceptions are grounded in early processes of socialization. For example, women may be socialized to be more fearful of strange environments than men (Maccoby, 1966).

Rengert and Pelfrey (1998) found perceptual differences applied equally to a sample of police cadet recruits in a US city that they knew well, as it did to a sample of students. Using research techniques that included cognitive mapping and knowledge of the area in 1994 (a time when this area was generally viewed as unsafe), the focus was on how preformed opinions or 'faulty impressions' about the characteristics of an area impacted upon the way cadets perceived problem neighbourhoods. The cadets perceived the centre of the city to be safest with a ridge of decline in either direction moving away from it, but this was directly opposed to the known spatial distribution of violent crime. Perceptions of neighbourhood ethnic concentration also had an impact on their perceptions of relative safety, with predominately white areas viewed as safer than minority ethnic ones. This and other studies (Newman, 1972) raise the suggestion that preconceived ideas of an area among police workers has the potential to impact on how they might approach community problems.

However 'faulty' or divergent from spatial indicators of crime neighbourhood perceptions may be, they are powerful in contouring both public and policing behaviours. Perceptions may drive territorial social control, police patrol boundaries, and reputational ascriptions in ways that may function to restrict access in terms of 'who and what belongs where'. There is also some evidence that perceptions of a dangerous neighbourhood increase poor mental health outcomes amongst adolescents, with greater rates of depression, anxiety, and defiant disorder (Aneshensel and Sucoff, 1996). These are all issues discussed below in relation to a specific small area case study carried out during the development phase of the Neighbourhood Policing approach in England.

A case study of policing tensions and cohesion

All of the themes and issues rehearsed in the preceding sections were brought together during fieldwork conducted in Oldham, Greater Manchester, as part of the National Reassurance Policing Programme (see Chapter 2). The area concerned had been the scene of significant public disorder a few years prior to the start of this research, namely the 'Oldham riots' in 2001. These disturbances were the first in a wave of social unrest in the summer of that year that spread to nearby Bradford, Leeds, and Burnley. All were reported by the mass media as the culmination of longstanding ethnic tensions between groups in the local white and South Asian-Muslim communities, with UK General Election results at that time recording the biggest polling success ever for the British National Party (BNP) in Oldham (Tetteh, 2009).

The most violent conflict centred on the Glodwick area of Oldham, situated in St. Mary's ward, south east of the centre. This area was home to a sizeable Pakistani community (38 per cent) accommodated in post war, back-to-back housing, not far from the predominately white occupants of the nearby St. Mary's estate. These two areas were well understood locally as being highly segregated along ethnic lines, with the former having a reputation among local white people as a 'no-go' area for fear of racially motivated attack (Vasagar et al., 2001). In May 2001, up to 500 Asian youths fought against riot police, throwing petrol bombs and other missiles at a local pub and newspaper headquarters, injuring at least twenty people. Shortly after these events, the government's 2001 'Cantle Report' highlighted the 'depth of polarisation' that existed between segregated communities in and around Oldham, and warned of further violence if government, police, and community leaders could not address this problem and facilitate more positive interaction between groups of residents.

It was against this backdrop that fieldworkers arrived in St. Mary's three years later and interviewed thirty-four residents (twenty-two of whom identified as white and ten as Asian, two did not provide this information) about their perceptions of neighbourhood, crime, and security. These in-depth data were augmented by a telephone survey of another 300 local people. Not surprisingly, the ethnically divided neighbourhoods that had erupted into violence in 2001 remained deeply ingrained in 2004, both physically and symbolically. When asked to map their neighbourhood, there was no overlap between the 'white' and 'Asian' neighbourhoods with clear boundaries demarcated by local residents to distinguish them.

The area as a whole was, and continues to be, troubled by the effects of significant material deprivation. Oldham was cited as the most deprived ward in England according to the Office for National Statistics, with 65 per cent of its areas in the most deprived 20 per cent of small areas (ONS, 2016). Within that area, distinct neighbourhoods have their own crime profile. In the ethnically 'white' neighbourhood in and around St. Mary's estate, drugs were a prolific problem associated with young males and were perceived by residents as the driver of many other criminal and disorderly acts in that locality. Some housing here had acquired a reputation as a 'rough estate' because of high residential turnover in council-owned properties in ill-repair. Hence, even within the white neighbourhood, there were areas that symbolized danger to people and characteristics ascribed to people living there as 'uneducated', 'unemployed', and 'lazy'.

In the Glodwick neighbourhood where the Asian population were concentrated, hate crime, verbal abuse, and harassment were commonplace. Its manifestation as street graffiti or English flags was important in demarcating areas occupied by different ethnic groups. It represented both a physical 'labelling' of areas and people in the environment and a symbolic warning tone; a 'them and us' tension among residents. During the interviews, all of the residents spoken to were able to tell the researchers exactly which areas had been claimed by different ethnic groups using graffiti. Moreover, the narratives that residents provided were consistently territorial in tone, with certain areas 'owned' by certain groups:

We have graffiti, but down in this area here. It's on the walls, 'whites keep out' … they have it up here, 'Pakis keep out'. (StM~278)

Graffiti was also used in a more personal 'attack' mode to deface people's properties: 'We had all our windows sprayed once, "National Front"' (StM 289).

The effects of these physical, visual signals in the environment were twofold. Firstly, they instilled fear and anxiety in people, and functioned to maintain and reinforce neighbourhood boundaries. There was fear on both sides that crossing one of these 'protected frontiers' would be a provocation for racial attack or abuse. Hence, a common behavioural response was to avoid such areas completely in everyday life, both at work and during leisure time, unless 'looking for trouble'. What this induces is inward-looking neighbourhoods that unite and cohere around a common 'enemy', the 'other', the outsider, and it is in this way that stereotypes and racial boundaries are maintained and the identity of the 'out-group' defined.

The second and related effect is that fear of 'no-go' areas perpetuates local reputational damage that is difficult to counter when rigid segregation often translates as minimal interaction with the 'other side'. This leaves little opportunity to undermine or dispel the meanings underlying collective reputations, and perceptions become temporally and physically fixed. As one resident put it:

Many people still walk through Glodwick … but they don't get any remarks. They don't get said anything, so I think it's all the reputation, it's in your mind as well … it's more the misconceptions we have of each other. (StM 186)

This is significant because it shows that people's perceptions of risk and their subsequent behaviour are not limited to their direct experiences, but are inflected by reputational stories, a number of which will be grounded in long-lasting memories and form part of the cultural legacy of an area. Area reputations can be fragile, and the comment of one resident highlighted a negativity bias in local appraisals of place:

You can do one bad thing and you can ruin the reputation. You can do 100 good things and it's not going to do the same effect. (StM272)

In Glodwick, reputations and divides were amplified by local media and political groups. It was the local newspaper, for example, that first introduced the term 'no-go area' into public parlance. The BNP made considerable symbolic capital following an incident of murder and assault inflicted on young white men by a group of Asian youths. These 'signal crimes' stirred up significant political action by the BNP in the area and their intention was to place a memorial stand on the place where the victim had died, a state of affairs that required police intervention.

More generally, residents in this ward often saw police as active agents, themselves afraid to cross symbolic boundaries and subject to abuse or intimidation if they did. This was reinforced by the stories people recounted of the police failing to respond to a call out: 'she phoned the police and they wouldn't come out'. A couple of incidents were recounted during the interview which illustrated the perceived futility of police action. For example, following police interventions there was 'blowback' resulting in criminal damage to police property (the theft of its blue light), or physical altercations between police and local youth:

... they might arrest an Asian youth and right away he's got about twenty of his mates there, all stoning them, kind of thing. (StM 268)

Conclusion

In seeking a nomenclature to aid the implementation of a new, highly localized style of policing, the UK police service readily adopted the concept of neighbourhood. With the benefit of hindsight, more thought should perhaps have been given to what such a construct actually means and what implications flow from connecting it to the delivery of policing services. Indeed, we would assert that even today much of the research literature has failed to attend sufficiently to the role of neighbourhood as an organizing and structuring concept for Neighbourhood Policing. One of the advantages of conducting a large-scale programme of research that spans multiple forces, such as that underpinning this book, is that it reveals the diversity of implementation models in terms of how Neighbourhood Policing has been delivered across different localities.

To partially redress this neglect of neighbourhood, a significant portion of this chapter has been given over to exploring empirical data on how citizens perceive and construct their understandings of neighbourhoods as spatial units, and how particular identities, reputations, and meanings come to be ascribed to them. The significance of this is that it starts to complexify existing models of 'neighbourhood effects' which attend to the ways the conditions of an area structure the prevalence and distribution of social pathologies that present therein. The analysis reported in the chapter has started to bring through how the very occurrence of crime influences and impacts upon what people think of as 'their neighbourhood'. At the very least, this suggests a need for neighbourhood effects models to incorporate feedback loops into their dynamics, to recognize the extent to which crime and disorder shape how people think about the constitution of what they view as 'their' versus 'other' neighbourhoods.

These interpretative processes were especially pronounced in the focused study of Glodwick in Oldham. Our extensive experience of mapping neighbourhoods across the United Kingdom using the methodology outlined in this chapter suggests that it is comparatively rare to identify 'bright line boundaries', where there is a high degree of consensus between residents about where frontiers between different neighbourhoods are situated. As such, where high degrees of consensus are detected, it can be diagnostic of deeper troubles. In the case of Glodwick, when fieldworkers went to observe what was actually happening on the ground, they found both material and symbolic expressions of the lines drawn in the cognitive mapping exercise, in the form of racist graffiti daubed on the pavements and walls. With further development, this implies that the methodology utilized has potential for detecting and understanding community tensions and where problems with cohesion are being felt.

More broadly, this analysis makes a unique contribution to the growing environmental criminology literature on crime and place.

There is now extensive and compelling evidence that crime clusters and concentrates in particular places and is not uniformly distributed spatially. As a reflection of this, many police forces have invested in 'hotspots policing' methodologies and technologies as a way to effect aggregate crime reduction. However, the limitation of many such approaches, and especially the analytics underpinning them, is that they pay insufficient attention to the hermeneutics of meaning at a neighbourhood level. If you want to understand how and why the occurrence of crime in certain places matters, it is misleading to just divide the world up into abstract spatial units and then map incidents on to these. Places and their people have histories, reputations, and identities that shape the significance and salience that is attributed to the occurrence of any troubles when they arise. The analysis reported herein has illuminated both a method for better understanding collective perceptions of neighbourhood, and how these are influenced and shaped by the occurrence of crime and disorder.

4

Policing Interactions

'Every contact leaves a trace' is an aphorism that, if you hang around with police officers for long enough, you will almost inevitably hear. First appearing in 1910, it was brought to public attention in later translations of Edmond Locard's (1877–1966) original papers, as a predicate of forensic science. For it articulated how every direct interaction between two or more sets of physical materials leaves some form of impression of this contact upon them (Pye, 2007). These traces may be almost imperceptible, but they are there, and when subject to forensic analysis can be used to evidence that contact occurred.

More recently, this notion has been somewhat ironically repurposed within police organizations. One usage of this term has been to refer to the bureaucratic 'traces' that police officers have to construct when any meaningful contact occurs between them and a citizen, especially when the latter are cast in a role of potential or actual victim, suspect, or witness. As Ericson and Haggerty (1997) identified, the documentary records of such encounters, resulting from the official forms police complete during and after any such interaction, provide an audit trail of police–citizen contacts that can be subject to a range of post-hoc interpretations about how well police work is being performed. A second related definition of 'every contact leaving a trace' seeks to articulate the importance of contacts and encounters between police officers and citizens in terms of the impacts that these can have upon the latter's perceptions of, attitudes towards, and confidence in the police.

What the public thinks of the police has particular salience within the traditions and values of UK policing. Certainly more so than found in other jurisdictions, with their quasi-militaristic conceptions of the police function. Even in the United States, where many agencies have dallied with community policing and

Neighbourhood Policing. Martin Innes, Colin Roberts, Trudy Lowe, and Helen Innes, Oxford University Press (2020). © Martin Innes, Colin Roberts, Trudy Lowe, and Helen Innes.
DOI: 10.1093/oso/9780198783213.003.0001

problem-solving operating models, the predominant accent has been upon them as modes of law enforcement and crime control, rather than sources of reassurance or legitimacy.

This idiosyncrasy of British policing can be traced back to the deep, structuring influence exerted by the much lauded so-called 'Peelian Principles'. Although these are actually little more than a part of the foundation myth of the British policing model, they do nevertheless gesture to the ways that the mission of the 'new' police was being thought about in the context of the early onset of industrialization and urbanization.[1] They capture some of the sentiments and values of those with political influence at the time, pertaining both to what the new police should be, but also what it should not.

Trace elements of this history can be detected in the contemporary interest in police legitimacy, trust, and public confidence. There is a rapidly growing scholarly literature gravitating around the concept of procedural justice and the ways that how police treat citizens in their encounters with them shapes aggregate levels of public trust and confidence. (Jackson et al., 2012b; Bradford and Myhill, 2015). Collectively these accounts are building a strong case about the extent to which the overarching public legitimacy of the institution of policing is tied to whether police are perceived to treat the public fairly when they come into contact with them (Bottoms and Tankebe, 2012).

It is worth noting of course that the scale and distribution of public encounters and interactions with police are not uniformly distributed. For the majority of the public, their actual interactions with police are 'brief encounters', consequential by virtue of their infrequency. Only a few citizens, whose attributes cast them as what Reiner (2000) labelled 'police property', have a more 'regular customer' status. Membership of either of these status categories plays a key influencing role in structuring the tenor and tone of any police interaction. This is relevant because, as Skogan (2006) identified, on average it takes between nine and fourteen positive encounters with police to offset the perceptual

---

[1] Labelling it a foundation myth captures how Peel never articulated the principles in this form. It also reflects how the dominant Whig histories downplayed the levels of resistance that the first several cohorts of officers encountered (Reiner, 1992).

and attitudinal effects associated with one poor interaction. More than this though, what the adherents of procedural justice neglect is the fact that although each individual police–citizen interaction can be well managed and thus deliver 'procedural justice', aggregated they can all be 'unjust' if they are disproportionately directed at one population sub-group.

This normative 'blind-spot' aside, what these studies have started to do is to identify the features of police–citizen interactions that are more likely to propagate and diminish levels of public trust, confidence, and legitimacy. Such considerations are especially pertinent to Neighbourhood Policing as they are pivotal outcomes that are being sought. Ultimately however, such attempts are constrained by the methods used to derive insights. Almost exclusively, the key studies in this area have been based upon secondary analysis of large-scale survey datasets. This involves police–citizen interactions being disaggregated into a series of variables used to discern patterns of correlation. What any such approach struggles with is the ability to capture the nuances, negotiated power dynamics, and mutual adjustments that occur when police and citizens encounter each other across a variety of social situations.

Accordingly, this chapter provides a high resolution, qualitative analysis of police–citizen encounters when they are physically co-present with each other. It seeks to really 'get into' what physical and verbal strategies are employed to order these interactions, as particular resolutions and outcomes are negotiated. Adopting such an approach has the capacity to enrich the kinds of understanding that the survey-based accounts of procedural justice have already set out. Even more importantly though, this perspective possesses the potential to develop a unique theoretical position on the conduct of community policing.

This more avowedly theoretical dimension will be directly framed by Erving Goffman's (1959) dramaturgical sociology, and in particular his concepts of the interaction order and 'face work' (Goffman, 1967; 1983). For Goffman, visible appearances matter in terms of people's ability to co-ordinate their actions and reactions when they encounter others. The impressions that people project when in the presence of others are 'read' and interpreted in terms of what they convey about intentions and motivations, leading to a series of behavioural adjustments as those engaged navigate their ways through the encounter. In particular, Goffman attends to how the impression management that is undertaken is situationally shaped and adjusted to the normative conventions associated with the setting. As a consequence of which, how people behave and the identities that they project will be contingent and contextual.

Informed by this understanding, this chapter documents four principal interactional modes directly involved in the delivery of Neighbourhood Policing:

1. Controlling—where the intent of police action is to explicitly control the behaviour of those they are involved with;
2. Confrontational—is a situation where there is clear resistance to the authority of the officer;
3. Collaborating—covers interactions where police adopt a more avowedly co-operative stance, working with others to accomplish an outcome;
4. Collective—in the context of Neighbourhood Policing, this recognizes the fact that not all key interactions are conducted on a one-to-one basis but can adopt a one-to-many format.

Attending to this micro-level of interactions between police and citizens possesses considerable potential for understanding Neighbourhood Policing as a set of institutional behaviours and for devising a deeper theoretical perspective on community policing more generally. In effect, and as will be posited, it shifts our thinking from conceiving 'police performance' as a set of instruments for guiding and evaluating police actions, to conceiving of community policing interventions as a set of public performances designed to communicate messages to an audience. In the next section, we develop a more detailed account of some of Goffman's key ideas and how they can be connected to conceptual themes in the extant community policing literature. These are then developed by introducing some empirical data, before the Conclusion attends to the aforementioned conceptual 're-purposing' of the notion of 'police performance'.

The craft and drama of Neighbourhood Policing

In his ethnographic account of community policing, Fielding (1995) argues the vast majority of studies conducted in this area have been prematurely over-interested with establishing 'does it work? His point of departure is different. Instead he is interested in:

… looking closely at the work, spelling out the tactics, looking at the negotiations, with the public and within the force. We need to know the phenomenon before we evaluate it. (Fielding, 1995: 1)

Elaborating this approach, he focuses in upon how decisions get made across the range of contexts and situations in which community policing interventions are invoked to negotiate order.

What emerges from this account is the sense of the craft of the community police officer. In his broader discussion of the idea of 'craftsmanship' Sennett (2008: 9) assigns it several defining attributes of skill, commitment, judgement, and a pronounced practical ethos.[2] Unlike 'science', where established theoretical principles and abstract predicates that determine how the work is to be conducted are prominent, a craft depends much more upon the skill, judgement, and practical expertise of the worker. It is precisely these qualities that Fielding's account of the work of community policing attends to. Framed in this way law becomes something that is not simply and unproblematically 'enforced', rather it is a set of resources to be mobilized selectively in trying to negotiate social order.

Through his painstaking and detailed ethnographic mapping of the work of community police officers, and contrasting it with the dispositions of their colleagues performing different policing roles, Fielding (1995) surfaces how neighbourhoods and their communities are understood differently by different police officers, and in turn, the police and police actions are understood differently by separate communities. The perspective of a community officer embedded within the rhythms and routines of an area for an extended period of time is considerably different from that of a response officer, whose concern is with 'fire-brigade' reactive policing tasks. This reminds us that although there is a tendency to talk about 'the police', as a wealth of research has now documented, in their day-to-day work police officers are cast in a range of very different roles. These roles are partly organizational constructions, but also reflect the requirements of the social and geographical situations in which officers are required to interject.

---

[2] Sennett (2008: 9).

Across a series of studies, Erving Goffman talked a lot about the requirements of performing particular roles. This was a pivotal part of his application of the dramaturgic metaphor to illuminate many seen but un-noticed features of co-present interaction. Goffman's empirical and conceptual interests centred upon the microstructural influences that collectively configured what he referred to as 'the interaction order'. Plotting out the constituent components of which, he attended to how people configure their identities and what they say and do, according to the conventions deriving from the situation and setting that they find themselves located in. The picture that emerges is one of a continual flow of reveals and conceals as those co-present with each other work their way through their encounters and engagements, in the process projecting and interpreting varied information.

Especially in his essay 'On Face Work', Goffman (1967) focused in high resolution detail upon how the process of co-present interaction depends upon collaborative activities by those engaged in the encounter. He casts the conduct of interaction as an 'expressive order' suffused with rituals. His analysis disaggregates a number of key components of these interactions, including: 'the little ceremonies of greeting and farewell'; the corrective 'interchanges' invoked when norms and expectations are breached; as well as the general 'savoir-faire' required for competent participation. It is a mode of analysis that leads him to conclude that the social identities that people seek to project are edited according to the contingencies of the situation they find themselves in. As he famously concluded:

> ... societies everywhere, if they are to be societies, must mobilize their members as self-regulating participants in social encounters. One way of mobilizing the individual for this purpose is through ritual; he is taught to be perceptive, to have feelings attached to self and a self-expressed through face, to have pride, honour and dignity, to have considerateness, to have tact and a certain amount of poise. (Goffman, 1967: 44)

Whilst Goffman's conceptual toolkit offers much, its focus upon dissecting mundane social interaction means it cannot be automatically transferred into an analysis of interactions involving the police. For very often such encounters are premised upon the fact that someone has violated the code of self-regulation to which he refers. More than this though, as the physical embodiment of state power, the position of authority that police officers inhabit alters the dynamics of interactions with citizens, whether the latter are cast in roles of suspect, victim, or witness. Extending this logic, the stance and poise that officers adopt when interacting with citizens is necessarily shaped by their role as 'law enforcers'. In effect, across a range of settings and circumstances, law supplies police with an outline 'script' in terms of 'the line' (in Goffman's 1967 terms) that they will act out.

With its focus upon the rules, rituals, and rhythms of how individuals and groups engage, and the ways of regulating, accommodating, and adjusting to each other's behaviours, it seems that Goffman's work might offer a unique conceptual frame for guiding a detailed analysis of how police and citizens interact under the auspices of Neighbourhood Policing. There are hints of how this might work in some of the classic texts on the nature of police work (see Manning, 1977). More recently, O'Neill (2017) has deployed a dramaturgical lens to explore how Police Community Support Officers (PCSOs) 'stage' their performances in the context of Neighbourhood Policing Teams. She found that in terms of their connectivity to their police colleagues, PCSOs in different areas had very different experiences. In some areas, PCSOs were highly integrated with their colleagues, whereas in other sites they were more distanced. Pivoting around Goffman's concept of 'performance teams' where he attends to the ways that groups of co-workers have to actively collaborate to construct a coherent performance, O'Neill (2017) focuses in particular towards how PCSOs construct their primary conception of 'audience' around their police constable colleagues.

In this chapter however, we adopt a different focus. We are less interested in the internal team dynamics and performances than with how both PCSOs and police officers orient their conduct to a public audience. This is justified on two grounds. First, and as has been rehearsed in the preceding chapters, being visible and engaging with communities is positioned as the pre-eminent focus of a Neighbourhood Policing officer's role, whether they are a PCSO or constable. As such, understanding how they seek to conduct their public performances towards their primary audience possesses particular value.

Second, as Reiner (2000) elucidates in his seminal analysis of the politics of policing, engaging in 'contempt of cop' can be fateful in terms of the policing outcome that a citizen experiences.

When interacting with police, members of the public whose de-meanours fail to display due 'deference' to the symbolic authority of the office of constable are liable to be subject to harsher treat-ment than those who comply with the ritual order that police as-sume such interactions should conform to.[3] In his account, Reiner only hints at how we might theorize these links and possibilities. However, by drawing in Goffman's work far more explicitly, in particular some of his ideas about the micro-structuring of face-to-face interaction, the following analysis demonstrates how his theoretical sketch, blended with a close reading of some empirical materials on community-police interactions and encounters, af-ford new insights into how Neighbourhood Policing gets done.

A recurring insight of Goffman's approach was that appear-ances matter, and should not be lightly dismissed in terms of understanding the ordering of social interaction. Conceptually, the connection that can be made with Neighbourhood Policing resides in its accent upon officer visibility. As noted in the previous chapters, accentuating levels of police presence and visibility was a key component of Neighbourhood Policing as a strategy, as part of an overarching approach to influencing public perceptions and reassurance. Evidence in support of this general disposition, as well as some of the complexities associated with it, were illumin-ated by a short experiment conducted in an effort to test some key aspects of public reactions to policing. This involved several very large photos of police that varied the number of officers in the pic-ture and how they were dressed. Each photo featured either one, two, or four officers, dressed either in standard police uniform or in fluorescent high visibility jackets. Different combinations of these photos were then shown to a random sample of members of the public, who were asked a series of questions about their thoughts and feelings having viewed each picture.

What this revealed was that there was a roughly fifty-fifty split between those who preferred uniformed officers to those mem-bers of the public who were more positive about officers in high visibility clothing. For the latter group, they accounted for their preferences typically on the grounds that it made the police easier to see and they were more aware of them. Contrastingly, those inclined to prefer the standard blue uniform pictures intimated

[3] In using some of these terms we are explicitly linking to another of Goffman's (1967) essays 'The Nature of Deference and Demeanour'.

that high visibility jackets connoted sensations of 'emergency' or 'danger' to them. What all respondents agreed upon though was that they did not like seeing multiple officers clustered together, as that definitely implied something must be wrong. This effect was especially pronounced for the picture of four officers all in high visibility jackets.

Developing the interactionist thrust of the analysis, a further finding that can be inferred from this experiment is the importance of officers patrolling on their own to increase their perceived 'accessibility'. In some of the qualitative comments provided there were suggestions that officers on their own were perceived as more approachable. To understand why this might be we can re-introduce Goffman's work to the discussion. One of his abiding themes was how, when two people are co-present, then this adjusts the expected norms and conventions of conduct. Many of these are seen but unnoticed, but they are, according to Goffman, pervasively influential. Consequently, when officers patrol on foot in pairs, as they seem to prefer to do, a prototypical social situation is already formed into which a citizen has to interject if they are seeking a direct interaction.

Accessibility, at least in terms of how it has tended to be understood within the police recently, has come to be a surrogate term for 'contactability'. That is, making sure officers' telephone numbers, email, and sometimes social media details are publicized. These are not unimportant. However, what the above analysis has sought to suggest is how there are some social-psychological rules and rituals of co-present interaction that might shape how accessible officers are perceived to be by members of the public in particular situations. In the process, such findings illuminate just how attending to the micro-physics of police–citizen interactions can provide new insights into how public perceptions are formed.

Controlling interactions

A defining quality of police interactions with members of the public, variously cast in victim, witness, and suspect roles, is how officers are engaging in such encounters as corporeal embodiments of the state with the authority to invoke their legally endowed powers at almost any moment. This is something that ineluctably frames how any such encounters are conducted. Police participants have to project the authority of the state and decide whether to introduce their legal powers into a situation (or suggest that this is a possibility), and there is a power asymmetry involved when they do so. Unsurprisingly therefore, they often experience varieties of 'reactance' from those they are involved with. Given how important such face-to-face interactions are to Neighbourhood Policing and its delivery, it is appropriate to consider how they are used to elicit control and how the almost permanent potential for confrontation is managed.

A recurring theme across empirical studies of community policing is how many officers struggle with it, and the role and performance it requires of them. One possible reason for this is that it goes against the grain of so much of their basic training. After all, when being instructed as emergency responders and crime fighters, roles that retain high levels of symbolic capital within police agencies, they are indoctrinated with the need to take control of the situation. When responding to potentially conflictual and violent encounters with members of the public, police training inculcates an imperative to dominate the scene.

This assuming of control even stretches to giving a statement. If you have ever done this, you will recall how officers do not just let you tell your story. Rather, they pose specific questions and explicitly introduce particular legal terminology into the witness statement. Law structures their approach inasmuch as the witness' account is broken down into specific points to prove for demonstrating that a defined legal offence (or offences) has taken place. It is an approach that is learnt and emphatically reinforced during initial police training. Extending the dramaturgic metaphor outlined earlier, in this sense, law provides the key components of the script and plot that interviewing officers build their interview interactions around. Similarly, when interviewing suspects in custody, as Richard Leo (2009) has compellingly documented, the whole situation is suffused with micro-techniques of power intended to endow the officer with a dominant status and position.

Some of these themes were surfaced in the early research data when we asked people about local policing. For example, one resident from London recalled:

I saw on Portobello Road, I saw them in action in a very good way, where a very big, a very aggressive black guy was ... he was basically screaming abuse at two police officers who were remarkably calm and remarkably sort of together in dealing with him ... so I think the police officers were very good in calming the situation, which I think in the area can become explosive quite quickly (Col- 201)

In many ways, this is an ideal type description of the police role and the 'dirty work' they undertake. Maintaining a calm outward demeanour, projecting an air of authority, and acting professionally to diffuse a situation threatening violence resonates with many of the themes that classic accounts of the democratic police function have taken to be its defining capacities and capabilities. It is a particularly focused example of the kinds of impression management and face work that Goffman elucidated. But what this account particularly neatly draws out is the ways that such mundane policing actions communicate messages to a wider social audience. This man telling the story, after all, was not involved in the encounter, he was an observer, an onlooker. But the impression that it left upon him was to frame a positive perception of the local police. What the person threatening violence thought of the police may be very different.

To invoke the title of this chapter, across a range of situations then, we can detect how police engage in 'policing interactions'—that is controlling, directing, and choreographing much of what happens when co-present with victims, suspects, and witnesses. Fundamentally, they are trained to project authority and to take charge of what may be a chaotic, unsettling, and/or uncertain social situation. The intriguing thing about this breeding in of a particular approach to policing interactions, in the sense of regulating and directing them, is how community policing expects them to interact rather differently with citizens. Indeed, under certain formulations, police are explicitly expected to cede power and for their work to be responsive to the needs and wants of local communities. There is then potentially a genuine condition of cognitive dissonance between the role of response and Neighbourhood Policing officer, at least in their 'pure' incarnations.

Such role-identity tensions may be potentially amplified by the fact that, as possessors of community intelligence, local police officers may be 'wise' in the Goffmanesque sense of the term. That is, aware of hidden but discreditable information about some of those they encounter. In keeping with Goffman's conception of strategic interaction, when in possession of such materials, Neighbourhood Police officers often make decisions about whether to disclose, or at least 'hint', at what they 'know' on the basis of holding clandestine intelligence about those they are interacting with. Such measures can be helpful in influencing the conduct of those they are engaging with, in terms of overcoming any recalcitrance and securing compliance.

As was intimated in the previous example, there are of course multiple audiences for these kinds of routine police actions. How these different audiences 'read' policing interventions will be shaded by their standpoint, attitudes, and values. Recognition of such factors starts to move us into a more nuanced and subtle understanding of how police interventions are interpreted and perceived, a particular striking exemplification of which was evident in a story told about a drugs raid mounted by the police.

In terms of understanding why the community 'read' the police behaviours in the way they did, it is important to know that this was an area of London with long-standing and serious concerns about the impacts of drug dealing. Consequently, when the police raid was launched, a number of the local residents turned out on to the street to observe proceedings. Initially pleased that their concerns had been recognized and action was being taken, as the respondent recalled, the impression management of how police were seen to be interacting with those arrested as they were led out of the crack house totally changed the observer's perceptions of what was occurring:

I: I tell you what, one thing that was extremely annoying was to see the police laughing with the drug addicts … All smiling and interacting with them. Extremely annoying.

R: Why?

I: Because it felt like they were on their side. Everybody mentioned it. Everybody got annoyed, 'Just look at them, they're smiling at them', got annoyed. But when you think about it, that's what happens between the police and their regular clientele … But the perception, the community perception, was one of absolute fury. It seemed as if they were colluding in some way. (Col–206)

As was recognized in the latter parts of this extract, the suspects and police were well known to each other. Moreover, the police officers were probably using interactional strategies with the arrestees to try and manage and defuse a potentially volatile situation. To appropriate Goffman's (1952) well-known phrase—they were 'cooling their marks out'. But from the point of view of the wider audience, such behaviours sent a rather different message to that intended:

It sends you a signal that somehow, it's acceptable to the police for that drug substance abuse to be allowed in the neighbourhood and I don't think they understood that. (Col 206)

These extracts clearly convey the extent that who is present as the audience watching the action 'on stage', in even relatively routine policing interventions, is consequential in shaping the meanings that emerge and the definition of the situation that is constructed.

In terms of the meanings that are ascribed to police interactions of this kind, it matters who is on the public stage delivering the performance. At the time when the data were collected, as part of the National Reassurance Policing Programme, PCSOs were being rolled out nationally as part of the new Neighbourhood Policing teams. There was uncertainty amongst senior police leaders about the role that these officers were to perform, and how they would be received by members of the public. Such concerns were manifestly amplified by lots of mass media commentary about them being 'plastic police'.

Confounding such expectations however, in St. Helen's on Merseyside, we found that some young people in the area actually stated a preference for the PCSOs when compared with the uniform constables. As they described it, the response officers who drove around in car were much closer to their own age, and typically interacted with them in a relatively aggressive manner, using threats of legal action to establish compliance. In contrast to which the PCSOs, who were middle aged and had children of their own, were seen as having a much more empathetic 'kerbside manner'. Unlike their younger response colleagues, they did not feel a need to project their authority, but were far more likely to negotiate compliance in securing order with the young people.

A second example, also focused upon the work of PCSOs, further illuminates how the interaction order frames their work. Especially when they were first introduced into some of the higher crime, high disorder neighbourhoods, a number of Neighbourhood Policing Teams encountered quite vociferous verbal resistance from older groups of teenagers, who local residents referred to as 'gangs'. The more perceptive of the PCSOs recognized this kind of behaviour as a signal of something salient, posing the pertinent question 'why were these groups so agitated by the new local policing presence in the area?' As a consequence, they self-tasked to research the police intelligence system about what was known about these 'gang members', their circumstances, and social networks, quickly building a rich picture of these individuals and their lifestyles.

Collection of community intelligence about private troubles and local public issues is a key function of local policing officers. In the process though, some officers become important repositories of intelligence about local criminality. For example, one sergeant in London had built up a formidable understanding of the local gangs and their members in his patch of London. He knew all of their street aliases, real names, and faces, and could identify them all fairly accurately at distance. He made a point of finding out who the new joiners were when they appeared on the streets. As a consequence, when officers from the pan-London Operation Trident were looking to identify suspects from this neighbourhood in London, for murders and attempted murders, they often 'borrowed' the sergeant as their 'spotter'. His field intelligence skills and the knowledge he had built up was an asset that the other cops valued. His was 'face-work' of a different kind to that described by Goffman, in that he could recognize by sight, name, and know elements of the criminal histories of a large number of individuals of regular interest to his colleagues.

The ability of patrol officers to visually identify known 'villains' has long been identified as a core skill within the occupational culture of policing. It is something that continues to be valued by those engaged in Neighbourhood Policing. Building up knowledge about the rhythms and routines of an area, and who and what can be expected where and when, and thus what are matters out of place, and especially being able to connect names to faces, and to a working biography of possible villains, is a key ingredient of the craft of successful Neighbourhood Policing work.

Confrontational interactions

A key element of Goffman's analysis of the interaction order is the accent he placed upon how elements of situation and setting shape and steer conduct and behaviour. There are contextual conventions and pressures that are highly influential in terms of how those who are co-present with each other relate and interact.

As he pithily described it, it is not so much 'men and their moments, but moments and their men' (Goffman, 1967). These self-same social mechanics and dynamics pertain to the conduct of Neighbourhood Policing, where the prevailing social order exhibits an important influence upon how police–public encounters are enacted, and what 'dosage' of police intervention is deemed both acceptable and necessary. By way of example, in the extract below, taken from an interview in Moss Side, Greater Manchester, a respondent explains how policing in a high crime area with historic gang problems has to 'compete' with, and is judged against, other forms and agents of social control:

Q) Was there also a reaction against the gangs?

A) No, not really because the gangs were being seen to be doing something about it. For instance the guys that were thought of doing this to [Billy], not too far after it I mean the guy had been kneecapped. I mean we knew [Billy's] brother had plans because he is inside, he was doing a six year stretch and he was going to come out and see to the guy. But we heard all these rumours whether they were true or not it didn't really bother but at least something was being done. Then the police on their side were doing nothing, so I mean there was no negativity towards the gangs because they were being seen to be doing something. It sounded like the gangs were trying to sort out what was going on and get retribution and clean up their act, but the police weren't doing nothing, nothing at all.

Q) So overall the negativity is directed at the police?

A) Yea, yea … You would think the police would have heard it as well but until this person tells the police are they going to hear about it? But nobody will tell the police because nothing will get done.

Q) And nobody would want to be the first to tell the police?

A) Exactly, as soon as they tell the police somebody would hear about them telling the police and it would get back and that persons a grass, keep away from him, don't let him know nothing … As soon as people label yer, that's it your damaged goods.

(MS 0901)

This account gives a quite telling depiction of how in deprived, high crime, urban neighbourhoods police are not the security providers of 'first resort' for all citizens. In this case police were not only mistrusted, but seen as less effective, responsive, and timely than the informal social control exerted by the established gangs. Talking to the police, even being seen with them risks breaking the normative rule of 'not grassing'. One PCSO working in a

Neighbourhood Policing Team described the interactions encountered early on in an area:

There is an intimidation factor still there. It's a long process to end that completely. If it had been going on for one or two years it might be different, but this has been going on for 20–30 years, for a very long time. Especially for older people I talk to, they see it as a way of life, something they have just got to get on with. To get on with it they have just got to keep their heads down and don't do anything that might anger the gangs. (CPol-MS5)

In his work on the ironies of social control, Gary Marx (1981) infamously described how certain overlapping structural neighbourhood conditions can induce a 'policing vacuum' which can be filled by other agents of social control, as intimated above. For our purposes herein however, such conditions are important because of how they support a climate of confrontation.

Resonating with many of the prior issues highlighted, in the next extract, a PCSO describes how their interactions with some local young people were frequently highly confrontational:

They are quite negative and aggressive. I would say that the older lads who hang around in gangs pretty much blank you. They turn around and head away. They will always stare at you. If you say hello to them they just look at you blankly and look away, they always try to get that 'presence' thing. The younger ones get very aggressive in the way they talk to you. They shout stuff like 'plastic PCSO. What you doin round here. You're not commin round here, fuck off' They are always trying to intimidate you; they are letting you know that you are in their area. (POL-MS6)

For many ordinary members of the public, such behaviours are intimidating and indeed, from the point of view of their protagonists, this is what they are intended to do. As part of the tradecraft of street policing however, confrontational interactions can be 'read' and interpreted. For as the previous officer elaborated:

They don't realise how much we get to know about them. Them being them, they always want to make their presence known, even if they don't want to talk to you. So they will make themselves known to you. They have a habit of doing it. I find it very useful. They may think they have got one over, because they have been giving us all this shit and that. But what we are doing is writing down exactly what they said to us, looking at exactly what they are wearing, exactly where they are, who they are hanging around with, and that goes straight into the intelligence system. (POL-MS6)

In effect, what this officer was describing is how they sometimes seek to 'engineer' confrontation with gang members as a way of getting them to reveal information that may have intelligence value to police. Reading behaviour in this way is a key craft skill of street policing.

Collective interactions: collaboration through public meetings

The focus of this chapter so far has been upon individual level interactions between police and public. However, in terms of how Neighbourhood Policing is delivered and experienced by communities, there are also important collective interactions that take place. Most notably, these include community meetings organized by local police, which are intended for local people to come along and share their concerns about any troubles and to find out about policing activity. Under the auspices of Neighbourhood Policing these tend to be referred to as PACT (Police and Communities Together) meetings, although a variety of monikers are used across individual police force areas. Although predating the formal inception of Neighbourhood Policing by a number of years, as part of the national roll-out of this approach, these meetings were institutionalized as the principal vehicle for police–community engagement in many parts of England and Wales.

Across the life-course of the research programme, a number of variations of police–community meetings were studied. One especially interesting example was in the London Borough of Lambeth, where the group met monthly and a researcher observed each meeting for more than a year. The original forum had been established (as were many in inner-city areas) in the wake of the Brixton Riots in 1981, principally in response to recommendations of the Scarman Inquiry (1982). Every meeting was attended by the Metropolitan Police Borough Commander and several other senior officers from the local policing teams.

This group was studied in detail on the grounds that it might provide insights into how PACT meetings might operate in areas where police–community relations were challenging and frequently highly confrontational, and how the resulting interactions were used to foster a contingent form of collaboration. As described in more detail below, the group occasionally functioned as a 'safety valve' enlisted in neighbourhood-level conflict resolution.

From first attendance at public meetings of the Lambeth Community Police Consultative Group (CPCG) it was evident, to use Goffman's (1959) term, that there was a 'front stage' and 'backstage' to the business being transacted. The interactional dynamics of the 'formal' meetings were frequently chaotic, with people intervening in ways that deliberately breached the conventions and protocols associated with the conduct of such public occasions. Moreover, the demeanour of key participants was often highly emotional, with frequent angry exchanges between those in the room. In terms of the dramas being acted out on such occasions, they functioned as little 'power plays', showing how the meetings were not just an opportunity to hold the police to account, but to show the audience that the police *could* be held to account, and importantly *who* and which faction within the community had the power to do it.

In part, this reflects how the notion that there was one community in Lambeth that police were trying to engage with was an artifice. There were instead, a complex of shifting allegiances and agendas infused with a history of difficult and challenging relationships between the public and police in the area, as well as between different segments of the public. As a consequence, these complexities and the power relations that they induced were regularly manifested in the conduct of the CPCG meetings.

One of the important findings of following these meetings over an extended period of time was to understand how there was a regular cast of actors who attended and participated in every meeting, but also a shifting 'supporting cast'. One of the original purposes of establishing the group from the police point of view had been to try and create an alternative channel for grievances to be shared, without recourse to direct public violence and protest of the kind seen in the past. Indeed, all core participants acknowledged this as being part of its function:

I was a resident but I was also chair of the National Black Caucus at the time and we were organising demonstrations outside the police station around deaths in custody ... in fact the rioting in Brixton in 1995, was a consequence of the demonstration. Now the reason why we had that demonstration is we went to the Consultative Group (CPCG) the day after [Name 1] had died in hospital. [Name 2] was in the chair and I asked for the matter to be discussed and put on the agenda. Now [Name 2] said 'no, we can't do that'. He said 'no, it's not on the agenda, it's not here, no way'. And I said 'if we're not going to discuss it here we'll discuss it on the streets of Brixton'. And we left. And we discussed it on the streets of Brixton and the rest is so much history you know. Front page headlines in the Mail and so on. But soon after that I think the Consultative Group and I realised that it was a mistake, to not take on such a significant issue. They invited us back and we then began to have a real dialogue about it. (APM5L)

What this account conveys is the extent to which, in an area challenged by serious crime issues including high rates of gun violence and a history or racial tension, the perceived need to 'control the police' can retain a unique power and salience. In effect, policing was seen as part of the problem, rather than inherently being the solution. It was with this set of dynamics that the introduction of Neighbourhood Policing into the area had to grapple. In practice however, this history and context meant that the meetings of the group frequently orbited around 'live' or recent policing incidents and their community impacts, rather than being able to engage in a sustained manner with more mundane neighbourhood security issues. Each time a critical incident occurred, in effect 'the clock' of police–community relations was set back a little, or a lot.

These issues notwithstanding, the police–community relations did prove adept at preventing mass civil disorder. This capacity was demonstrated during the middle of the first year of observations. Unlike previous meetings attended, there was a large foot and mobile police presence both outside the Town Hall and in the streets surrounding it, with helicopters buzzing overhead. The meeting room was packed with new faces that had not been observed at previous meetings and journalists.

It transpired that there had been a large but peaceful public demonstration outside Brixton police station at 4:30pm, organized by 'Movement For Justice by Any Means Necessary' (MFJ).[4] The protest concerned the perceived failure to bring criminal charges against, or dismiss, a police officer who had run down and seriously injured a young black man. The public demonstration was

---

[4] A neo-Marxist group based in South London who described themselves as an anti-racist civil rights movement. They emerged in Kingsway College Student Union in 1995 and state in their own media content that they were the most 'active and militant union in Britain'.

timed to end so that participants could attend the CPCG public meeting. The Town Hall was crowded with people and tensions were clearly running high. Some in the audience were choosing to shout abuse at the police even before the meeting started. On the dais sitting alongside the police Local Borough Commander was a Deputy Assistant Commissioner (DAC) who, the Neighbourhood Inspector announced before the meeting commenced, had come to publicly offer his apologies to the victim and his family for the way he had received his injuries, the way he had been treated, and the time it had taken to arrive at the present stage of a resolution.

It seemed that the intent of the MJF was to render the incident as another example of institutionally racist policing, similar to that of the Stephen Lawrence case. After the DAC had apologized to the victim's mother, with her now disabled son next to her (providing a powerful visual symbol of the violence of the event), the mother stood up and called for the named driver of the police car to be sacked. The Chair of the CPCG then immediately echoed her call, which visibly calmed the audience. Some of the faces of the MJF and its supporters registered shock at this. It was as though this act of agreement was unexpected.

Next, a young black man from MFJ, who perhaps sensed the meeting was going the wrong way, stood up and gave a detailed, forceful, and highly articulate analysis of the case. He emphasized several key points painting the police as racists, linking to past similar acts. He ended by saying angrily that the police had 'No authority to police our community' and that it was 'now legitimate to use cars to run over black people'. He then called again for the officer to be sacked and ended with 'we want justice!' It was clear that when he used the phrase 'our community' he was talking in the political sense of the black community as a whole, not necessarily the black community of Brixton.

By this point, the atmosphere was incredibly tense, with an almost tangible sense that it would take little for the meeting to break down into immediate public disorder. Then, a senior figure in Brixton from the Dominos Club, who had become a familiar face from previous meetings, stood up to speak. He was a deeply articulate man and had often supported the police over day-to-day crime control issues in previous meetings. This time however, his message was slightly different and seemed to be shaped to connect with the new radicals present in the meeting. However, subtly he also conveyed a sense to the audience that relations with the police had got a lot better over the intervening years and there was now a lot to lose.

When he spoke, he turned and directly faced the MJF representative across the room, saying, 'There has been great improvements in the police, are you going to let it go back?' He then turned to face the police and went on to carefully dissect the case from the perspective of whether or not the police officer's actions represented reasonable use of force. The law relating to the use of force is a complex area of study, yet the speaker's analysis showed a comprehensive understanding of its finer points. He pointed out that no threat had been made and as a consequence there was no right to use the car as a weapon. He also noted that officers were equipped with CS spray, radios, and batons and 'there was no evidence that the officers were in danger'. He then ended his intervention by commenting on the evidence presented that the officer was laughing as the victim lay severely injured on the ground with a major wound to his leg from which he could have bled to death—a point that resonated with the death of Stephen Lawrence who had bled to death with police in attendance. The speaker finished on a note of incredulity, turning back to the senior Metropolitan Police officers present saying, 'Are you really telling us you can't get rid of this officer?'

What can be seen here is how group members had learnt through their interactions with the police to present counter arguments in the 'special language' of the police discipline system. The argument had been shaped so as to present a case for 'criminal conduct' for which an officer can be dismissed under Police Regulations. By this point in the meeting the tension in the room had risen to a new level. Someone shouted out that this was like the Derrick Bennett case and others, and said 'If this continues, we will not be here, we will be on the streets like the past!' In response, the DAC reiterated his line of deepening public contrition. A woman in the audience, not satisfied with this, interrupted and said with a tone of derision:

We know the story. This tells us of police brutality and racism. It doesn't change the truth we know. A panel sitting somewhere doesn't change that. We know what's true. If you want to be a racist and crush black people against a wall, join the police! You want to be a racist join the police!

By this point, all of the police officers, some of whom had had nothing to do with the case, were looking flushed and uncomfortable. More pressure was then applied by the MFJ representative of the victim's family, who skilfully drew a parallel to the death of Stephen Lawrence by saying there had been a deliberate conspiracy (as in the Lawrence case) by senior police officers in the Borough to cover up the evidence. He went on 'This was a young black man so it didn't matter. This is a racist attitude that exactly mirrors the death of Stephen Lawrence.' Turning to the audience he said accusingly, 'He didn't want the blood of a young black man in his car.' A woman began to chant repeatedly, 'racists, racists, racists'. A young black activist from the MFJ came and stood between the dais and the audience and shouted abuse into the faces of the police barely two feet away. This looked like a deliberate attempt to provoke a response from the police, but none came.

At this point the Chair intervened, told the young man that he was out of order, and calmly summed up all the points made in a way that was clearly oppositional to the police and thus difficult for the MFJ to find fault with. He said that the whole incident 'served to undermine public confidence in the police' and that the Independent Police Complaints Commission would be consulted on how to change police regulations, and that the group would make a submission that would call for the officer to be dismissed. He then made it clear that he was about to move onto the next 'important' item regarding youth services and provided an opportunity for the victim and his family to leave if they wished. The family and all the MFJ people, the assembled press, and the DAC left the room, and the agenda was resumed as though nothing had happened.

This was one moment in the stream of police–community relations in London, albeit an especially 'acute' one, where there was clear potential for significant trouble. It warrants an extended case study treatment in the context of a broader discussion of Neighbourhood Policing because of the way it condenses together a number of key issues. First, it gives a sense of some of the complexities and structural forces that have to be navigated and negotiated when delivering Neighbourhood Policing in some settings. There are now several scholarly accounts of Neighbourhood Policing that provide details about what might be referred to as the 'mundane governance of neighbourhood security', reflecting how they have been conducted in relatively stable settings and conditions However, Neighbourhood Policing was delivered across England and Wales and as such it is important to capture how the prevalent situation framed what policing services were actually delivered across different circumstances. For what this case study captures is how, in stressed communities, where police–community relations were far more challenging and confrontational, experiences of Neighbourhood Policing were very different from that pertaining to other places and spaces.

Second, the case study articulates the power of collective interactions in the delivery of Neighbourhood Policing. With some justification, many police have become quite sceptical about the value of community meetings. Under more 'normal' conditions, the evidence collected by this programme of research does suggest that they can tend to be poorly attended, and fairly perfunctory in terms of what is achieved. Equally however, there is evidence that there are exceptions to this general pattern. At moments of crisis, such as those described in the preceding sections, public meetings can play a critical role in exorcising the potential for significant violence and disruption. This 'episodic' form of social control was 'conciliatory' and 'meditational', or even 'arbitrational' in nature.

Thirdly, this case study serves to remind us of the 'inconvenient truth' that the notion of there being one 'community' is something of a fiction. Especially in more challenged urban areas, there are frequently multiple and contested viewpoints and agendas that have to be negotiated and taken into account by police and other public service providers. As a consequence, understanding whose needs and concerns are being represented becomes an important consideration.

Back stage routes to activism

On the surface, the CPCG group was apparently convulsed for more than a year by very public infighting and conducted very little actual business. It was a period when there were several brutal homicides involving guns in the area. Most meetings would fail to get through the set agenda and the police, in particular, rarely got a chance to even give a report on their activities. However, this front stage appearance, which was frustrating for many of those involved, belied less publicly visible activities taking place 'backstage'. Indeed, it was these more veiled and less visible aspects of the work of the meetings that enabled the kinds of community impact management functions described previously, and that sustained many peoples' involvement with the group.

The backstage work of several of the CPCG 'actors' was significantly different from the front stage role they adopted. For behind the scenes, the meetings were being used to exchange information and arrange problem-solving interventions. This could be in the form of bringing particular issues to police attention, or facilitating contacts between key actors in the local community without the involvement of the police. Through repeated observations, it became clear that before and after most meetings, small groups of attendees, members, and police officers, sometimes including the Chair, would be huddled in deep conversation. Later one-to-one interviews with some of those involved revealed the level of collaboration that was being brokered:

Yeah. Well as [a board member] you manage about 4 or 5 agendas on the day. You're managing a police agenda which you know about. You know what their concerns are, you know what their senses are. You are managing the business of the group, which has its own particular dynamic. And then you're managing a sort of community intelligence brief where people are coming to you and saying, 'I can't say this publicly but blah de da de da'. What you've got to do is assimilate that information and then try to push it back out into the appropriate place that gets our required action. (AMP5L)

Similarly, the periphery of the meeting was also an opportunity to meet a particular person to facilitate other forms of collective action. For example, on one occasion, some regular participants agreed to distribute leaflets across the neighbourhood for another member. In another case, one participant was suggested who may be able to help another with a problem. In this sense, the meeting was acting as an informal infrastructure for arranging collective action in the community.

Outcomes of these backstage discussions would sometimes reappear in the front stage business of the group at a later point, giving a view of how private troubles could be translated into public issues. An example of this was an issue disclosed by a member of the black community who privately, through one of these seemingly innocuous encounters, had raised with a Police Superintendent a concern about young black men publicly drinking, using violence, and dealing drugs in a local public garden. Behind the scenes, the Superintendent went away and ordered an intelligence gathering exercise in the area and found that there was cannabis dealing, public drinking, and guns being 'flashed' in the area. After consultation with SO19 (armed police), it was decided to conduct an operation in the area targeting violent dealers and public drinkers. Importantly, it was learnt that the person who had raised the issue had explained that the older Caribbean men who had regularly met for years to talk and drink beer in the gardens were not causing a problem. This enabled the police to use coercive social control to settle the dispute through repressive pacification of the problem in a way that reduced any potential for collateral damage to community support. 'Policing clever' as they called it. At a more theoretical level of analysis it is coherent with the principles of what Carr (2003) labels 'new parochialism', with leverage over a problem of community self-regulation enabled through a covert mechanism. Furthermore, it illustrates how the interventions of Neighbourhood Police officers can interface with and support other forms of police intervention.

The possibility of passing community intelligence and steering police interventions in a low visibility manner was important in an area where being labelled a 'snitch' or 'grass' was freighted with serious consequences. Members of the group were frequently 'bridges' for communicating intelligence, with others using them to route information to the police without having direct contact themselves. Importantly, the information involved was frequently not inconsequential, involving threats to kill and similar. An interview was conducted with one of the members engaged in this role, about how they decided what to do:

It's never neat, because even when you've got good information about a particular thing and you put it into the [system], sometimes you don't recognise what comes out the other end. So there is a constraining factor almost on what you can actually say or how to say it, you know, to the police and the authorities, because the way in which you give information can often dictate the outcome, so you've got to be very precise in your words and very sensitive to make sure that this is what is required, you know, not an overblown response but a precise response. (AMP5L)

As this respondent captured, acting as a 'bridge' between police and his fellow residents was a skilled role involving 'filtering' and 'focusing' the process, where personal identifying items were removed and the data presented to police in a way intended to

achieve the optimum social control outcome for the original pre-
senter of the information and the community. 'Editing' the information was an essential element to provide the necessary level
of trust and security for the participants in the network. The respondent was then asked to describe this editing process:

Q) So you find yourself censoring the information as it goes into the
formal structure. Am I right to say that they don't get all the information
because you probably can't give it to them, is that accurate?

A) That's precisely what I have to do, that's it precisely and what I do
is get the trust of the police and others that what I'm telling them is the
best thing that can be told. So I am able to say 'this is the information but
you've not been told it, or this is the information and it is contextualised
in this way and this is what I want you to do, or this is the information
and I don't want you to do anything' and you know we sort of negotiate
it along those sorts of lines ... (APML5)

Explicit in this account is the import of trust between those involved. Building these trust relations was not aided by the turnover
in police personnel, and was something that the instantiation of
Neighbourhood Policing was intended to redress. Also intriguing
was the idea that some items were passed to police because they
'needed to know', and others because a policing response was
desired.

Fundamentally then, the value of attending to the conduct of police–community meetings in this manner resides in
illuminating how public appearances can be deceptive and
collective interactions can occasion the performance of less
visible functions. Of equal salience is how the discussion has
blended together a number of themes to show how collaborative, confrontational, and collective interactions can overlap
and coincide.

Conclusion: police performance or the performance of policing

Adopting a high-resolution focus upon how police seek to manage
their interactions with citizens cast in a variety of roles and the
face-work they conduct in doing so, tunes us into the performance
of Neighbourhood Policing. Invoking the concept of performance
in this way is deliberately ironic. After all, the notion of 'police
performance' is one that has achieved considerable traction over

the last two decades, albeit defined in a very different way to how it has been used in this chapter.

The orthodox formulation of police performance has been used to refer to a way of steering and managing police behaviour at both the organizational and individual levels. It is an approach that involves applying multiple data collection and analysis instruments to appraise the relationship between policing inputs and outputs, and rendering judgements about effectiveness and efficiency based upon these (Savage, 2007).

The more dramaturgic conceptualization of the performance of policing that has undergirded this chapter is in many ways the antithesis to this approach based upon performance metrics. For it brings to the surface the craft skills that are used by officers when 'doing' Neighbourhood Policing. This close reading attends to how police behaviours function as instruments of influence and persuasion situated within the context of citizen encounters. In so doing, it reproduces and reiterates one of the recurring findings of research upon the police. That is, although the work of the police is regularly referred to as 'law enforcement', in fact they frequently tend to enforce compliance only as a 'last resort' (Hawkins, 2002). This does not mean that legal powers are irrelevant to police conduct in such situations and settings. Just that they are not necessarily foregrounded. They do though have a structuring role for how policing interactions take place. Extending the dramaturgic metaphor, law provides a kind of outline script for police–citizen encounters. Of course, officers work around theses scripts, improvising and fitting the requirements of law to the situated contingencies of the events that come to their attention. The script that they draw upon will depend upon whether they are framing the citizen(s) they are engaging with as enacting a 'victim role', 'suspect role', or 'witness role'.

Possibly we might think of this as elucidating the 'kerbside manner' of Neighbourhood Policing. Just as it has been demonstrated that the 'bedside manner' of doctors matters to patients and the levels of satisfaction they express with their treatments, so it seems that how police interact with citizens matters in terms of their perceptions of confidence and legitimacy. There is a general consensus within the policing studies literature that public confidence is something that is easy for police to 'lose' and difficult to 'win' (Sturgis, Sindall, and Jennings, 2012). Consequently, if we want to understand how and why some police interventions, performed in some neighbourhoods, deliver enhanced public trust, confidence, and legitimacy, but not others, then attending to the micro-dynamics of police–citizen interactions may yield some important insights, above and beyond those that can be inferred from the discreet variables of large-scale surveys.

The particular contribution of this chapter to this book and the academic literature more generally is in providing a close reading of the interactional skills and strategies that police perform when engaging with members of the public cast in a variety of roles. In so doing, we have sought to work out the principal tenets of a dramaturgical analysis of Neighbourhood Policing. This has in-cluded considering how forms of face-work and the management of impressions are part of the art and craft of street policing. As part of which, it is possible to entertain the idea of reframing the concept of police performance from its orthodox usage, referring to a set of measurement instruments applied to gauge police ac-tivity, to a more dramaturgically sensitive understanding of how and why police behave in particular ways in their interactions and encounters with citizens that have altering effects on localized social order.

5

Police Support versus Community Support

In Chapter 4 we saw how particular insight into the work of Neighbourhood Policing officers is derived from casting them as engaged in a form of dramaturgic performance that seeks to persuade and influence their various public audiences about levels of local safety and security. In this chapter, we want to further develop this framing with reference to a specific role within Neighbourhood Policing Teams—that of the Police Community Support Officer (PCSO). Although originally conceived outside of the development work associated with Neighbourhood Policing, these uniformed, non-warranted officers were rapidly assimilated into the Neighbourhood Policing system, and to a degree became almost synonymous with it. This is because in many areas PCSOs took on a number of public-facing duties associated with the performance of Neighbourhood Policing's 'on-the-ground' delivery.

In providing a detailed examination of the role and work of these core members of Neighbourhood Policing Teams, the analysis pivots around a defining tension in terms of their core function and purpose. This tension is highlighted by the legislative renaming process undertaken via the 2002 Police Reform Act, when the former job title of PCSO was revised to Community Support Officer or 'CSO'. This intimates a question about the extent to which these roles are principally envisaged as supporting police officers in their work, or as providers of social support to communities to bolster their levels of cohesion, social capital, and collective efficacy. It is this conceptual and operational ambiguity that lends the chapter its title and also persists today as the titles 'CSO' and 'PCSO' are used inter-changeably.[1]

[1] For the purposes of this chapter and throughout this book, we adopt the title 'PCSO' unless specifically referencing Welsh Government funding of the

Neighbourhood Policing. Martin Innes, Colin Roberts, Trudy Lowe, and Helen Innes, Oxford University Press (2020). © Martin Innes, Colin Roberts, Trudy Lowe, and Helen Innes.
DOI: 10.1093/oso/9780198783213.003.0001

Prior to engaging with these matters in any more depth though, the chapter starts by setting out a high-resolution case study of a particular PCSO and her activities. This is helpful in terms of continuing to develop the sense of the 'craft work' involved in performing Neighbourhood Policing that was commenced in the previous chapter. Especially salient is how, despite not being able to invoke the 'hard' legal powers of her warranted police officer colleagues, the PCSO concerned nevertheless accomplished a lot through creative 'softer policing' means. Indeed, this juxtaposition between the implementation and accomplishments of 'soft' and 'hard' policing is an important recurrent theme for the chapter overall.

Some of the key aspects of this case study are then explained and accounted for by introducing details about the policy context, setting out how and why the PCSO role was originally introduced. This is further elaborated by the introduction of some comparative analysis looking at differences in the activity patterns of Welsh CSOs across several police forces. These data reaffirm how Neighbourhood Policing has been conceived of and implemented very differently across different contexts and settings. The chapter concludes by seeking to develop two important theoretical strands of argument. The first concerns this tension between performing 'police support' and 'community support' functions. The second theme attends to the importance of 'soft policing'. A lot of political and public commentary on policing in general focuses upon the exercise of formal police powers and whether they are sufficient to enable police to do their job. In contrast, the most sophisticated and nuanced academic studies of police have all accented the craft skills of street policing and how the most effective practitioners are able to accomplish most of their aims without recourse to invoking their formal powers of coercion. As Keith Hawkins (2003) so memorably put it, they turn to law as a 'last resort', more often resolving conflicts through a blend of charismatic authority and specific techniques of influence. This account of the role and work of PCSO/CSOs is very much aligned to this position.

Community Support Officer role since the latter is via budgets for community safety rather than policing in Wales.

A case study of the craft of community support work

Prior to taking up her post as one of the first PCSOs, 'Jane'[2] had been a social worker. Her first assignment upon joining her local force was as part of a neighbourhood team serving a population of nearly 8,000 people. The area where the team was focused was highly deprived, with people living there routinely encountering and experiencing a multitude of social problems. Although crime was relatively high, part of the reason for introducing a PCSO was that public complaints about social disorder and antisocial behaviour had been escalating.

However, when she first started working in the ward, her presence was not especially impactive. When interviewed about her early forays into the area she recalled how:

In the first month, possibly longer, no-one spoke to me. I used to walk around and I used to say 'hello' to them and some said 'hello' back or turned away, didn't even answer. (Jane, PCSO)

Interviews conducted by the research team at around the same time with members of the community revealed that these reactions were not driven by personal animus. Rather, they reflected how local residents were angry and felt let down by police because of long-standing and ongoing problems experienced on the estate not being resolved. One particular episode served as a condensing symbol for their concerns. It involved a local man who had a reputation for indiscriminate violence and whom police had advised local residents to avoid contact with. One Sunday afternoon, the individual concerned and a number of other young men got drunk, went swimming in the canal, were swearing at residents, and then started trying to gain access to a number of nearby properties. Several residents tried to call 999 for immediate assistance as they had been told to do. However, according to them:

[We] rang 999 and asked them to come down and they refused, the police absolutely refused to come. (Estate resident)

Allegedly, this was not the first time police had refused to attend incidents on the estate. Even when they did arrive, people felt that their actions were largely ineffective: talking to groups of youths,

---

[2] Name has been changed.

moving them on, only to have them reappear soon after they'd left. As a consequence, anger and mistrust of the police were high. Issues were amplified by the fact that people were fearful of the potential for repercussions if they were seen to be interacting with police:

People did not trust the police and did not trust that they would not get their windows broken if they spoke to the police. (Estate resident)

Confronted with these kinds of challenges, Jane engaged in a sophisticated example of problem-solving. She established a routine whereby every day when she checked in for her ten-hour shift, she would start by walking through the estate at around the same time, following roughly the same route. As part of this routine, she would stop and visit anyone who had reported trouble to the police the previous night. What these regular activities did was make her increasingly visible, accessible, and familiar to the local populace. As she described it, what she was having to do is try and overcome the cynicism that had grown up:

I think what also helped was that they saw me a lot in the first couple of weeks. The first couple of weeks they thought 'fly by night, another one of these hair brained schemes that they bring up' and 'here we go' and 'they'll be gone tomorrow'. (Jane, PCSO)

Although it was never clear whether it was a deliberate part of her strategy or fortunate happenstance, it transpired that her regular foot patrol route through a local park was of especial significance in affording a place where people felt safe to interact with her, away from informal surveillance mechanisms on the estate:

I got most off people chatting to me there because they felt as if they were not being watched and off the estate ... I got notes passed to me like 'take that and I'll meet you there'. (Jane, PCSO)

As outlined in the above quotation, through a subtle, nuanced approach that encapsulates much of the trade craft of street policing across the ages, Jane had established herself as a conduit for community intelligence to be passed to the police. This in turn allowed her to build up a 'richer picture' of what was happening on the estate in terms of its problems, but also who her potential allies might be. This latter dimension should not be underestimated and indeed, in subsequent months, she utilized this understanding to help establish a residents' committee and to trigger a range of problem-solving initiatives.

In her own account of how and why she was successful, it was clear that she very much understood her role as being principally involved in supporting the local community and residents. With her background experience of dealing with local agencies, she positioned herself as able to bridge the gap between them and residents:

I fill the gap between the Residents' Association and the police. I think if they hadn't formed the Residents' Association there could have easily been a vigilante group, because some of the residents have been having problems for years and feel that nothing was being done about it and felt angry about it. (Jane, PCSO)

However, as will be detailed below, not all PCSOs, police officers, commentators, or members of the public see this as an appropriate or legitimate role.

Background

The initial introduction of PCSOs into the 'police family' in England and Wales followed the edicts of the Police Reform (2002) Act and predated a national Neighbourhood Policing strategy by some three years. At that time, the government saw an opportunity for such a role to help relieve some of the pressure on front-line policing by carrying out basic patrol, providing a visible presence in communities, and dealing with antisocial behaviour (Home Office, 2001). Uniformed, but without the full legal powers of arrest and detention available to police officers, the new civilian recruits were first employed by police authorities and were under the direction of individual Chief Constables. They were able to: issue fixed penalty notices; seize alcohol and tobacco from a minor; and enforce no public drinking. In addition, Chief Constables were endowed with the authority to provide them with additional discretionary powers if needed. Historically then, the exact powers of a PCSO have always been tied to police force area boundaries and have always been finite, in contrast to the Special Constabulary of volunteer staff who are sworn officers able to exercise full police powers (Police Act 1996). PCSOs, whilst permitted to use reasonable force where necessary, have always been required to execute their duties in a non-confrontational manner that does not expose them to undue personal risk (College of Policing, 2015a). There also exist variations within the PCSO role; the power to detain is a discretionary one for neighbourhood PCSOs and is limited to thirty minutes, whereas those engaged on the British transport network are universally permitted to do so.

This change to the make-up of policing was met with fierce and sustained criticism and opposition. The Police Federation were amongst those extremely vocal in voicing their concerns about the new breed of 'numties' and 'blockheads' *replacing* 'real' police officers on the streets (Caless, 2007). The *Daily Mail* (2009) and several other newspapers ran infamous campaigns and stories referring to them as 'Plastic Police' (Daily Express, 2010). Indeed, the idea that PCSOs were a cheap alternative—a pale imitation of 'traditional policing' lacking any distinct role—led some police authorities to refuse to recruit any (Police Review, 2004) and to date the Police Federation of England and Wales (PFEW) excludes unsworn officers from its membership. Referred to as 'semi-trained auxiliaries' by a former Metropolitan Police Commander in 2007, the limited enforcement powers of PCSOs were assessed as wholly insufficient for the task of patrolling neighbourhoods and ensuring public compliance (Gilbertson, 2003). This kind of resistance and ridicule is not unique to British policing. In the United States where community officers are full-fledged police officers, critics refer to them as the 'grin and wave squad', dismissing their activities as little more than 'social work' (Trojanowicz and Bucqueroux, 1992).

Despite such reputational tribulations, by the time PCSO powers were made statutory in 2007 (Home Office, 2007) their role was inexplicably tied to the implementation of Neighbourhood Policing throughout England and Wales and seen as central to its delivery at a grass-roots level. Some £50 million of new government money was allocated to a Neighbourhood Policing Fund in 2004 to deliver and support PCSOs or wardens to underpin 'solid professional police work' across the whole of the country (Home Office, 2004). Between 2003 and 2010 there was a national year-on-year increase in PCSO numbers; from 1,100 to a peak of nearly 17,000 in March 2010 (Home Office, 2015). Throughout this period, the Association of Chief Police Officers (ACPO) repeatedly emphasized the importance of their role in 'reassuring the public' through the heightened visibility, accessibility, and familiarity that resulted from them being physically and consistently situated in neighbourhood teams, or at trains and stations on the railways as part of the British Transport Police workforce (ACPO, 2007).

That the PCSO role was integrated into Neighbourhood Policing Teams is an important, yet under-appreciated, dimension of how Neighbourhood Policing was designed to be delivered. For unlike previous iterations of community policing, this was not being undertaken by individual officers, but a small group of locally focused police workers. The fact that they were part of a team explicitly recognized that different participants had different roles and contributions to make. From the outset, Neighbourhood Policing Team priorities were centred on negotiating and engaging with local communities, and joint intelligence-led problem-solving to identify and act on community concerns (Turley et al., 2012). At the level of policy, it was envisaged that it would be this two-way process that would help build community capacity, public trust, and co-operation with the police service in tackling crime and antisocial behaviour (Home Office, 2004), not reliant on heightened police visibility and familiarity alone (Tuffin et al., 2006).

It is in this context that the specific role of the PCSO can be positioned as a 'connector' or a mediator between public and police. By *being there* and *being known* by community members, and not just acting as a visible policing deterrent to acts of crime and antisocial behaviour, the idea was they would 'build bridges' (Casey, 2008; Flanagan, 2008). Fundamentally then, the work of the PCSO within a neighbourhood team was always understood as much broader than cutting crime. And whilst some people never 'bought into' this vision and concept, with the onset of public sector austerity and associated reductions to police funding following the global financial crash of 2008, others began to question whether, in policing terms, such a role was 'a nice to do' as opposed to a 'need to have' (Foster and Jones, 2010). Some of the ways in which these pressures and debates played out can be illuminated by providing an extended case study of what has happened in Wales over the lifespan of CSOs.

Especially intriguing was the decision by Welsh Government to make a policy commitment to financially support 500 additional Community Support Officers (CSOs)across the four Welsh Police Forces at a time when police forces in England were cutting these roles following reductions to their funding. The reasons for this initiative reflect some of the complexities of the Welsh Devolution settlement whereby responsibility for most public services is devolved to Cardiff, but policing and criminal justice is not. As such, the Welsh Government could not legally fund police officers, but working with local Police and Crime Commissioners, they could fund CSO posts under a 'safer communities' banner. Based upon an analysis of Home Office police workforce data, Greig-Midlane (2014) reports that all Welsh forces *increased* PCSO/CSO numbers at a time when the majority of forces in England experienced staff reductions across all sectors of their workforce. Other forces, most notably in London, incurred a disproportionate reduction in their PCSO numbers, post 2010. As such, the research on the introduction and impact of Welsh Government-funded CSOs was akin to a 'natural experiment' that, in the context of a longer research programme on Neighbourhood Policing, provided an almost unique opportunity to ascertain what kinds of difference a community support role makes across a range of outcomes.

In a report published in 2014, Her Majesty's Inspectorate of Constabulary (HMIC) estimated that the challenging funding environment for policing would lead to an average reduction of around 10 per cent in the number of PCSOs across England. This was on top of the national contraction in police officer numbers since 2010 across England and Wales (Home Office, 2015). In Wales, however, the additional investment meant that the number of PCSOs per 1,000 population stayed steady, albeit total police officer numbers decreased between 2012 and 2015 (Home Office, 2015). Ultimately the consequence of this policy decision was that, for a period at least, the trajectory of Neighbourhood Policing in England and Wales was slightly different. Notably, in Wales there was a slight rebalancing with PCSO/CSOs taking a more prominent public-facing role.

In assessing these changes it is important to note that they were undertaken in a period where recorded crime rates were declining. Illustrating this long-term trend, Figure 5.1 tracks the number of recorded crimes per officer for the decade up to 2014.

These national statistics between 2003 and 2014 show no obvious demand for PCSOs to 'substitute' for police in relation to crime management work. Over this period, there was a sustained fall in the crime rate that outpaced reductions in the police officer workforce. However, it is important to note that a measure of total crime volume is likely to obscure marked variations in the

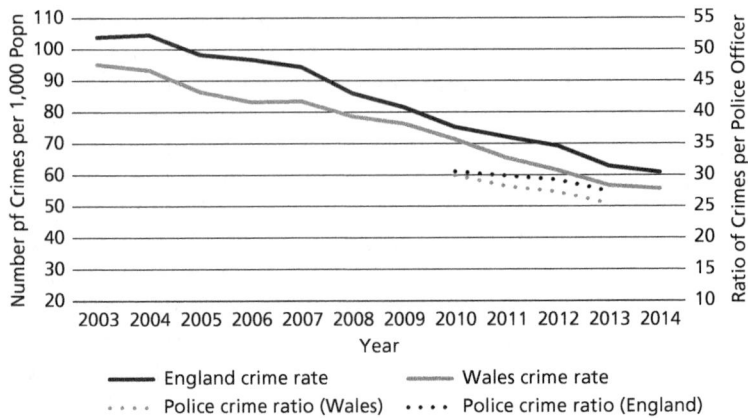

Figure 5.1 Crime Rate for Wales and England, 2003/14 Showing Ratio of Crimes per Police Officer

Source: Office for National Statistics

amount of police resource and time spent on different types of crime, as well as non-crime activities (College of Policing, 2015b).

The 500 additional Welsh Government-funded CSOs were introduced over a two-year period. As part of an attempt to track what, if any, impact they were having, two public surveys were commissioned by the Welsh Government in 2012 and 2013. These surveys suggested some positive gains in public perceptions associated with additional CSOs on the streets. Between the surveys, reported 'regular' sightings of CSOs on foot patrol increased, as did the percentage who felt that visible patrol made them feel safer (Lowe et al., 2015). However, because the CSO role was conceived in different ways in different areas, there was considerable variation at a police force and unitary authority level (the closest survey approximation to neighbourhood).

The extent of local area variation is further illuminated by a more qualitative comparison of how the CSOs were deployed in two different areas of Wales. In one of the largest commercial and industrial centres, five of the new CSOs were offered part-time hours to enable them to cover Thursday, Friday, and Saturday evening shifts. The rationale was to provide a visible, uniformed boost in policing resource for the city centre at peak times for its thriving night-time economy. This particular centre has a number of bars, pubs, and clubs where, since 2005, premises have been able to apply for twenty-four-hour alcohol licensing that has subsequently been linked to a rise in antisocial behaviour and public drinking.

On paper, the idea of boosting visible policing presence at peak demand times has many merits and was lauded by HMIC (2013) as 'forward thinking resource management'. However, the resultant focus on preventing, and responding to, antisocial behaviour associated with the night-time economy was sometimes at odds with the community-facing role of CSOs. Part-time working hours also induced some issues in terms of the officers concerned feeling that they were not fully-fledged members of the local Neighbourhood Policing Team.

As stated earlier, CSOs are not expected to intervene in conflict situations and indeed lack the necessary powers and protection to do so with minimal personal risk. However, 'dropped' into a busy and relatively demanding urban context, there were inevitably situations when they were called upon to react. One of the officers recruited into this role stated how:

The issue we have got is people see a uniform and they expect you to deal with it. They expect you to help, you know. They do not see you are a PCSO … We do not really have a choice, there is not enough time, for even us to call and wait for someone to come … We have to deal with it, by virtue of the fact we are there. (CSO16)

As this officer and several of his colleagues recounted, on occasions, members of the public were aware of their inability to intervene, and they were told: 'oh, you're only PCSO mate, go away!' With time-limited powers to detain, CSOs in this situation often reported feeling both vulnerable and frustrated in terms of their ability to properly perform their role. Several recalled encounters where they felt they had no option other than to withdraw and observe from a distance. It was acknowledged that these demands are a difficult balancing act because many CSOs did not generally support or want increased powers, believing them to hamper the development of community relations. However, they felt that observing and not acting in adversarial situations compromised public trust and confidence in their role.

A very different picture was obtained, however, from field observations and interviews conducted in a seaside town on the west coast of Wales. Here, the additional CSOs supported by the

Welsh Government investment were integrated into the existing Neighbourhood Policing Team, allowing it to double in size. The 'surge' in capacity was very much directed towards increasing levels of visibility and enhancing the quality of community engagement. As one of the officers supervising the newly expanded team explained:

Before we would have a PC and potentially one PCSO covering [the area]. Now we have got four PCSOs covering [the] town ... so they're on foot there in town. They're meeting businesses, licensees—interaction is far better than we have ever had before. So they are visible and more involved in the community. (LMT3)

By embedding themselves, the officers concerned had developed a number of problem-solving mechanisms to tackle neighbourhood issues through engaging with residents, businesses, and tourists. The team spent a considerable amount of their day understanding and getting to know their 'patch' and the individuals within it, playing an active part in school and community events, such as fetes, creating a community garden, and participating in a youth cycling scheme. In focus groups, officers told how getting to know young people paid dividends if they were subsequently required to enforce any sanctions against them, such as confiscating alcohol or tobacco:

I think we've got a better approach to talk to them from the offset because they know who we are. And then more often than not they'll listen to us. (CSO1)

The CSOs largely took responsibility for organizing local public meetings with police. Some felt that the insight and skills that they had acquired were qualitatively different from that of a police officer in the same locale:

We see different faces than a police officer would see ... maybe the drunks or whatever, those that are sitting on the benches in the summer time, the old boys ... the only people they [police officers] know is the people they've arrested ... We see the same people every day, stop and have a natter with them. They're the people that tell you things. (CSO4)

As alluded to in the last comment, this was engagement with a purpose. It was through these regular and routine interactions with local people that the kinds of trust were established that encouraged the passing of community intelligence.

Community engagement and relationship-building is complex and its success less readily quantified than reactive or 'response' policing. It takes time and persistence. CSOs are, in theory, ideally situated to act as what Kretzmann and McKnight (1993) term 'community connectors': by functioning to mobilize local assets from individuals, groups and organizations, community problems, and actions to resolve them, are shared. Such community liaison is at the heart of the joint working and problem-solving approach advocated by the Neighbourhood Policing ethos. It is also significant in building social capital or community cohesion in an area through the process of bringing people together (Putnam, 2000); not only people like each other ('bonding capital') but also diverse groups of people who don't know each other well ('bridging capital'; Szreter and Woolcock, 2004). When and where this does occur, research shows that inter-personal trust and community resilience can be bolstered (Poortinga, 2012). Informal social control can be strengthened so that communities feel better able to involve themselves in helping to prevent crime and disorder. That said, it is equally important to highlight that such outcomes are not always achieved, particularly for neighbourhoods experiencing detrimental effects associated with local deprivation.

CSOs must have, as Kretzmann and McKnight (1993) suggest, 'capacities beyond their ability to respond to crimes ... to use their skills and assets to help build a safer and strong community'. Trojanowicz and Bucqueroux (1990) argue this requires a qualitatively different kind of officer to be successful; a generalist, an outreach specialist, a mobilizer, and a mediator, someone able to release community assets from residents, local institutions, and businesses that otherwise would remain under-utilized.

In areas such as the one above, where proactive police–community engagement activities were 'normalized', local public perception surveys found a healthy alignment between community concerns and the activities of CSOs. Interventions focused around traffic and environmental problems, for example, were responding to those issues that mattered most to the communities being served. Officers' familiarity and visibility was noticed by members of the public, albeit older members of the public, who, when surveyed, were more likely than younger age groups to make an unfavourable distinction between sightings of 'just' a CSO and a 'proper' police officer (Lowe et al., 2015).

From how to why

So how can we explain why these differences in CSO deployment and citizen interaction arise? Taking a step back from the detailed investigation of individual sites to look across the various contexts where the work of CSOs has been studied, there is certainly some evidence that it was in the 'less stressed' communities where the community support element of their role was most readily translated into everyday practice. Typically, these were places where crime and disorder problems were less acute, where Neighbourhood Policing Teams covered smaller, more accessible areas, and were well resourced with staff.

The contours of an area and the local deprivation context are fundamental in shaping demand for policing services (Longstaff et al., 2015). The volume of police recorded crime and incident statistics show area variations across forces in England and Wales (ONS, 2017) that translates into demand for policing services in terms of reacting to local crime and disorder. But as has been repeatedly rehearsed now, such statistics omit many other types of time-consuming work that police perform, including acting out of protective statutory duty or undertaking more proactive preventative, problem-solving or Neighbourhood Policing activities (HMIC, 2015).

CSOs working in deprived neighbourhoods, when describing their work, strongly accented the importance of developing relationships with key local people. This was understood as part of their role, to break down long-standing barriers between the public and the police where historically public attitudes were anti-police—something that previous research suggests is vital to the success of policing more disenfranchised communities (Wake et al., 2007).

When PCSOs were first introduced and deployed in deprived areas, Innes et al. (2004) found evidence that they were sometimes regarded by residents as little more than 'police snitches'. Over time, however, as their presence was 'normalized' and their interactions with the public more numerous, residents reported 'behind the uniform is a human being' and ultimately compared them favourably to police officers. However, the challenges and effort associated with this work should not be underestimated. Observational fieldwork conducted during the early days of Neighbourhood

Policing suggest that relationship-building with those who are 'highly disengaged' from the police is often reliant upon the skills of individual officers. These individuals are especially proficient in befriending alienated groups and establishing rapport; something that nearly half of those officers examined in a study by Cosgrove and Ramshore (2013) were lacking.

A corollary is that statistical analysis of data from the Crime Survey for England and Wales suggests that how the public interpret the visible presence of uniformed officers (police and/or community support) is sensitive to the local deprivation context and is more complex and nuanced than just 'more equals better'. There is then, what we might label a 'dosage effect' of police visibility. Our analysis of the Crime Survey found that, in areas of high deprivation, perceptions of highly visible foot patrol were most strongly associated with public reassurance about antisocial behaviour and crime (Lowe et al., 2015). However, the same perceived 'dose' of foot patrol for people living in areas of lesser deprivation had a converse effect. That is, rather than reassuring them, it was associated with heightened concern and anxiety, fuelling public perceptions that there must be some form of local problem to warrant this amount of policing activity.

This survey-based finding concurs with the logic of Innes' et al. (2004) insight derived from local fieldwork, that the presence of uniformed and visible foot patrol in neighbourhoods functions as a symbolic 'control signal' that people interpret as an indicator about the crime risks within their local area. However, visibility alone does not necessarily transform public perceptions and renew police confidence, it requires reinforcement by engagement or changes in police behaviour (Scribbens et al., 2010). 'Too much' visibility in a particular location can amplify public feelings of insecurity, rather than provide reassurance that social order is being maintained (Innes et al., 2004). It can even serve to antagonize sections of target communities whose previous contact with the police has been negative (Foster and Jones, 2010).

Levels of visible patrol risk being undermined if the public do not witness officers engaging in worthwhile activities or interactions. This has clear implications for a neighbourhood CSO whose local knowledge and familiarity with residents and their concerns is likely to be invaluable in understanding the optimal dose of visible patrol appropriate to the needs and wants of their community.

CSOs can, and do, perform an important role in the delivery of Neighbourhood Policing when they are deployed and utilized appropriately at a local level. Yet despite this, a certain sense of ambiguity and uncertainty about their value continues to attach itself to many discussions about them. In part this reflects a fear of the potential for 'mission creep' (Caless, 2007), where CSOs are used as substitutes for and to infringe the police constable role. Much of the initial hostility to PCSOs stemmed from a failure to provide clarity on its role and that of police constable (Boden and Slack, 2008) between the two roles. This was only ever resolved to a degree by the Neighbourhood Policing model which sought to give PCSOs a 'distinct and complementary' role engaging with low-level problems of concern to local people (Home Office, 2008), permitting police officers the time and focus to respond to crime. Moreover, with the onset of austerity, the clarity of distinction between the two roles has arguably lessened.

HMIC first reported in 2014 that a number of police forces in England and Wales had responded to a contracting workforce by broadening the remits of their Neighbourhood Policing Teams. Some teams were taking on tasks previously carried out by police response officers and/or investigators. HMIC expressed concern at that time that neighbourhood police officers were increasingly being expected to respond to emergency calls and investigate crimes. This is supported by research with PCSOs in the same year, where over three-quarters of thirty-two PCSOs participating in focus group discussions said they were carrying out criminal investigation work into auto-crime in the area, but hadn't received any specific training on how to do this (Rogers, 2014).

Similar sentiments were expressed in a series of in-depth interviews we conducted with CSOs working in Wales over this period. Many of them described how their days were increasingly filled with investigative tasks including house-to-house enquiries, reviewing CCTV footage, and response calls. In respect of the latter, this involved not only lower-level incidents but on occasions to priority (grade 1) calls. Capturing the general tenor of many of these interviews, one CSO described having to assume responsibility for aspects of investigation pertaining to a potentially more serious offence that they felt ill-equipped to deal with:

I've got one on my workload ... the attempted burglary and it keeps coming back to me. I don't know what questions to ask. I'm not saying I'm thick, I've asked questions, but it keeps coming back to me.

Developing this theme, they elaborated their frustration that community-facing aspects of their role were being marginalized.

It's gone, it has. They've killed community. What it boils down to, like what I said, we are now second tier response. (CSO33)

Longer-serving CSOs in particular tended to recall when more of their efforts could be directed towards integrating into their communities for the purposes of developing cohesion and resilience. In Wales, some of those newer in post expressed confusion about the intended focus of their role. An increasing workload, coupled with the time needed to cover a large geographical area, meant that even ostensibly community-facing tasks often required them to travel outside of their allocated communities. In 2014, nearly half of Neighbourhood Beat Managers in South Wales agreed that CSOs were regularly 'abstracted'—that is, removed from their own areas to cover duties in other areas (Rogers, 2014) in order to meet regular and increasing demands. This is an experience shared with police staff in other countries, who report tensions in meeting the expectations of police and local communities (Cherney and Chui, 2010). Regular abstractions risk undermining the objective of delivering to the public meaningful engagement with a familiar local officer and was something that the early iterations of Neighbourhood Policing sought to guard against by setting out stipulations against it in key policy documents (HMIC, 2017). However, in the face of police workforce reductions, these stipulations proved unsustainable.

The balancing act

In terms of its theoretical policy construction, the role of CSO blends a delicate balance between community-focused proactive interventions and reactive 'police tasks'. Based upon the data collected and analysed, we would conclude that in different areas the accent upon these two dimensions has tended to vary. In some settings the work performed is better described as that of a 'police support officer', whilst in others the focus is more avowedly upon supporting community cohesion and resilience. One of the consequences of austerity is that it seems to have sharpened this divide and created a pressure for CSOs to take on more and

Police Support
- House to house
- Crime prevention
- Administration
- Public order
- FPNs
- CCTV

Visible Patrol
Victim Support
Intel gathering

Community Support
- Reassurance
- Organise or
  participate in
  community events
  and meetings
- Do outreach work
- Schools and youths

Austerity weights scales towards police support
at a time when CSOs substitute for declining
officer numbers.

Figure 5.2 The CSO Balancing Act

more police support functions at the expense of their community support work.

The kinds of activities associated with these different aspects of the CSO role are depicted in Figure 5.2. The community support operating model focuses upon engagement activities, nurturing and supporting community cohesion, and is more preventatively minded. This is counter-pointed by more reactive tasks, traditionally carried out by police officers, that form the basis of the police support operating model. Between these two 'pure types' is a grey area where there are activities and tasks that by nature are community focused yet are associated with the investigation or policing of crime and antisocial behaviour. Figure 5.2 shows that the multitude of challenges associated with long-term and ongoing economic austerity across the public sector weight the scales towards a police support modus operandi for the CSO. Community-facing aspects attract a lower status than enforcement under conditions of financial constraint and increasing demand.

CSOs and the future of Neighbourhood Policing

These challenges and tensions associated with the CSO role are consistent with ethnographic studies (O'Neill, 2019; De Camargo, 2019) and have started to key us into some of the ways Neighbourhood Policing has evolved over time. It has both matured and had to be adapted to respond to exogenous political and economic pressures. There are three pre-eminent influences that can be detected in this regard: economic austerity; the changing nature of crime and crime management; and how these feed through into the organization of Neighbourhood Policing and its constituent roles.

Most of the budget allocated to police forces across England and Wales is for staff costs, and consequently as central government funding for policing has reduced following the 2008 financial crash, they have grappled with difficult decisions about how best both to support and protect front-line policing and maintain a public-facing service to the public and victims of crime. For instance, in 2015, the Metropolitan Police Service considered scrapping all 1,000 PCSOs in London neighbourhoods in order to help meet savings of £800 million by 2019 (Beake, 2015), albeit they did not ultimately action this. A number of other larger police forces have cut the number of neighbourhood PCSOs from their workforce (Grieg-Midlane, 2004) and allocated fewer officers to roles that are visible to the public (HMIC, 2013), in what could signal a 're-prioritization' of police functions towards crime management.

Ongoing austerity across the public sector has been, and is likely to continue to be, a key factor that shapes the work balance for PCSO/CSOs away from community support to police support functions. The attendant risk with such moves is that incremental improvements in public confidence in the police that were so hard-won over the last decade will be undermined or lost completely if the resource-intensive work of building and maintaining local community relationships is eroded.

Such pressures are afforded additional impetus given how front-line police are subject to 'collateral demand' arising from similar cuts being applied to their public sector partners in health, social services, housing, and the voluntary and community sector (HMIC, 2014). In 2013, between 15 and 20 per cent of incidents reported to the Metropolitan Police Service were linked to mental health, which if scaled nationally, equates to some 4 million incidents in 2012/13 (Independent Commission on Policing and Mental Health, 2013). Embedded in local communities, PCSO/CSOs are particularly likely to encounter a large amount of mental health and social care needs as part of their day-to-day role. Arguably, they would be ideally situated for early intervention, signposting, and connecting vulnerable people to local support services to help combat social isolation if their presence could be maintained. Given police officers' reported preference for 'action-oriented' police work over 'pink and fluffy' engagement work (Reiner, 2010), the danger is that a more personalized delivery of policing would be lost or neglected if PCSOs were not part of the future police family.

But the most common approach has been the adoption of a more explicit crime management focus, using PCSOs to provide a targeted visible policing presence in crime hotspot areas. In a systematic review of forty-four international studies, Bowers et al. (2011) reported that targeted policing strategies in crime hotspots can be effective in reducing crime and disorder without displacing it elsewhere, a tempting prospect for police managers when finances are low, staff numbers reduced, and data analytics can predict where crime will occur. Having PCSOs focus their presence in such areas is understandably alluring for senior officers, but the trade-off is that this tends to be at the expense of the more nebulous 'soft policing' tasks that can do so much in propagating public trust and confidence (McCarthy, 2013), but whose effects are less easily read.

A related issue of course is the fact that the crime profile is changing, with a marked increase in online 'cyber-enabled' offences, including fraud (College of Policing, 2015a). These changes in aggregate offending patterns signal the need for at least a partial shift away from policing 'conventional crime' in a physical neighbourhood setting. As well as the digital impetus, recent years have also seen a number of high-profile sensitive cases involving vulnerable victims, both current and historic, which now demand a considerable amount of police time and effort (HMIC, 2015). Identifying, protecting, and supporting those at risk of crimes such as domestic abuse, sexual exploitation, and trafficking is difficult and complex work that increasingly takes up police resource across the country.

Whilst bearing such trajectories of development in mind is important because of how the digital dimension to social life is becoming so significant, it is equally vital that the police as an institution do not forget the 'analogue'. There is a definite trend of police and PCSOs seeking to exploit social media as an engagement tool to help maintain a virtual presence in communities. However, research suggests that the proliferating number and dominance of virtual platforms in no way represent a panacea for effective community support work. Stapleford (2017) reports that traditional communication methods for younger age groups, such as a police presence in schools, are more highly valued by them in terms of feeling safe and reassured than social media, which is used more for awareness raising. When surveys ask the general public which forms of communication make them feel safer in their local area, face-to-face interaction with a police officer is the dominant response and, for just under half of people, this includes interaction with a community support worker on patrol (HMIC, 2014).

Given this confluence of influences and pressures, it is perhaps unsurprising that there have been a number of attempts to revise who PCSOs are and what they do. By 2016, a number of police forces were making significant changes to the organization and duties of their PCSOs, overlaid upon cuts to their number. In West Mercia, selected PCSOs were being trained as retained firefighters as part of a joint pilot in 2016, released from police duty for training over a five-week period (Hereford Times, 2016). Sussex Police have geographically re-organized their PCSOs so that they respond to issues from a shared base rather than being responsible for a particular area. They are also purportedly recruiting for a 'new type' of PCSO with enhanced enforcement powers (The Argus, 2016). Both of these developments feed through into problems with retaining and developing staff in PCSO roles where new and different skills and training are required.

One consequence of the central government squeeze on police funding in 2010 was a freeze on new police officer recruitment throughout England and Wales. Employment as a PCSO came to represent an indirect entry route (along with being a special constable or police cadet) to the police officer profession, and one that was actively encouraged by the police service (Cosgrove and Ramshore, 2013). It was justified on the grounds that it allowed those with such an ambition to gain valued experience within a police force and a 'foot in the door' to transfer internally. However, this was at the detriment of establishing long-term relationships between police and communities brokered by individuals committed to the community support role. It was reflected in the demographic profile of the new cohort of officers taken on in Wales in 2012. They were more likely to be young and male, fewer were from a minority ethnic background, and they were drawn from a fairly limited number of occupational backgrounds. This contrasts with the traditional demographic profile of PCSOs nationally, which was more diverse in terms of gender and ethnicity than any other part of the police service (Home Office, 2007). Such findings are a reflection that PCSOs who come to the profession later in life, bringing with them considerable life experience, skills, and learning beneficial to the role, are becoming increasingly fewer in number (College of Policing, 2015a). More subtly, these recruitment patterns and the lack of a formal career development pathway as a PCSO have buttressed a perception within the police service that the 'good ones' go off to become 'proper' police officers. This is inflected by the higher premium and credibility attached to crime work over community work within cop culture (Cosgrove and Ramshore, 2013). Taken together, these factors have contributed to a high turnover or 'churn' of CSOs, with all the risks this entails.

Conclusion

The title of this chapter makes reference to a defining tension about the purpose and functions of a particular policing role that has become integral to, and almost synonymous with, the delivery of Neighbourhood Policing, that of the (Police) Community Support Officer. Are they principally concerned with performing support functions for police officers, in effect directly increasing their capacity and capability? Or, is their function to engage in activities that might promote levels of community resilience, cohesion, and collective efficacy, shaping public reassurance, trust, and confidence to contribute more indirectly to the prevention of crime and disorder? The nature and salience of this uncertainty about precisely what these officers can and should be doing is reflected in their shifting nomenclature. They started out as Police Community Safety Officers, only to later be revised to Community Support Officers, with or without the Police prefix.

Significantly, this ambiguity about whether 'police support' or 'community support' functions constitute the proper role for police auxiliaries resonates with deeper, more philosophical arguments about the fundamental mission of the police. Indeed, it is one of the profound ironies of the contemporary scene that many officers are now talking openly and at length about how their role is 'so much more than crime', involving responding to various kinds of vulnerability. Foregrounding this change necessitates sustaining investment in Neighbourhood Policing Teams, albeit that their focus may require reconfiguring. This was precisely the conclusion of a number of the early seminal ethnographies of police work that were largely ignored or disputed by many police officers at the time. Contesting the more dramatic portrayals of police as pure 'crime-fighters', authors such as Reiner (1978) labelled police as 'blue coated workers' and Punch (1979) 'a secret social service', to capture the mundane and heterogeneous nature of much of the order maintenance work that is performed by officers when out in the community and on patrol. These are jobs that do not require a legal power of arrest and as such are absolutely the kinds of tasks PCSOs are well placed to take on. As such, there is a 'deep' connection to the fundamental mission of the police as a social institution, even though the PCSO role is not that of the police constable.

In seeking to clarify and understand how and why the CSO role is different to that of the police constable, and how this plugs into the conduct of Neighbourhood Policing, the empirical data has highlighted an important conceptual point—how Neighbourhood Policing is conceptualized and performed in different areas varies. Across England and Wales, different forces have designed and delivered their services to the public differently. In some areas, CSOs have been deployed in ways that are more clearly aligned with the idea that they are to provide support functions for the work of their warranted colleagues. Moreover, there is some evidence to suggest that over time, especially as the effects of public sector austerity and reduction in police funding were felt more acutely, this disposition became more commonplace. That said, there are other areas of the country where the accent for PCSOs was more avowedly focused upon public-facing community engagement and support.

In some ways this should not be unexpected. A strategy such as Neighbourhood Policing is, after all, intended to be responsive to local needs and harms, and thus flex to local contexts and conditions. That said however, the empirical data do speak to the fact that there is often a relatively 'loose coupling' between policy and practice in policing. The former does not determine the latter. In the case of Neighbourhood Policing, informed principally by research evidence distilled from the National Reassurance Policing Programme, but also other work in the community policing tradition, there was a reasonably detailed delivery model with associated principles and rationales set out. However, in establishing how they would configure these locally for their particular areas, individual Chief Constables maintained greater and lesser degrees of fidelity to the originating model. As a consequence, Neighbourhood Policing accomplished different things in different communities.

Cutting across these variances however, there is little doubt the figure of the (Police) Community Support Officer was an integral element of Neighbourhood Policing, whether performing more police support or community support functions. Framed by the empirical analysis reported herein, the particular importance of this role was its recognition of what could be accomplished through the invocation of 'soft power'. Unlike their warranted colleagues endowed with legal powers to invoke arrests as a form of coercive 'hard power', PCSOs were far more reliant upon their powers of persuasion and influence to get things done. They were also critical in establishing conduits for the passing of community intelligence, through 'normalizing' the process of police–community engagement.

6

The Cardiff Community Engagement Experiment

Reassurance policing, and the systems and processes derived from it for Neighbourhood Policing, were predicated upon the idea of local neighbourhood officers working to diagnose and understand the problems that really matter to individuals and communities. Indeed, notwithstanding their differences, a golden thread connecting the two models was the idea that prior to developing and delivering interventions, police need to engage systematically with communities in order to understand with precision any problems they are encountering. In so doing, there are clear affinities with the accent upon 'scanning' to be found in Problem Oriented Policing (POP). But equally, and as rehearsed in the opening chapter, integrating engagement into these arrangements introduced something unique. Specifically, it afforded an opportunity to enrich the police viewpoint of what the key problems and issues actually are, on the grounds that it circumvents the well-documented tendency for some crime and disorder problems to be under-reported to, and under-recorded by, police.

There is, however, a strikingly consistent finding in the literature on community policing—that officers do not tend to value or see particular significance in engagement activity (Herbert, 2006). There is a litany of research studies, recording police–community engagement activities as fairly perfunctory and ritualistic undertakings, with little accomplished in terms of discernible outcome. Over the fifteen-year period that we have been working on Neighbourhood Policing, only a relatively small number of officers have ever grasped the potential power of community engagement if conducted well. Relatedly, the willingness of police organizations to undertake engagement comprehensively and in a systematic and structured manner has proven to be the exception rather than the rule.

Neighbourhood Policing. Martin Innes, Colin Roberts, Trudy Lowe, and Helen Innes, Oxford University Press (2020). © Martin Innes, Colin Roberts, Trudy Lowe, and Helen Innes.
DOI: 10.1093/oso/9780198783213.003.0001

In this chapter we discuss a particular project that, embedded within the overarching research programme, sought to challenge this disposition in police occupational culture, as well as general organizational resistance. It involved work whose principal aim was to test, quite rigorously, what benefits could be attained by police adopting a systematic community engagement methodology. The key features of this approach were incorporated into a bespoke, computer-assisted interview instrument. This was aligned with a set of procedures to collect community intelligence data from each neighbourhood, analyse it, and then use the insights it generated to inform the design and delivery of policing interventions reflecting the diversity of neighbourhood needs. Compared with the police–community meeting Police and Communities Together (PACT) and public surveys which were the predominant vehicles for these kinds of police–community contacts at the time this work was conducted, the approach described provides a considerably richer picture view of a community and the issues assailing it.

To capture and articulate these qualities, the chapter is built around a case study of work in Cardiff. This is salient as it represented an attempt to deliver an innovative approach to police–community engagement 'at scale', where most prior innovations have either tended to be based upon relatively small areas or, when delivered across larger territories, reliant upon fairly conventional methods. In contrast, herein we are talking about a city-wide experiment. It was 'experimental' in the classical meaning of the term, inasmuch as a particular variable—the quality and quantity of police–community engagement—was manipulated and compared with more established and orthodox police approaches to this element of their function. Moreover, and in keeping with this experimentalist orientation, working on a city-wide scale enables an ability to understand how different local community contexts structure and 'colour' engagement processes and practices.

The chapter starts by sketching a brief outline of Cardiff as a place and the approach adopted to delivering Neighbourhood Policing across the city. This is followed by a brief recitation of the key principles embedded within the SENSOR engagement methodology. These are developed by comparing and contrasting them with the reach and coverage achieved by a postal survey to a local Citizens' Panel and PACT meetings, which were South Wales Police's preferred engagement mechanisms at the time. The penultimate section of the chapter then sets out some of the key community intelligence insights generated by operationalizing the methodology across the city, together with a discussion of what police did in respect of some of the issues identified. By way of conclusion, we describe what lessons were learnt from the Cardiff experiment.

Cardiff: context and community

As the capital city of Wales, Cardiff is the largest population centre in the South Wales Police force area. The administrative area of the city is covered by twenty-nine electoral wards and a total of 1,010 Office for National Statistics 'Output Areas'. In 2008, when the study was conducted, the city was managed by South Wales Police as six Neighbourhood Management Areas (NMAs), which were units also used by the local authority in an attempt to harmonize aspects of their service delivery across agencies. In policing terms, each NMA had an assigned local Neighbourhood Policing Team, comprising sworn neighbourhood police officers and relatively newly recruited and trained Police Community Support Officers (PCSOs).

The resident population at the time was estimated at around 330,000 and relatively young (according to the 2001 Census 24 per cent of residents were under twenty years), exacerbated by the fact that students from two large universities live in the city. Ethnically, the population was and remains predominantly white British, with a smaller minority ethnic population composed of significant Asian/Asian British and Black/Black British communities. Although it has its prosperous areas, and parts of the city have benefitted from considerable economic investment, overall, many areas remain relatively deprived: 46 per cent of local authority Lower Level Super Output Areas (LSOAs) were among the top 50 per cent of most deprived LSOAs in the Welsh Index of Multiple Deprivation (WIMD) 2014, of which 17 per cent were in the 10 per cent most deprived areas in Wales (Welsh Government, 2014).

To contextualize a number of the issues that will be highlighted and discussed, it is important to note that, in the years immediately prior to the Cardiff Community Engagement experiment, levels of recorded crime had fallen, although they were beginning to creep back up towards their previous level. However, this fall had not brought about reductions in fear of crime. South Wales

Police survey data recorded at that time revealed high levels of public worry about certain crimes (violence and burglary in particular), clearly suggesting a widening 'reassurance gap' in the city (Innes et al., 2009). To put it another way, although the trend in aggregate recorded crime was flat and stable, public concern about it was rising.

Police awareness of these perceptual trends at the time was largely based upon their use of a 'Citizen's Panel', established and run by Cardiff Council and comprising a representative sample of 1,400 members of the public living in Cardiff who had volunteered to receive regular opinion and attitude surveys. South Wales Police and other local Community Safety Partnership (CSP) agencies were regularly consulting these individuals about various public safety and wellbeing issues, principally through structured survey questionnaires.

Data and insights from these consultations were supplemented and augmented by information generated through local PACT meetings, conducted under the auspices of South Wales Police's delivery of Neighbourhood Policing. At the time, most areas had PACT meetings being organized, albeit with varying degrees of regularity, by officers from the respective local Neighbourhood Policing Teams. Critically, because of the localized delivery structures pivoting round the Neighbourhood Management Areas, no-one really appeared to have a comprehensive overview of how much police–community engagement was being conducted, nor its quality. As such, one of the key objectives of the 'Cardiff Experiment' was to compare the reach and richness of the intelligence gained from adopting a more proactive and innovative approach to engagement with these more established, passive measures.

The experiment

'SENSOR' Neighbourhood Security Interviews

The principal engagement methodology utilized in the Cardiff work was the intelligence-orientated Neighbourhood Security Interview, or 'SENSOR'. Originally developed by the research team as part of their work on the National Reassurance Policing Programme (NRPP), the methodology is based on the Signal Crimes Perspective (Innes, 2014), described in detail in the Appendix.

In essence, it provides a structured approach to conducting pro-active, in-depth interviews with members of the public regarding their experiences, knowledge, and perceptions of problems in their neighbourhoods. The interview instrument typically runs on a laptop or computer tablet, allowing maps of the local area to be shown to interview participants to aid data collection. Thus, a particular sampling logic integrated with a set of analytic and inter-pretative procedures are used to identify those signal crimes and disorders that are having greatest impact on collective thoughts, feelings, and behaviour in the target area.

A key innovation of the SENSOR methodology is the selection of 'Neighbourhood Sentinels' as respondents. Neighbourhood Sentinels can be defined as local residents who, by virtue of their social networks or familiarity with an area, have developed es-pecially high levels of knowledge about key places and people associated with them. In effect, they possess enhanced situational awareness. They are particularly well placed to provide informed insights about the prevalence and distribution of any issues in an area.

For the Cardiff experiment using this approach, a total of 746 SENSOR interviews were conducted over a ten-week period be-tween January and April 2008. This was 74 per cent of the target originally set for the project to conduct one interview in each of Cardiff's 1010 Output Areas. Most of the areas where an interview was not completed were lower 'demand' ones according to a pro-file of local area crime rates and deprivation that was used to sup-port the work (Innes et al., 2009). The majority of the interviews were conducted by a team of PCSOs seconded full-time to the work, who were supplemented and mentored by a small team of experienced university researchers. The former were trained in the interview methodology, with regular 'dip check' samples of work made by the researchers in an effort to ensure that the interviews were being conducted in a consistent manner. In addition, several features were built into the computer software used to guide the interviews and record data to help with quality assurance.

As an aside, these quality control measures uncovered some interesting insights into the staff performing a front-line commu-nity engagement role for South Wales Police. Whilst some dem-onstrated an aptitude and appetite for this aspect of their work, others were reluctant and clearly lacked the appropriate skills. Intriguingly, it appeared from these data that some of the least experienced staff, who felt neither confident nor competent to engage with the public, were assigned to areas where such skills and contacts were most needed. For instance, two young white men, on their first police assignments as PCSOs, were assigned to ethnically heterogeneous areas of the city where community tensions were heightened due to concerns about the implementation of the PREVENT counter-terrorism strategy.

Citizen's Panel Survey

At the time when the work in Cardiff was being conceived and considered, the police's approach to engagement gravitated around two main methods: police community meetings of the type described in Chapter 3 and a survey of local residents administered by the local council. In an effort to try and understand what benefits, if any, the SENSOR methodology might afford as a public engagement mechanism, a systematic assessment was simultaneously conducted of the Citizen's Panel postal survey and local PACT meetings. The idea was that, by running these three methods in parallel with each other, it would be possible to compare and contrast the respective insights yielded.

A well-documented methodological problem with postal surveys is that of non-response bias: whilst the original sample may be representative of a larger target population, this does not necessarily mean that the replies received will be. With this in mind, a structured postal survey instrument was designed and sent to all 1,400 members of Cardiff Council's existing Citizen's Panel. The instrument contained questions spanning a number of public safety topics. Consistent with findings from the established social research methods literature, it transpired that the non-response rate was quite high—only 301 completed forms were returned. This constitutes a response rate of 21.5 per cent, which is what one would typically expect for a postal survey.

Respondents were asked to include their postcodes as part of their survey returns. This information was used to ascertain whether people who chose to participate in the Citizen's Panel were more likely to live in certain areas of the city than non-responders. When these location data were geo-coded and plotted on to a map of the city, it was clearly evidenced that the majority of the 301 survey respondents did not live in those areas predicted to have high demand for policing and other public services.

Indeed, it was notable that a sizeable proportion of them were living in areas of the city that historically had a reputation for being relatively affluent and with few crime and disorder problems. The inference drawn from this distribution was that the citizens being engaged by police via the Citizen's Panel methodology were not living in the areas where public safety problems were especially acute. When compared to the geographic distribution of the completed SENSOR interviews, this relationship was reversed. The PCSOs and researchers were more likely to complete interviews in the harder-pressed neighbourhoods across the city, and least likely to conduct them in the low crime areas.

A second point of comparison for the two methods was to examine the demographic profiles of respective participants. Clearly evident was how respondents to the Citizen's Panel were dramatically skewed towards older age groups (particularly those aged sixty and over), meaning that the overall profile was not at all representative of Cardiff's population as recorded in the 2001 Census. The sample achieved through the systematic engagement of Neighbourhood Sentinels was far closer to the age profile recorded in the Census.

Further divergence between those who replied to the Citizen's Panel survey and the demography of Cardiff is evident when we consider ethnicity. The 2001 Census recorded that 13 per cent of the population of Cardiff were from visible ethnic minorities. Only 9 per cent of the respondents to the Citizen's Panel self-defined in this way, compared to 11 per cent of the SENSOR participants. As such, even this 'first cut' of the data generated from the more proactive SENSOR process suggests that it was proving more successful in extending the reach and coverage of South Wales Police's engagement into and across different communities than the Citizen Panel survey.

PACT meeting analysis

As rehearsed in the preceding sections, South Wales Police were not just using the Cardiff Citizen's Panel to engage with local communities in the city, they were also conducting community meetings. PACT meetings were organized and led by local Neighbourhood Policing Team officers, intended as vehicles via which police could access community concerns and report on how they were responding to these. At the time the research was conducted, PACT meetings had become established as one of the key mechanisms for engagement utilized by Neighbourhood Policing Teams. Indeed, in many areas, they have retained this prominence to this day. This is despite suspicions that they tend to afford a 'narrow' form of engagement, attracting participation from only a small band of 'usual suspects' and capturing a limited diversity of viewpoints. This is problematic given their purported role in steering the establishment of priorities for local police action.

Framed by such concerns, a defined strand of the research activity compared the reach and depth of one-to-one public engagement via the SENSOR methodology with that of the community meeting approach. A key finding in this respect was that, of the 746 individuals who engaged in the SENSOR process, 73 per cent stated that they had not previously attended a PACT meeting. To develop the implications of this insight, ethnographic observations were conducted at twenty PACT meetings held in and around the more central areas of Cardiff in an effort to discern who was attending the typical PACT meeting. This revealed that, once you discounted the presence of those attending in an official capacity (such as police officers, local councillors), together with those representing institutional interests (such as estates and facilities managers and so forth), the average PACT meeting was being attended by 10.9 ordinary members of the public. Behind this headline average, there was considerable variation. One meeting saw thirty-three members of the public present, whereas the lowest attendance was four. Over half of the meetings sampled (eleven out of twenty) were attended by fewer than ten members of the public.

In an effort to further understand whether this pattern of attendance was leading to these police–community meetings being 'captured' by a narrow range of interests, the documentary records of all PACT meetings held in Cardiff between March 2007 and the same month in 2008 were collected and analysed. The priorities set at each of the meetings were extracted from the minutes and aggregated across the number of meetings to establish the top three priorities for each PACT over this one-year time period. In total, the priorities from 124 separate PACT meetings were collated and aggregated. This aggregation was necessary because different neighbourhood areas appeared to have held PACT meetings with different frequency and records were missing or not publicly available from a number of the meetings. The priorities were calculated using a simple scoring system: each time an issue was placed as the top priority it was scored three points, when it was a second priority two points, and a third placed priority one point. The scores for each individual problem that was identified in a series of PACT meetings were then summed to establish what the key priorities for the meetings held in that ward were. This procedure enabled us to construct PACT priority profiles for eighteen of Cardiff's twenty-nine wards.

Informed by these data, it was concluded that the PACT meetings in a number of areas appeared to have become fixated upon particular local issues, with the same priorities being set recurrently. For example, in one area of the city, the PACT meeting appeared to have fixed upon a link between drug-dealing and anti-social behaviour locally. Across the eight PACT meetings sampled, in all but one drug-dealing was set as the number one priority.

This tendency to 'fix' on particular problems could be symptomatic of one of three things. First, it may be that the authorities were not willing or able to respond to expressed public concerns about a chronic problem, thus the repetition reflected a desire for a solution to the issue to be implemented. A second explanation is that the agenda of these groups was effectively being hijacked by the particular 'single issue' concerns of a minority of regular attendees. Alternatively, a form of 'group-think' had set in, wherein the collective dynamic of the PACT process continually led them to formulate the causes of local problems in a similar way.

Taken together, this analysis of the more established and orthodox approaches to police–community engagement adopted in Cardiff illuminated the constrained and narrow nature of the input South Wales Police were receiving via these methods. Set against this backdrop, the investment in the SENSOR methodology was intended to change engagement from being a 'reactive' function to a 'proactive' one. The vast majority of contacts that police have with ordinary, law abiding members of the public tend to be initiated by the public themselves. This applies not only to one-on-one contact but also public meetings where police arrange and convene a gathering but are dependent upon individual citizens turning out to participate. The SENSOR methodology, on the other hand, places the onus on police to proactively 'reach out' and research people's concerns. The difference between these two approaches can be captured quite succinctly. The rationale of the former is 'come and tell us your problems'; the latter, 'we are coming to find out what your problems are'. This second approach conveys a subtly different message about how police are construing their relations with the public.

Community intelligence insights

Having outlined some of the key attributes of the methodology underpinning the experiment, we now describe some of the community intelligence derived from its operationalization in Cardiff. These data provide insights into which issues and locations were especially influential in shaping citizens' experiences of safety and security across the city.

From the 746 SENSOR interviews conducted, respondents identified over 2,000 signal crimes and disorders across the city, falling within thirteen thematic groups. Table 6.1 below shows the top ten problems ranked by a simple count of the number of times that category was mentioned by the total sample.

Table 6.1 Signal Crimes and Disorders Ranking

Signals	Count	Rank	Associated Expressions	Count	Rank
Groups of youths	525	1	Groups of youths	820	1
Inconsiderate parking	155	=2	Litter	492	2
Burglary (domestic)	155	=2	People shouting	490	3
Graffiti	142	4	Public drinking	464	4
Speeding	139	5	Graffiti	432	5
Theft from vehicles	113	6	Verbal abuse	430	6
Damage to vehicles	97	7	Broken glass	408	7
Litter	91	8	Threatening behaviour	381	8
Drug dealing (public)	69	9	Damage to vehicles	350	9
Damage to bus shelters	64	10	Damage to buildings	325	10

In an effort to capture the complexities of how people make sense of the risks and threats they perceive in their social environments, this approach to the analysis differentiates between the highly visible 'Signal' and other problematic issues associated with that signal. On the right of the table therefore, a similar ranking of the total number of 'Associated Expressions' are reported.

Overall, what these data convey is how the principal public concerns about public safety and security in the city gravitated around sixteen types of problem. Consistent with the findings from the NRPP, these comprised a blend of crimes, social and environmental disorders. Specific incidents relating to these problem categories were responsible for over half of the issues that respondents indicated were inducing a change in how they were thinking, feeling, or acting in relation to their security.

Perception 'hotspots' and recorded crime

In a practical register, a signal crimes-oriented approach to neighbourhood security is designed to detect those events that really matter to a community by virtue of the impact they have on how people think, feel, and act in relation to them. This event-based logic does not then seek to catalogue every occurrence of crime and disorder, but rather to focus in upon those that appear to have capacity to shape and influence levels of harm and the ways people construct their sense of safety. As detailed above, analysis of the data collected in Cardiff was able to clearly identify that there were certain types of crime, social disorder, and physical disorder that were having a definitive influence upon many people's views about their neighbourhood and the city more generally. A key component of the SENSOR interview methodology is not just identifying what problems are triggering public concern, but also where these are located. This is both a way of trying to validate issues brought forward by interview respondents so that they do not just talk about abstract worries and concerns, and a way of eliciting useful intelligence for police in terms of which locations they should focus upon when making any interventions. Subjecting this dimension of the data to geo-spatial analytics techniques affords understanding about the geographical distribution of these impactful problems. Mapping these data in Cardiff illustrated clearly that the signal crimes and disorders detected in the city were not uniformly distributed, but tended to cluster and congregate in particular locations.

This approach to processing and depicting the data has clear affinities to the suite of analytic techniques associated with the 'hotspots' oriented version of intelligence-led policing (Ratcliffe, 2016). As a model, hotspots policing is designed to direct and steer police attention and resources towards 'crime attracting' locations, informed by analyses of the geo-spatial aspects of recorded crime and incident data (Weisburd, 2015). The key innovation introduced in the Cardiff engagement experiment was applying similar principles and techniques to hotspots policing, but in relation to perceptual data. A key finding deriving from this application is that, just as crime clusters and coagulates around certain places, so too do public concerns and worries. Importantly however, and as described in more detail below, the physical locations of recorded crime hotspots and perception hotspots are not always aligned.

Mapping the geographic spread of signals in this manner gave a sense of how, from the citizens' perspective, risk was seen to be distributed across the city. There were particular areas that were seen as being places where worrying and troublesome events occurred regularly and, attached to these 'hot signal' locations, were particular effects, such as people being genuinely fearful and actively avoiding them. In policing terms, representing the geographic distribution of signals in this manner rendered them as intelligence. It identified those precise localities where South Wales Police needed to target assets and effort to attempt to address the public's subjective perceptions of risk.

There are important differences between the approach operationalized in Cardiff as part of South Wales Police's delivery of Neighbourhood Policing and more orthodox constructions of POP. What the police in Cardiff were doing was using the systematic and structured citizen engagement process to scan for issues having a detectable public impact, and using the empirical data generated from these interactions to drive the problem-definition work that precedes the implementation of problem-solving interventions. It was, in effect, deployed as a 'problem-finding' methodology, setting up the potential for meaningful 'problem-solving'.

Intriguingly however, further analysis revealed that the areas of highest signal density, where signal crimes and disorders were most abundant, were not always the same places as those that historically had a reputation amongst city residents for being especially problematic. Nor were they always those with objectively high recorded crime and disorder profiles. In an attempt to concisely represent some of these complexities, Figure 6.1

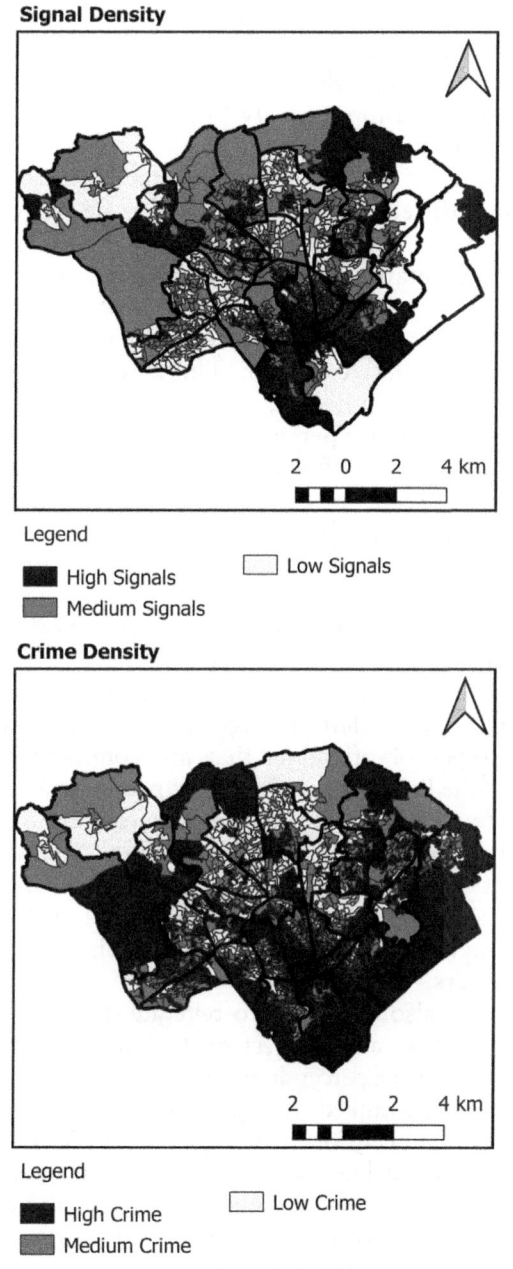

Figure 6.1 Signal Crime and Disorder and Recorded Crime Density

compares the signal data with recorded crime data. The first map divides the city into thirds according to the relative density of signals. Those areas shaded black are in the top third in terms of having a comparatively high signal density, the grey areas are the middle density locations and the white areas have the lowest levels of recorded signals. The second map depicts a similar procedure, but this time displaying police recorded crime data.

Viewing these maps alongside each other, several key features can be observed. There are a number of areas that feature as 'high' or 'low' for both datasets. Equally important however, are the differences between them. There are some regions that feature high for one indicator, but not the other. So there are neighbourhoods that are perceived as problematic and troublesome by residents, but this is not necessarily supported according to police recorded crime data. Equally, there are areas where crime appears fairly common, but for whatever reason, public perceptions do not appear to be unduly influenced by such behaviour.

It would appear then, that whilst the perception of risk does track levels of recorded crime to some extent, its association is not always completely aligned. In some areas, people seem to either accept and tolerate a relatively high level of crime and disorder. Perhaps the types of offending that are commonplace in such places are not the kinds of problems that people tend to register in terms of shifting how they think, feel, or act about their security more broadly. Conversely, in a number of other areas, a high perception of risk does not seem to correlate with levels of police recorded crime, perhaps reflective of the kind of problems that do not tend to make it into crime statistics, such as environmental physical disorders.

That said, it is also important to reiterate that there were areas where the 'objective' and 'subjective' Cardiff datasets coincided. Figure 6.2 integrates the perceptions and police datasets, highlighting in black those areas ranked as 'high' across both measures of recorded crime and publicly identified signal events. In effect, this combined approach was delineating areas with relatively high volumes of crime and disorder, where these incidents were also causing high levels of public harm. For local police, this afforded a relatively sophisticated intelligence picture that could be used to prioritize how

Signal and Crime Density Difference Map

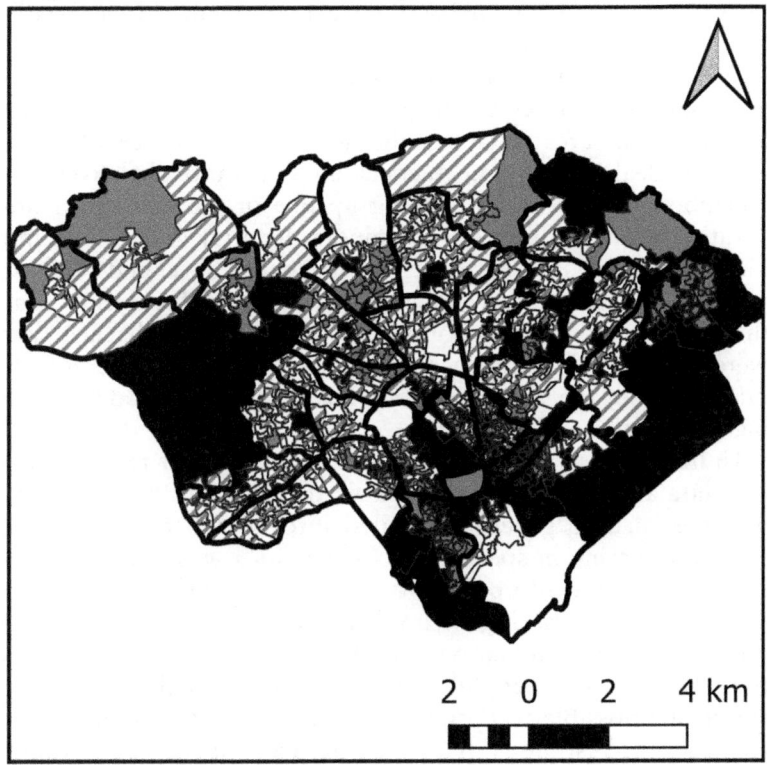

Legend

■ High Crime and Signal Density
□ High Crime Density Only
▤ High Signal Density Only
▨ Low-Medium Signal and Crime Density

Figure 6.2 Signal and Crime Density Differential

they organized and delivered their Neighbourhood Policing interventions. The signal crimes approach to diagnosing key issues allowed largely shorter-term acute crime problems and longer-term chronic disorder problems to be distinguished, ensuring that the right kinds of resources and assets were made available to tackle the spectrum of risks and threats that combine to impact upon how citizens experience neighbourhood security.

Whilst visualizing data in this way can prove useful to police managers in terms of planning an operational strategy across a large area, it is arguably less useful to officers 'on the ground' dealing with the tactical and operational delivery of Neighbourhood Policing. Picking up one of the theoretical imperatives from Chapter 4, it is important to try and understand Neighbourhood Policing in terms of what it does, and not just what is said about it in policy statements and documents. It is thus significant that the kinds of community intelligence that were being sought and generated by the engagement interactions undertaken by the Neighbourhood Policing Teams in Cardiff were highly granular and detailed.

Unlike more typical community surveys which tend to collect data at a fairly aggregated level, the SENSOR methodology was designed to generate detailed information about specific events occurring in specific places. The idea was that it should be possible to 'drill down' into the detailed circumstances associated with these high-crime/high-signal areas. By mapping out the recurring and co-occurring crime and disorder incidents that disturb local people's sense of security in these areas, it should be possible to design multi-faceted, contextually sensitive policing responses that take into account the varied range of issues involved in rendering a place troublesome or worrisome. Accordingly, this section of the chapter provides a detailed, high-resolution case study of what exactly this focused community intelligence work enabled in relation to a key microlocation in Cardiff.

Cowbridge Road East (Figure 6.3), lying just west of the main city centre, emerged as the most 'coherent' location for signals of insecurity across the whole of Cardiff. The term 'coherence' is used here to denote the highest level of agreement between multiple respondents about the signal crimes and disorders occurring therein. In addition to Cowbridge Road East itself, the analysis was extended to include a number of adjoining roads that were identified as being beset by similar kinds of problems.

A variety of strong and coherent signal events were present at the time of the data collection, many of which were associated

Significant Location: Cowbridge Road East

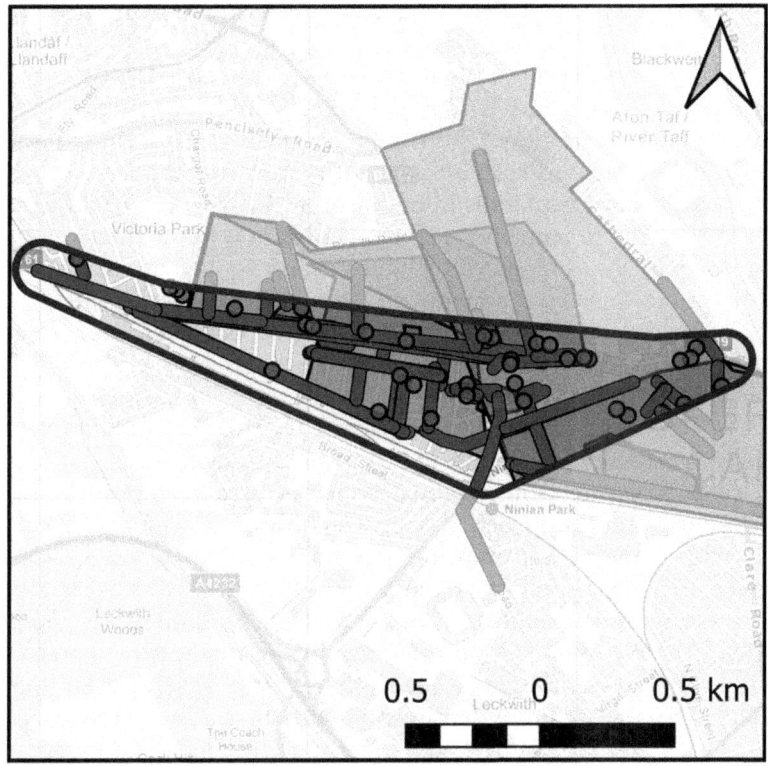

Legend

☐ Area Highlight   ▬ Linear Signals

● Signal Points   ▨ Signal Areas

Figure 6.3 Cowbridge Road East, All Signals

with the activities of young people in the area. Repeated references were made to the public consumption of alcohol, public violence, verbal abuse, broken glass, and litter, as well as various forms of criminal damage. Relatively strong signals were also identified in relation to drug use and supply and a small number of respondents also mentioned incidents of racist hate crime and knife possession. Viewed in aggregate, these kinds of issues were reported to be particularly prevalent on Fridays and Saturday evenings.

Turning to the individual and collective impacts of these problems upon people's sense of safety and security, the analysis revealed a range of emotional, cognitive, and behavioural reactions to them. Of those who intimated that their exposure to these kind of problems in and around Cowbridge Road East was troubling in some way, 19 per cent said it made them angry and 17 per cent referenced feelings of fear. Sixteen per cent indicated it had triggered a heightened sense of a threat to safety in their outlook, whilst others suggested that occurrence of these problems led them to conclude the area was 'degenerating' (15 per cent).

Overall, the detailed data generated from across public interviews conducted in the area indicated Cowbridge Road East was an area suffering from ongoing issues of alcohol-related youth disorder. These issues were having a significant impact on the perceived personal safety of local residents.

How the local policing team used this analysis was especially interesting and insightful about the value of community intelligence to Neighbourhood Policing. In the qualitative material collected during the interviews, there were several mentions made by separate individual respondents that a lot of the issues congregated around the local supermarket. The store in question had a car park with no lighting and was not covered by any CCTV cameras. It also contained quite a lot of overgrown weeds and shrubs. As a consequence, local young people hung out there, creating a nuisance of themselves by engaging in lots of relatively minor forms of antisocial behaviour. It was also sometimes used by local drug users as a space where they could inject themselves out of the public view. Armed with this community intelligence, the police responsible for the local area devised a multi-dimensional response. This included adopting a more assertive intervention posture in respect of some of the recurrent antisocial behaviour issues in the area, by, for instance, taking out Anti-Social Behaviour Orders in respect of a small number of individuals whose behaviour was especially problematic.

In addition, they also leveraged a series of situational crime prevention measures. Quite creatively, members of the Neighbourhood

Policing Team took the community intelligence analysis to the managers of the supermarket to try and persuade them to do something. It worked. The car park was tidied up and lighting and security cameras installed. Staff in the shop took greater 'ownership' of the public spaces surrounding the store, for instance sweeping up litter and so forth. At the same time, they tightened up on selling alcohol to people who appeared underage. Collectively, these changes had a discernible impact upon the local disorder problems. Over a period of three months, public calls to the police to report incidents of antisocial behaviour declined dramatically. Even more interestingly, the manager of the store reported to police that they had seen a marked increase in their 'footfall statistics'.

Implicit in this case study is a sense of how the integration of the signal crimes perspective into the delivery processes for Neighbourhood Policing effectively provides a demand management tool. What the analysis was indicating was how the police did not need to attend equally to all crime and disorder occurring in an area. Rather, it was by understanding which incidents were having a disproportionate impact upon public perceptions and experiences that they could steer their attention and efforts towards those problems where interventions were most likely to enhance levels of reassurance and neighbourhood security.

In addition to the operational policing benefits accrued from being able to understand how multiple troubles and problems connect and reinforce each other in particular defined micro-locations, there were further insights gleaned from collecting these kinds of data at a 'whole city' scale. As Taylor (2015) amongst others has noted, how one defines the geographic 'unit of analysis' in any empirical study serves to simultaneously illuminate and obscure particular dimensions of the data involved. To put this another way, it is quite likely that public perception priorities at the scale of a city will differ from those in its constituent neighbourhoods.

With this in mind, Table 6.2 lists the top three signal crimes and disorders identified via the SENSOR methodology for four of the NMAs in Cardiff. This suggests a relatively variegated picture in terms of comparing across the areas, whilst simultaneously identifying some fairly common problems. Alongside

Table 6.2 Comparison of Top Signals and PACT Priorities

Neighbourhood Management Area	PACT Priority		Top Signals
Canton & Ely	1	ASB	Youth disorder
	2	Drugs	Theft from vehicles
	3	Parking	Drug dealing
Llanishen & Llanedeyrn	1	Parking	Youth disorder
	2	ASB	Graffiti
	3	Speeding	Inconsiderate parking
Roath & Cathays	1	ASB	Inconsiderate parking
	2	Parking	Theft from vehicles
	3	Car crime	Litter
Rumney & St Mellons	1	ASB	Youth disorder
	2	Speeding	Graffiti
	3	Underage drinking	Burglary (domestic)

the signals data, we have included the PACT priorities for these four NMAs to facilitate a second form of comparative analysis of the two engagement methodologies. This will discern the extent to which similar issues and problems were being highlighted.

'Eyeballing' these data suggests that across the four units of analysis there was a reasonable degree of correspondence between the two methods, but also important points of departure. Notably, the crimes of burglary and drug-dealing were picked up through the signal crimes-based analysis but did not feature as PACT priorities. Similarly, graffiti was a salient issue in two of the areas according to the SENSOR approach, but was not highlighted in the PACT meetings. Where the signal crimes analysis undoubtedly 'adds value' though is in the level of granularity that can be achieved through the analysis. This significantly aids the calibrating and targeting of interventions to those issues causing public harm at a local level.

Conclusion: a base for democratic policing

Fundamentally, the Cardiff community engagement experiment was designed to test, 'at scale' whether the delivery of Neighbourhood Policing could integrate a structured and systematic engagement methodology, and what benefits and unique insights could be accrued from doing so. The project and methodology described probably represents one of the most ambitious and extensive attempts to systematically deliver and test the capacity and capability of police and their partners to generate, analyse, and act upon community intelligence that provides a diagnostic of the drivers of neighbourhood insecurity. An important aspect of this work was comparative analyses contrasting SENSOR with police recorded crime and incidents, and with the priorities derived from the police–community meetings.

Two conclusions can be distilled from these comparisons. First, the empirical data tends to confirm that the neighbourhood security risks and threats that shape public experiences and perceptions vary at a localized level, albeit there are also some commonalities between them. A second key learning point was that different engagement methodologies can potentially generate very different priority issues. This should not be especially surprising, but it is important to have it empirically validated. So whilst there were some similarities and consistencies across the insights deriving from the Citizen's Panel, PACT meetings, and SENSOR interviewing method, there were important differences also. These became especially apparent when taking into account the geographic scale of the unit of analysis. An important, but hitherto unremarked, feature of the empirical analysis presented in this chapter is the way that it deliberately moves between different geo-spatial units. It demonstrates how the kinds of material generated can be amalgamated or disaggregated to provide different views of any situation and its attendant problems. This is important because Neighbourhood Policing Teams operating at street level will typically want to know different things to inform their work than managers working at a more strategic level.

Arguably more important was the demonstration that Neighbourhood Policing, if appropriately configured, could operationalize a systematic and structured proactive community engagement methodology. This methodology has potential to generate community intelligence that affords a more textured and nuanced understanding of what crime and disorder problems function as triggers for concern among particular communities in particular settings. In turn, this enhanced understanding sets up the potential for more precisely calibrated interventions that can respond in a more accurate fashion where they are really needed.

Many of the most trenchant critiques of Neighbourhood Policing and other approaches in the community policing tradition have been based around the notion that whilst considerable accent is placed upon the public value of engaging communities, in practice it often tends to gravitate around little more than consulting a small group of 'usual suspects'. What the Cardiff experiment evidences is that it doesn't have to be this way. The SENSOR approach introduced a more democratic and deliberative feel to the engagement that was taking place, capturing how differing local situations induce different security wants and needs that Neighbourhood Policing can be responsive to. By understanding and evidencing these differences and enabling 'smarter' more precision approaches to intervention in respect of them, there was an embedded form of demand management being enacted.

In this sense, one might describe the approach as integrating some of the discipline of information and knowledge management associated with intelligence-led policing models into the systems and processes of an avowedly community policing oriented approach. Indeed, precisely this quality has been implied by the repeated invocation throughout this chapter of the 'community intelligence' construct. As a term, this strongly denotes how the principal concern here is with issues and problems that are troubling to and harming a local community. There is also a collective dimension to the sourcing of the material, which is part of how it is validated.

This notion is that there should be some kind of democratic input and steering in terms of what the focus of police activity should be. That police should have a regulated responsiveness to community concerns is a defining principle of the community policing tradition. It is certainly something that distinguishes it, for example, from problem-solving, where it is all too easy for police to assume the 'primary definer' role by relying upon their judgement about what 'counts' as a problem warranting their attention.

In engaging with such considerations, in this chapter we have largely adopted a 'cross-sectional' approach to discussing the engagement methodology and its results on the grounds that this enables us to compare and contrast it with other options. However, in the next chapter, the application of this structured methodology is put to test over an extended period of time.

7

Policing and Changing Perceptions of Neighbourhood Security

The preceding chapter showed how a systematic and structured methodology for investigating community perceptions of crime, disorder, and policing can illuminate the extent to which key public concerns vary across space. Implicitly, it concerned how context matters in terms of what problems present as community priorities and where. In this chapter, we describe a project in which the same method is applied, but this time longitudinally. The purpose is to track and trace how the issues that people see as impacting upon their sense of neighbourhood security change and adapt over time. In the process, we can draw some inferences about the extent to which Neighbourhood Policing-based interventions can help to shape local perceptions and experiences of crime and disorder.

This focus is important given the aforementioned empirical limitations with much of the community policing literature. Studies monitoring how such models of policing are implemented over time, and how they mature, remain extremely rare. This is salient in starting to think about whether the quality of interventions practised 'drifts' over time, and the extent to which any impacts or effects attributed to Neighbourhood Policing might be sustainable over the longer term.

In framing such an analysis, it is pertinent that both nationally and locally, the policies guiding and governing the implementation of Neighbourhood Policing have been subject to almost continual refinement and revision. Layered on top have been shifts in governmental ideologies, including significant public sector funding reductions. Although it is not its principal focus, the analysis does provide some insight into how the policy context has fed through

Neighbourhood Policing. Martin Innes, Colin Roberts, Trudy Lowe, and Helen Innes, Oxford University Press (2020). © Martin Innes, Colin Roberts, Trudy Lowe, and Helen Innes.
DOI: 10.1093/oso/9780198783213.003.0001

to influence the ways in which Neighbourhood Policing is experienced by members of the public in their local areas.

To engage with these themes, this chapter presents a case study based upon an extensive programme of work conducted within the London Borough of Sutton (LBS) with the Metropolitan Police Service (MPS). Over the course of more than a decade, SENSOR, the same intelligence-oriented Neighbourhood Security Interview methodology used in Cardiff, has been undertaken annually by MPS officers and Police Community Support Officers (PCSOs) from the Borough's eighteen ward-aligned Safer Neighbourhood Teams. Each year they have interviewed around 600 members of the public living in all of wards in the Borough. These interviews have focused upon understanding what incidents and events are shaping their sense of neighbourhood security at a fine-grained and very localized level. In practice, the resulting data have been used by the MPS and Sutton Council to inform their selection of targeted tactical interventions and for strategic community safety planning purposes. Herein though, we slightly 're-purpose' these data. They provide us with an almost unique opportunity to explore how community perceptions and priorities have adapted and evolved over an extended period of time, and the role of policing interventions in shaping these patterns.

The chapter starts by describing the setting for the research, positioning it as one specific area within the largest police force in the United Kingdom. This flows into an outline of the volume and nature of data collected. Moving on to the data itself, we set out some of the key materials and findings, with particular accent upon presenting it as time-series material. This includes describing how it was used to inform interventions at a local level. The discussion considers both the crime and disorder problems presenting as key shapers of public perceptions and experiences across Sutton, as well as local citizens' views of policing. This latter aspect in particular is used to develop an analysis of factors driving public confidence. Again, the granular nature of the data is important, inasmuch as it suggests that at least to some degree, how the public interprets the state of policing varies over time according to a range of political and economic influences.

The London Borough of Sutton: the place, its people, and its police

Twelve miles south of central London, Sutton is a relatively affluent part of the county of Surrey. Much of its resident population of around 200,000 people consists of younger, working age people. In terms of its ethnic mix, this population is predominantly White British, although there are relatively sizeable established Asian/Asian British and Black/Black British communities (UK Census, 2011). The Borough incorporates Sutton Town Centre, one of four Metropolitan Centres within South London, as well as six district centres, a large number of smaller local centres, and many small and dispersed parades of shops.

The Borough is policed by the London MPS and is one of the safest boroughs in London, with recorded crime consistently ranking in the bottom decile of London boroughs in relation to total notifiable offences over the last decade. Upon implementation of the Neighbourhood Policing Model in 2006 and consistent with what happened across London, each of Sutton's eighteen electoral wards was given a dedicated Safer Neighbourhoods Team (SNT). The teams initially comprised a police sergeant, two police constables, and three PCSOs, the aforementioned '1-2-3 model'. An additional Town Centre SNT was merged with one for Sutton Central ward during the early part of 2010, creating a new, much larger team, staffed with three sergeants, eleven constables, and eight PCSOs.

Since the onset of austerity and considerable reductions in public funding for policing from 2013 onwards, the MPS has significantly reconfigured the make-up of its SNTs. For a while sworn officers undertook a dual role, tasked with responsibility for what had previously been cast as 'response policing' activities. This included investigating some crime types and 'early to late' calls-for-service coverage. Since 2018, a greatly reduced number of constables and sergeants have been dedicated to neighbourhood functions, alongside those PCSOs that remained. At the time of writing, most wards now have just one or two dedicated constables or PCSOs, with sergeants working across ward boundaries within five larger 'neighbourhood management cluster areas'. Over time then, there has been a noticeable diffusion in the 'dosage' of Neighbourhood Policing applied across London.

The MPS in Sutton work closely with the local authority on community safety issues under the auspices of the Safer Sutton Partnership. This involves senior neighbourhood policing and council community safety staff being co-located with response officers at Sutton police station in an effort to facilitate close working relationships.

Although relatively prosperous overall, there are some localized areas of disadvantage in the Borough that are ranked amongst the most deprived in the United Kingdom. Data on levels and distribution of community cohesion collated from all SENSOR surveys since 2007 consistently show people generally enjoy living in their neighbourhood, perceiving it to be safe and considering their quality of life to have been stable, or improved, over the preceding two years. Consistently, most people feel that those living near them will pull together to improve their neighbourhood and that all or most people can be trusted. However, it is notable that a significant minority (around 15–20 per cent) say there is a very or fairly big problem with respect and consideration within their community. Taken together these factors make Sutton a good vantage point from which to construct a view of Neighbourhood Policing and its changes, on the grounds that Sutton is a fairly typical and broadly representative area of England.

Neighbourhood security over time: the Sutton programme

The SENSOR process was first conducted in Sutton during 2006 as a pilot in the two town centre wards of Sutton Central and Carshalton Central. The following year, the methodology was rolled out across all of the Borough's eighteen wards. Officers and PCSOs from each of the SNTs were trained to recruit members of the public and conduct interviews using the SENSOR methodology. More details about this aspect of the work are provided in the Methodological Appendix. The interviews were conducted ward-by-ward on a rolling basis.

The process was repeated annually between 2007 and 2018,[1] resulting in a total Borough sample of between 532 and 653

---

[1] With the exceptions of: 2012, when the hosting of the London Olympic Games significantly stretched police resources; and 2016, as a consequence of local operational priorities.

respondents each year over the twelve-year period. Each ward's data were collected during a similar period of the year, with annual interviewer training or refresher sessions for all staff involved. Data were then analysed by the academic team, first on a ward-level and then again on aggregated basis to provide a Borough level view. This dual-level analysis produced individual ward-level community intelligence reports for tactical use by each SNT, and a more strategic Borough report to inform wider strategic assessment and resource allocation.

Public perceptions of crime and disorder

At the start of each interview, respondents were asked an orientation question about whether, overall, they 'perceive crime and disorder in their neighbourhood to have got better, worse or stayed the same in the last 12 months?' Figure 7.1 displays the combined responses of all respondents across the Borough between 2007 and 2018. These data show that there have been some important shifts over the twelve-year period.

Over the four years immediately following the introduction of SNTs, the proportion of residents who perceived a worsening situation reduced significantly on the preceding year before stabilizing at around 15 per cent until 2015. This mirrored a downward

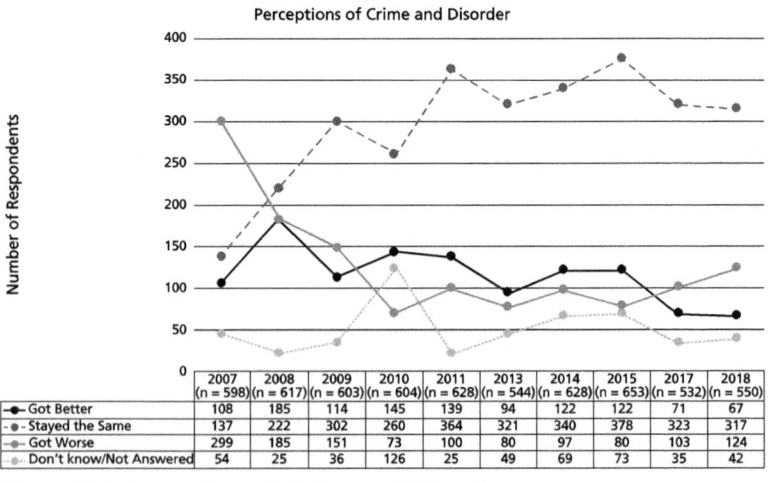

	2007 (n = 598)	2008 (n = 617)	2009 (n = 603)	2010 (n = 604)	2011 (n = 628)	2013 (n = 544)	2014 (n = 628)	2015 (n = 653)	2017 (n = 532)	2018 (n = 550)
Got Better	108	185	114	145	139	94	122	122	71	67
Stayed the Same	137	222	302	260	364	321	340	378	323	317
Got Worse	299	185	151	73	100	80	97	80	103	124
Don't know/Not Answered	54	25	36	126	25	49	69	73	35	42

Figure 7.1 Perceptions of Crime and Disorder

trend observed in the Crime Survey for England and Wales (formerly the British Crime Survey) over the same period, although it was considerably lower than the national average of around 30 per cent (British Crime Survey, 2009/2010). Equally, this was accompanied by a modest reduction in the proportion of people who perceived things as having 'got better' over the same time period. The most striking trend was a significant increase in the number of people who believed things had 'stayed the same', suggesting public perceptions of security had stabilized.

Interestingly, in the 2017 sweep, there were indications of a worsening trend compared with the previous two years. The proportion of respondents perceiving things had worsened rose above that of those thinking things had got better for the first time since 2009. This was the first time in eight years that the two views had 'crossed over' in this way and the trend continued into 2018. In interpreting these trends, it is relevant to recall that they were set against a backdrop of marked reductions in the amount being spent on community safety services and interventions.

What's the problem?—changes in Sutton's signal profile

Across the period under review, there was a remarkable consistency in the problems being identified by the public as the strongest signals of crime and disorder across the Borough. Notably, two issues stand out as ranking in the top two every year—'groups of youths hanging around' and 'speeding'. The former is a category that has been used in a large number of crime survey instruments. It has proven contentious on the grounds that it is somewhat nebulous and ambiguous as a category; young people being present in public spaces does not intrinsically mean they are engaged in uncivil behaviour (Burney, 2005). Such debates notwithstanding, people seem to use and interpret it as an adequate proxy measure for capturing the presence of a range of social disorders.

This interpretation is bolstered by looking in detail at the data collected via the interviews and teasing out what issues respondents associated with the 'groups of youths' signal. It is an approach that aids our understanding of why the behaviour of groups of youths should emerge as such a strong and entrenched problem. Noise, abusive language, and threatening behaviour; the misuse of alcohol and drugs in public space; and various forms of physical detritus generated by such activities were all consistently linked to the presence of young people. That said, amongst this collection of associated problems, there were some important and insightful movements over time in terms of which issues were brought to the fore. For instance, public drinking dropped out of the top five concerns in 2008 and graffiti in 2009. Neither has returned since, implying that whilst the congregation of young people in public spaces is still of concern to residents, these aspects of their behaviour are being adequately managed in the eyes of the community.

Worry about the volume and speed of traffic was also a significant issue throughout the twelve-year period and overtook groups of youths as the top signal from 2015 onwards. This is perhaps unsurprising given the suburban nature of the area and a reduction of recorded youth nuisance over the study period. The associated road safety problem of 'inconsiderate parking' emerged as significant in 2008, functioning as a recurring cause for concern ever since.

Various environmental disorders have also featured strongly and repeatedly among the public's top concerns, most notably litter but also, for a period between 2010 and 2013, dog fouling. Because the method used to diagnose these issues has been relatively consistently applied, it suggests that these shifts reflect subtle changes to the kinds of issues the public are attending to. These may not be especially evident because of more consistent 'headline' concerns, but 'below the surface' movement does appear to have taken place.

For instance, in 2009, an 'undesirable groups' signal emerged. Interrogating the detail of the qualitative data collected as part of the interviewing interaction suggests that it was predominately related to homeless people drinking and begging in Wallington Town Centre. This was a problem that then declined in profile the following year, potentially the outcome of a concerted approach by the Safer Sutton Partnership to tackling the issue as a result of the SENSOR intelligence. In 2017, the issue of homelessness re-emerged in a different location, with a strong 'undesirable groups' signal identified close to Sutton rail station where a charitable food and treatment centre had been set up.

A notable absence among the public's concerns, when researched in this way, were significant crime issues. Only in 2013 did 'domestic burglary' emerge as a strong signal. In part this may have reflected a decision that year to 'boost' the sample of Muslim respondents following a period of targeted Asian gold burglaries (the focus of a subsequent community safety campaign). From 2014 onwards, the problem continued to move in and out of the top signals list and, despite a reduction in recorded instances over that period, remained a perceived threat for residents regardless of actual risk.

The analysis reported to this point gives a sense of the overall profile of the kinds of problems that were impacting upon the perceptions and experiences of the residents of Sutton. As prefaced in the preceding discussion, it is notable how this is dominated by forms of social and physical disorder, rather than crime. This is coherent with aspects of the urban criminology literature, which would suggest that such a profile is not atypical (Taylor, 2015).

However, whilst this approach to the analysis captures issues driving how local people think, feel, or act in relation to their security, it does not articulate how frequently they are concerned by such matters. In an effort to articulate this dimension, taking into account year-on-year variations in sample size, Figure 7.2 plots

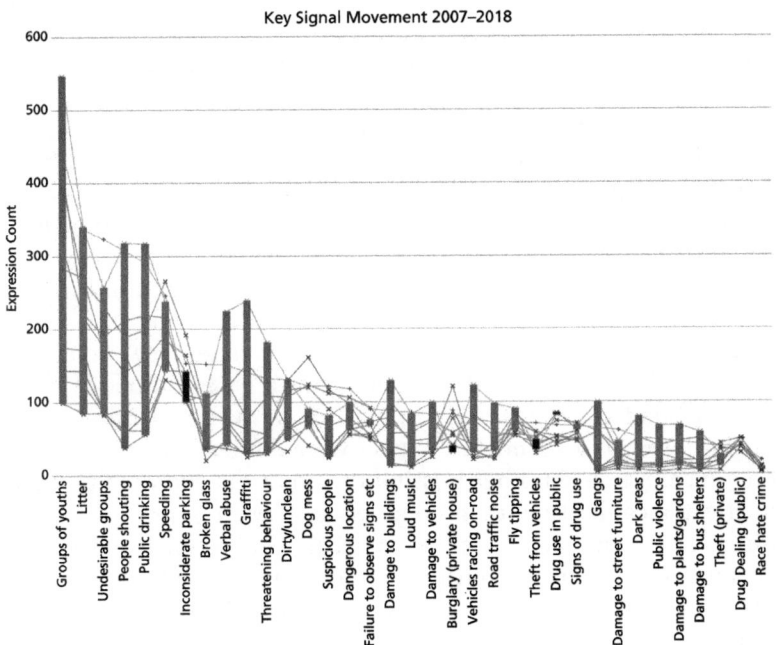

Figure 7.2 Key Signal Expressions—Twelve-year Movement, 2007 to 2018

the data so that indicative trends can be seen for each of the most significant signal event types across the twelve-year period.

Representing the data in this way clearly shows how the frequency with which most crime and disorder types were mentioned by people living across Sutton declined over time, and quite dramatically. The items denoted by a grey trend bar show where, over the twelve years, there was a reduction in the collective salience of the issue. This was the pattern for the majority of signal types. Youth-related disorder and public drinking in particular saw a marked decline, together with noise from people shouting. Road safety concerns, such as inconsiderate parking and speeding, remained consistent issues for the citizens of Sutton, with the former increasing in salience, as indicated by the black trend bar. Perceptions of environmental disorder presented a mixed picture, with litter showing a significant improvement and fly-tipping staying stable since 2007. Only two key crime types have worsened over the length of the study: domestic burglary and theft from vehicles, although drug use and dealing in public spaces remained fairly stable. By way of summary, the data shows that although public concerns consistently gravitated around the same problems, they were being mentioned less often in 2018 than in 2007.

Amongst the problems in decline are many that were targeted for police and partner intervention as a result of their identification by the analysis in earlier years. Other issues, most notably road safety and environmental problems, remained entrenched and continued to be generative of public concern despite interventions taken in respect of them. One possible explanation for this is that such issues were not entirely under the control of the Safer Sutton Partnership: Transport for London and New Scotland Yard's Traffic Command have significant responsibilities in relation to London's roads, for instance. As such, interventions that might have had a significant impact were difficult to achieve with only local assets. Another possibility is that the community were in effect 'recalibrating' their concerns as a result of improvements observed in other areas. For example, as youth disorder and litter declined in their neighbourhoods, concern switched to problems that were still very much evident, increasing the weight attached to them.

Location, location, location

As noted in the preceding chapter, an important component of the SENSOR interviewing methodology is its use of maps to help orientate the capture of geo-coded data from respondents. This can enable the identification of where incidents and problems are clustering in space in particular locations, or what are frequently labelled 'hotspots'. By extending the previous analysis in this way it became clear the same locations tended to feature strongly year-on-year as places where a variety of different problems were perceived by the public to co-occur. Consequently, they became prime candidates for multi-agency place-based interventions.

Sutton High Street was one such area, first identified as a significant location in the first wave of interviewing in 2007 and continuing to increase in salience as a result of the insecurity generated by a range of different issues there. By 2010, it was the top location for everything except road safety signals and its problem profile more or less continued through to 2018. Given the extensive interventions targeted at this area by both council and police over the period, this pattern was initially disappointing for them. However, an alternative interpretation is that it is a positive reflection of declining levels of concern about issues in more outlying areas of the Borough. Town centre locations are always perceived by the public as problematic and improvements are often slow to be recognized as reputation persists. As such, high use public spaces become more and more the focus of concern, particularly when problems in other locations are being reduced—a kind of 'recalibration' effect. The plausibility of this alternative explanation is somewhat supported by the data as it suggests a decreased 'coherence' for several more outlying locations associated with multiple signal crimes and disorders in the earlier years of the project, but which did not re-emerge as significant localities six or seven years on.

The declining importance of one such location, Wrythe Lane, provides a compact exemplar of the community intelligence-led strand of Sutton's Neighbourhood Policing operationalization. As a place where problems coagulated, at least in terms of local community perceptions, it showcases how such an approach can create a new perspective on problems that could not be grasped when viewed through other lenses and from different vantage points.

In 2008, the road was highlighted in the SENSOR surveys owing to the co-occurrence of multiple crime and disorder problems, the salience of which were being 'amplified' by the perceived impotence of the police response. According to the data collected, this was degrading public confidence in policing. As a long road spanning three wards within the Borough, the problem profile for Wrythe Lane generated through analysis of the community intelligence identified that people perceived and experienced particular problems with: drug use in public; youth disorder; and high levels of graffiti. Having established what was occurring in Wrythe Lane was an issue for a significant proportion of local residents, 'deeper' analysis of the problem was conducted. This included consulting police recorded crime and intelligence data. Looking across these data streams suggested two defined areas along the road where there were crime hotspots—St. Helier Hospital and the area around Rosehill Shops. Key problems occurring in these two sites according to police incident data included youth disorder, rubbish and graffiti, shoplifting, assaults and criminal damage.

The reason why previous interventions had failed to gain traction upon the problems was because of the length of the road and how the local SNTs were organized. Given Wrythe Lane traverses three wards, the various issues occurring along different sections of it were being addressed by different staff and thus not in a co-ordinated fashion. In effect, the police team assigned to one ward were trying to deal with the issues pertaining to 'their patch', but with little reference to the activities being undertaken in the other two wards. Informed by the community intelligence, a need to adopt a more joined-up and holistic approach to address the problems spanning these areas was identified. Adopting this perspective, it was apparent that there were a number of triggers for public concern. Taken individually these were not particularly high-profile issues, but packaged together as a 'problem', it was clear why such high rates of fear of crime and antisocial behaviour were being picked up in local surveys, and why people locally were dissatisfied with the police.

At Rosehill Shops, a small parade of retail outlets, there were three fast food restaurants and a licensed newsagent. These were all magnets for young people and their customers were also responsible for a high degree of littering in the area. As part of the response phase of the joint-partner problem-solving process that was initiated, all of these businesses were asked to sign 'responsible retailer agreements', and the police and council stepped up their ongoing monitoring of the licensed premises. A bit further along, there was a disused public toilet with graffiti-laden exterior walls. This was demolished as part of the response performed by the council. For their part, synchronized with these other actions, the police introduced high visibility foot patrols in the area, they undertook crime prevention campaigns at the hospital, and placed particular accent upon improving their investigative response to any reported crimes in the area.

When the impact of these interventions was assessed via the 2009 SENSOR consultation, it appeared the community intelligence informed joint problem-solving performed by the police and council had been successful. From a position where Wrythe Lane was an area causing residents across Sutton considerable anxiety in 2008, by 2009 it no longer featured in the top five most mentioned problematic locations across the Borough. It remained absent from this list for the next nine years. This case provides a useful illustration of how carefully collected data can both inform police 'problem-finding' and 'problem-solving' activity, as well as providing a useful instrument for gauging the community impacts associated with any interventions that are delivered.

That said, it is equally pertinent that not all of the problem-solving interventions implemented appeared to have been as effective. For instance, whilst the A237 London Road, Wallington was identified as a problematic location for speeding in the first few years, after 2010 it appeared to decline somewhat in significance and was replaced by other locations considered more concerning for this signal. None of these locations remained significant year-on-year, however, and in 2014 London Road emerged again, this time at its junction with Hackbridge Road, where a new road layout had been introduced the previous year. Designed as a traffic calming measure, a lack of signage, road markings, and lighting made the junction confusing for both drivers and pedestrians trying to cross. Whilst respondents suggested that the measure had slowed traffic a little, speeding on the London Road had once again become an issue and the 'chaos' at the junction added to the danger perceived by the public. Respondents reported being worried, fearful, and angry about the development: two respondents independently stated that 'it's an accident waiting to happen'. A year on in 2015, the same location was again being focused upon in the interviews, as evidenced by the following brief quotation:

The new road layout in Hackbridge is effective but the crossings are not effective for people to try and cross the road. People don't know what they are, they look like speed humps and are far too close to the round-about. (2015_wandlevalley)

This case of decline and re-emergence demonstrates how important it is for local agencies not to lose sight of the potential for unintended consequences when attempting to 'design out' specific problems.

Some specific problems identified by the local community have remained entrenched across the extended period of evaluation in Sutton. One striking example of this is Victoria House, a large commercial building in the Cheam area of the Borough, empty and boarded up since 2006. Year-on-year, the building became more and more derelict, a magnet for vandals and antisocial behaviour in the area, and a strong and coherent environmental signal for the local community in every SENSOR survey conducted. In the hands of private owners, there was little the Safer Sutton Partnership could do to influence what was to be done with the building and the site. Interestingly, in 2017, the site was acquired by a housing development group who submitted plans to demolish the building and erect a nine-storey block of much-needed new homes. Despite what the SENSOR data over the preceding decade might have suggested, local residents overwhelming objected to the proposal by way of a well-supported petition. Ultimately the proposal was rejected by council planners, citing that its height and mass were out of character with the area and that additional car parking and traffic issues would have a significant impact on the community. It would seem, in some instances, Neighbourhood Policing Teams can do little to impact upon residents' concerns even with multi-agency and commercial partnerships.

One final empirical example illustrates what can be achieved by acting on detailed, granular intelligence of the type obtained using the SENSOR methodology. In 2009, the exercise identified a relatively weak but coherent signal for race-hate crime outside a particular public house. A number of Asian Muslim respondents reported being verbally abused on numerous occasions by 'racist scumbags' who frequented the establishment. The business was already on the police's radar because of other co-occurring problems in and around the premises, but this detailed insight from a previously 'hard to hear' population enabled the senior

Neighbourhood Management Team to develop an intervention plan to tackle the problem once and for all. In a very short timeframe, their alcohol licence was withdrawn and the premises closed down. The local police Chief Inspector at the time described the reaction at a public meeting held shortly afterwards:

And I went along to the [Muslim Centre] and presented that as a success and they were absolutely over the moon. I had cheers from the back of the hall! It just goes to show! Thank you! Don't normally get that with a public meeting … certainly not with the BME community … you're normally on the back foot a little bit, hey! But my goodness they were really chuffed! (DG, 2010)

This case conveys just how public confidence in, and satisfaction with, policing can be dramatically influenced by Neighbourhood Policing Teams who target interventions informed by detailed, contextually relevant, and sensitive community intelligence. We now turn to a more generalized analysis of shifting public perceptions of policing over time.

Perceptions of policing

As well as affording insights into the changing salience of problems and places of concern within and across Sutton's neighbourhoods, the longitudinal nature of the data also illuminates important shifts in attitudes towards local policing and community safety in general over the decade. In summary, the general picture from earlier years is that interviewees were placing more import upon the work of SNT officers and the value of effective engagement. However, by 2017, this focus appeared to have been partially eclipsed by a greater accent upon police effectiveness at dealing with crime, antisocial behaviour, and public order. In effect, their 'needs' in terms of the policing services that they were ascribing particular value, has subtly shifted. There are several possible explanations for this. First, this shift away from a 'softer' public engagement role to 'harder' policing, focused more explicitly upon crime and disorder problems, may reflect a 'bedding down' of the SNTs' role in communities meaning that their availability and accessibility is now expected by the public. Alternatively, declining assets and resources, and the move to a dual neighbourhood/response role, as noted earlier in the chapter, may also have impacted. Finally, this pattern of development might reflect attitudinal shifts associated with a public discourse around austerity and the idea that policing needs to focus upon core service functions in an environment of less funding.

To explore this phenomenon further, some more nuanced data were examined on the performance of police. Collected as part of the SENSOR process, these data differentiated between local Safer Neighbourhoods officers and central response officers, as well as the council. Every time an individual respondent identified a signal crime or disorder during their interview, they were asked to rate the efficacy of each local agency in doing something about that issue.

The performance of the local SNTs was consistently rated the most positively out of the three. For over three quarters of the problems mentioned by respondents in 2007, SNT response was rated by the local public as 'very good' or 'good'. Given the well-documented sizeable reduction in police funding and the number of officers across this period, this level has since remained remarkably stable, albeit with a slight shift downwards in the last two years. This is not accidental, as it coincided with a significant disinvestment from Neighbourhood Policing by the MPS as they were seeking to cope with much reduced levels of funding.

Intriguingly however, public assessments of the uniformed response teams have improved considerably over time. The community safety services provided by the council fare well too. Whilst the proportion of reported signal events where the council's performance was rated as 'good' or 'very good' stuck at around one in five of respondents each year, there has been a marked shift in ratings from 'poor/very poor' to 'average'.

These data pose some interesting questions. From their inception, SNTs and officers were highly valued by the residents of Sutton and this has not diminished, as is sometimes the case with new initiatives. Furthermore, the performance of police response teams has improved in the public's eyes over the same period. Potentially this intimates that dealing effectively with all levels of crime and disorder becomes the primary focus for the public once local police accessibility and communication are normalized.

Between the 2009 and 2017 sweeps, a short series of items was integrated into the interview instrument where respondents were asked to describe anything that 'had happened in the past 3 months to increase or decrease their confidence in the MPS as a whole?' Interviewers were instructed to prompt respondents to think of things that had happened to them personally, something that they heard or read through the media, something that happened to a friend, family member, or someone else. A content analysis of the resulting qualitative data enabled some of the persistent drivers for increasing and decreasing confidence to be determined and their saliency over time to be charted. Figure 7.3 sets out some of the recurring factors identified as a relative proportion of all comments recorded year-on-year. It should be noted that many of the categories identified co-occur and interacted with others.

What coding these data in this manner helps to clarify is how improved confidence was associated with positive communication with, and feedback from, the police. Specifically, this involved officers listening and being sympathetic and helpful with regard to a respondent's problems. Although the data were often too ambiguous to definitively attribute these benefits to interactions with Safer Neighbourhood or response policing teams, engagement in positive interactions was clearly important. As one interviewee described:

Local safer neighbourhood team come 'round and chat to me. I like it when they visit, it makes me feel safe. (2010_shel)

As alluded to earlier, the other vital aspect of the policing role when it comes to public confidence is the effective management of specific crime/ antisocial behaviour incidents, and general effectiveness at keeping law and order. These factors interact with high patrol visibility and responding quickly and appropriately to calls for assistance. Charting these two drivers longitudinally across the dataset, an interesting pattern emerges. In 2009, still relatively soon after the introduction of SNTs, it was communication and

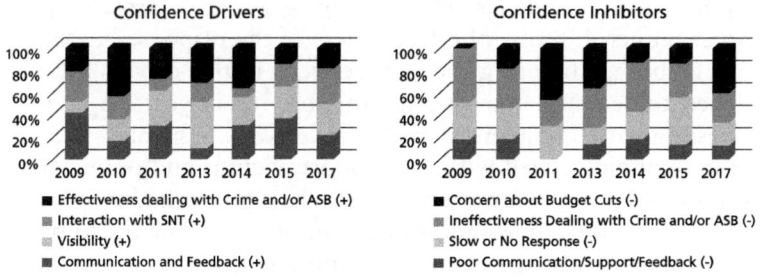

Figure 7.3 Changes in Confidence Drivers and Inhibitors, 2009 to 2017

interaction with officers that appeared most important to the public. Thereafter, as Neighbourhood Policing became more embedded and normalized in the routines and rhythms of local communities, there are signs of a shift towards policing effectiveness being of greater influence, only to reverse again in the latter two years as austerity took hold and local officer responsibilities were reconfigured. This is an important finding inasmuch as it suggests that, at a local level, what the public are looking for from the police may not be constant over time, but rather may flex and adapt, inflected by a range of exogenous influences. Significantly, based upon the empirical data available to this study, such shifts are not purely functions of crime and disorder rates. Instead, they appear to reflect wider political and economic currents.

That the public recognized diminishing resources would impact upon what they had come to expect from their community policing teams is borne out in the analysis of what led respondents to have reduced confidence in the police. Whilst the most significant issues reported across the time period were consistently related to police ineffectiveness, concerns around the impact of planned public spending cuts became far more prevalent in the 'free text' reply sections of the interview from 2010 onwards. By way of illustration:

Cutting police numbers, funding etc. Worried that if police officers are cut down there will be nobody on the streets at all. (2010_wnor)

Media reporting of the potential impacts of budget restraint on front-line policing were central to the articulation of this kind of public concern. It was noticeable that as these kinds of news stories became less frequent and intense, so these sentiments were appearing with much less frequency in the SENSOR returns. Worry about money and resources aside, other factors decreasing respondents' confidence in policing gravitated around poor service, either in terms of effectiveness of the response, its timeliness, or both. Mirroring the changes seen in the 'drivers' of confidence, these issues gain traction in more recent years. A handful of respondents commented that police were unhelpful and did not communicate well with, or support, victims and public alike. Equally, a number complained that when police had responded to a crime report, they had not been informed of the outcome, or of any actions taken. However, the more recent data suggest that instances of these confidence-decreasing occurrences have not increased in frequency over time, despite the significant reduction in Neighbourhood Policing resources.

Resisting engagement

Although the tactical and strategic products generated by systematically collecting and analysing community intelligence delivered valuable evidence and insights, the process as a whole did trigger cultural resistance amongst officers. That it did so potentially signals something about the value and worth that many officers ascribe to community engagement. Even specialist Neighbourhood Policing officers appeared reluctant to engage in an admittedly intensive, yet systematic, process to understand local communities' perspectives and needs.

In the first couple of years, it took some time and effort to build trust amongst potential police users of the data. There was an observed tendency amongst some local practitioners to suggest that the analysis was only telling them 'what they already knew', or indeed that it was simply wrong. The first of these was, to a large part, overcome by continually explaining and re-emphasizing the value of utilizing the 'signal crimes' approach to determine what, amongst all the known problems, should be targeted because they are causing most public harm. Whilst senior police and community safety staff quickly understood and recognized the potential in this approach, it is fair to say that it was often lost on those front-line officers tasked with interviewing members of the community. Existing alongside other priority tasks, the annual round of SENSOR interviews often became seen as an unnecessarily time-consuming exercise, which apparently generated little in terms of new knowledge and was not viewed as 'real police work'.

A high turnover of officers assigned to Neighbourhood Policing Teams exacerbated this problem over the years, with new interviewers being influenced by the negative opinions of longer serving colleagues who had 'done it before'. It must be acknowledged of course that as a methodology it is comparatively resource intensive, requiring far more effort than running a community meeting, and so its benefits come at a price. In the latter years of data collection, the reconfiguring of SNT resources compounded resistance levels.

Over the extended period of the work described in this chapter, we have also observed changes in relation to how rigorously the resulting data were used to inform interventions at an operational level. In the earlier years, all SNT sergeants were routinely tasked with reviewing their ward-level community intelligence report prior to developing a ward 'SENSOR Action Plan' covering key problems and locations in that area. These plans were 'owned' by Neighbourhood Inspectors and the sergeants were measured against them as part of their annual Performance and Development Reviews. Further, team resource allocation was driven by issues identified in their plan, with PCSOs tasked to patrol 'SENSOR hotspots' when they had no other ward priorities to attend to. However, with the onset of public sector austerity and consequent reduction and reconfiguration of Safer Neighbourhoods Policing resources, the robustness of tactical action planning around the annual community intelligence reports diminished, with structured action plans ultimately disappearing.

At a Borough level, the importance of the annual analysis in informing strategic resource allocation across community safety agencies has endured and remains a significant investment that continues at the time of writing. From the beginning, issues identified in each annual Borough-level report were included in a 'Control Strategy Appendix' to the National Intelligence Model compliant Strategic Assessment. During the early years of the programme, SENSOR data facilitated successful leverage of additional local government funding into the Neighbourhood Policing 'pot'. This enabled, for instance, the brigading of SNTs and the funding of two specialized Safer Parks Teams, both of which continue to be supported via the local authority to this day. Additionally, 'SENSOR Action Days' were established and continue to be attended by all partner agencies to explore ways of tackling the issues raised during each year's exercise.

The accusation that the analysis was 'wrong' was generally overcome by testing the findings against other data sources, most notably a representative telephone survey conducted by IPSOS-MORI in the Borough every two years. As a senior police officer, interviewed by the researchers to understand the implementation process, described:

They accept it now because when the [MPS standard survey] was done it said the same thing but didn't give you the detail ... The Council's own MORI poll said exactly the same things ... that's what gives credibility to the reports. (DG,2010)

The clear correlation across data sources and several higher-level indicators helped to convince a number of key local practitioners that community intelligence provided by the public is more often than not accurate. This validated its role in helping to steer and guide the delivery of Neighbourhood Policing services across the Borough. The same officer continued by emphasizing how the process of talking 'properly' and meaningfully with members of the public frequently elicited actionable crime intelligence:

We've found cannabis factories, we've arrested offenders, drug dealers ... these little snippets of intelligence come out of SENSOR. (DG,2010)

The acquisition of intelligence on these types of issues, which were more valued by police, was not routine. However, when it did happen, it was significant in building the credibility of the process, albeit there was still resistance. The implementation process of SENSOR also met more practical forms of resistance. Certainly, over the decade, it was evident that whilst the method was helping to understand community concerns, the process of 'bending' resources to service these needs proved more difficult. This replicates a pattern also observed in Chicago (Skogan, 2006).

Conclusion

This detailed case study analysis of Sutton, a fairly unremarkable part of England in terms of public safety issues, is designed to shine a light upon how Neighbourhood Policing is conducted in practice. Specifically, with its intense focus upon community engagement, it illuminates some wider patterns and trajectories. For example, in terms of its practical implementation and delivery, community policing type processes frequently blend with other policing styles, notably POP and intelligence-led policing. Whilst community policing 'in books' is often cast as separate and distinct from problem-oriented policing and intelligence-led policing models, in practice these can be far more closely aligned and integrated with each other. Indeed, possibly the defining quality of Neighbourhood Policing in Sutton was its systematic collection of community intelligence to engage in 'problem-finding' activity, then targeting 'problem-solving' interventions against those issues diagnosed as responsible for causing pronounced local harms. Labelling these data as 'community intelligence' is especially apposite because of how the collection and analysis process was designed to integrate the perceptions and experiences of multiple individuals in an area to present a collective view.

A second key insight that can be derived from the preceding discussion concerns what happens with innovations in policing as they mature and age. As was noted in some of the earlier chapters, this is something that has not been captured by many accounts. Typically, assessments and evaluations of policing models tend to be restricted to relatively short timeframes, more often than not focused around the earlier phases of their introduction. But such a disposition inevitably leaves a gap in our knowledge about what happens once initially exciting and innovative practices 'bed in'. How do they become 'normalized'? Do they lose their lustre and interest for practitioners? These are the kinds of questions that the methodology underpinning this chapter enables us to start engaging with. One of the key things we see is how it is not just what the police do that changes, but also how the world changes around them. In this case, wider and deeper social forces associated with the rise of a new information environment comprised of social media and big data, plus the onset of the effects of economic austerity, have shaped how Neighbourhood Policing is conceived and understood today.

A decade-long relationship between the research team and the Safer Sutton Partnership has painted a rich and detailed community intelligence picture for an area of suburban London where serious crime is relatively low and yet public perceptions of insecurity and expectations of their police force remain significant. By applying the SENSOR methodology over an extended period of time, it has been possible to track and trace how public priorities and concerns have evolved and adapted at a granular level. Identification of specific local problems and locations generating the greatest social harm from the point of view of the citizen allowed police to develop a succession of tactical plans to address the public's neighbourhood security needs. At a more strategic level, service provision has sometimes been able to be 'bent' towards theses public priorities to allow a more targeted use of ever-declining resources.

Longitudinal data affords insights into both the potentials and limitations of Neighbourhood Policing provision over an extended period of time. That the profile of the community's principal concerns has partially shifted suggests that, by 'gripping' problems at a local level, Neighbourhood Policing interventions can make a difference. However, the data simultaneously evidence that some problems can remain deeply entrenched or outwith local neighbourhood management control, indicating limitations to what can be practically achieved.

As particular problems or places are improved, it is not the case that the public become wholly unconcerned about neighbourhood security issues, rather they cognitively and affectively recalibrate what they are concerned about. In Sutton, over time, public concerns have increasingly gravitated around the High Street and, whilst this may be acceptable as a utilitarian benefit, this 'recalibration effect' warrants further consideration.

A more subtle and nuanced conclusion to be gleaned from the data is that perceptions of crime and disorder have declined, and assessment of the performance of community safety partners has improved, despite only limited progress being made over several of the public's self-defined problems. This may indicate that the very act of police engaging communities and being seen to be trying to address the concerns that they prioritize is actually an important facet of influencing their attitudes and perceptions, regardless of any outcome accomplished.

8

From Neighbourhood to National Security

In the wake of the cluster of terrorist attacks that took place in the first half of 2017, several senior police leaders went 'on the record' to publicly state the value and importance of Neighbourhood Policing assets to countering terrorism. It was, they declared, the local policing footprint and community connectivity afforded by Neighbourhood Policing Teams that established a channel for members of the public to provide community intelligence to the police about possible national security risks and threats.

Such arguments about the links between neighbourhood problems and national security responses have not always been made or accepted by senior police. Indeed, in the very earliest days of the National Reassurance Policing Programme (NRPP), several police leaders and academics argued against such an approach on the grounds that it would divert police capacity and capability away from the 'real intelligence work' of covert policing that is critical for tackling regional and national security threats. More recently, Manning (2010) has suggested that engaging local police in counter-terrorism work is risky because it will induce a mission drift, with officers neglecting their more routine and mundane crime responsibilities as they get wrapped up in the 'more glamorous' aspects.

Framed by increasing consternation about the ongoing impacts caused by the government's austerity programme and public sector spending cuts upon the police service, the more recent supportive interventions by senior officers undoubtedly possessed a political influencing intent. But they also raise an important question about the extent to which Neighbourhood Policing does provide a platform for generating community intelligence, and even perhaps community mobilization, useful to parts of the policing apparatus that are non-locally oriented. This issue is of theoretical

Neighbourhood Policing. Martin Innes, Colin Roberts, Trudy Lowe, and Helen Innes, Oxford University Press (2020). © Martin Innes, Colin Roberts, Trudy Lowe, and Helen Innes.
DOI: 10.1093/oso/9780198783213.003.0001

interest also given, as Brodeur (1983; 2010) has documented, there has been a long-standing 'bright-line' distinction between 'low policing' and 'high policing'. As such, if it could be demonstrated that the former explicitly and directly influences the latter in this way, then that would possess significant conceptual and operational implications.

It is precisely this issue that provides a centre of gravity for this chapter, which is explored through three case studies:

1. Preventing violent extremism in Birmingham
2. Countering violent street gangs in London
3. Drug dealing and distribution in Cardiff

Collectively, but from different angles, these studies explore how neighbourhood officers were engaged in tackling 'non-local' security problems and evaluate the contribution made by Neighbourhood Policing to the broader police mission. The analysis commences by looking in detail at the contribution made by neighbourhood teams to countering violent extremism. This is followed by a change of focus to consider the role of Neighbourhood Policing in tackling street gang violence. Several analytic themes are then developed by examining a third case—Operation Michigan, a study of organized crime policing.

Although their substantive focus is different, what all three case studies share is an interest in eliciting details of the street craft of Neighbourhood Policing and its social dynamics. That is, providing 'high resolution' descriptive accounts of how aspects of the work gets done. In turn, this approach is used to distil some key insights into what determines the success, or otherwise, of neighbourhood police attempts to work with the public, to manage especially complex crime and disorder problems, normally viewed as beyond the role and capability of Neighbourhood Policing. Accordingly, the penultimate section of the chapter translates these 'richer' more grounded discussions into a more theoretical register to consider the wider implications for ideas about the co-production of social control.

Countering violent extremism

Following the London bombings in 2005, the United Kingdom's national security posture was radically revised. The cross-government CONTEST counter-terrorism strategy was devised and implemented in an effort to provide a more holistic and comprehensive response framework to the kinds of international and domestic terror threats that were now presenting (Omand, 2012). But whilst the policy intent and prescription were defined, how this should be translated into practical interventions and actions was less clear. Especially in respect of the more innovative strands of CONTEST, such as the Prevent Strategy, there was striking lack of practical details as to what agencies such as the police should actually be doing. Indeed, it is not unreasonable to assert that Prevent was little more than 'an empty box' at the time.

Set against this backdrop and building upon the relationships built through the NRPP and Neighbourhood Policing studies, in 2007 the research team were commissioned by the Home Office to conduct a study of how police in different parts of England and Wales were operationalizing Prevent. Based upon observational fieldwork and interviews with practitioners and community representatives, the evidence generated suggested that very different levels of progress were being made across the country. For the purposes of this discussion, we will provide a case study of one region that was particularly interesting and progressive in its approach.

The West Midlands is a region of the United Kingdom with an especially diverse resident population, including large Asian and Black communities, spanning different ethnic and religious affiliations, in its major urban areas. Although most people from these different backgrounds get along well, there is a history of inter-community tensions, with a series of crime and public order events manifesting as a result. Given such a backdrop, it is perhaps unsurprising that high profile extremist groups such as Al-Muhajiroun (ALM) and its surrogates, led by Anjem Choudhary, have repeatedly sought to build and sustain a presence in the area, their aim being to try and secure localized social support and recruits from the Pakistani and Bangladeshi communities, in particular. Over the years, they have organized a large number of public and private events in order to proselytize their message and radical interpretation of Islam. As a group they have been of particular concern to UK counter-terrorism agencies because of the large number of individuals who have had contact with the group and then gone on to be involved in terrorist plots and attacks, both in the United Kingdom and overseas (Wiktorowicz, 2005; Nesser, 2016).

Confronted by the challenging ongoing presence and provocations of individuals associated with this group, West Midlands Police sought to engage the capacities and capabilities provided by their Neighbourhood Policing presence to craft a response. In policy terms, their commitment to this approach was triggered by two influences. First, there was the difficulty posed by how, although a lot of the activities of affiliates of ALM were troublesome and worrying, they were frequently not illegal. Indeed, their ALM adversaries were often quite skilled in knowing where the boundaries of criminal activity were and ensuring their actions did not cross such a threshold, thus rendering it tricky for police to do anything, much to the consternation and frustration of local community groups. As such, engaging Neighbourhood Policing type processes was envisaged as affording opportunities to formulate more creative and innovative responses to locally presenting national security risks.

The second driver for adopting this approach was less positive, however. Under the auspices of 'Operation Champion', police and their partner agencies had attempted to establish a new CCTV surveillance system in an area of Birmingham, upon the pretext that it would enable improved crime prevention. However, shortly after its establishment, it was revealed that the scheme had been financed by funding from the counterterrorism budget. This fed into an established narrative within the local Muslim community that they were being cast as a 'suspect community' (Awan, 2012). The resulting public outcry had profoundly deleterious consequences for community trust in the police, with a number of community organizations and high-profile leaders in Birmingham publicly withdrawing their co-operation. This was just at a time when police knew it was vital that they were engaging meaningfully with this community and working with them.

Confronted by this situation, West Midlands Police decided they had to adopt a radical alternative, built around some of the principles and processes familiar from the Neighbourhood Policing doctrine. To facilitate this shift in approach they introduced a new role, which was defined as follows:

Security and Partnership Officers based locally in communities, in uniform, but overtly counter terrorist. They will state who they are, so that whoever we are talking to, whether a partner or a member of the community, they know that we are from the counter terrorism unit. (XO424CT Insp)

Conceived as a hybrid of a traditional neighbourhood patrol officer and counter-terrorism intelligence officer, the position of a Security and Partnership Officer was innovative. As a second officer elaborated, it was viewed as:

a difficult, but necessary way to be upfront regarding CT policing in Muslim communities. (XO89CT)

The concept was that because these were uniformed counter-terrorism officers, there was an important symbolic message to be conveyed by their presence. They were not plain-clothes 'spies' undertaking covert surveillance. But rather were performing work directly connected to the core mission of policing.

In addition to the unorthodox notion of having 'overt' front-line counter-terrorism officers, the individuals performing these roles were not recruited from the ranks of detectives or intelligence officers—the more usual 'breeding ground' for entry into counter-terrorism work. Instead, the profile for recruits to these positions were:

Good communicators from uniformed ranks, who above all understood how to work in a community, to make something happen, and communicate effectively at different levels within that community. (XO424CT Insp).

As an approach, this was viewed with some scepticism internally at the start. Also, as far as we know, no other police force adopted the model—although many came to West Midlands to see and discuss it. This notwithstanding, twenty-five Security and Partnerships Officers across different ranks (including PCSOs, constables, sergeants, and two inspectors) were recruited and deployed across the force, with some grouped into teams in areas with the highest perceived risk.

Initially individuals performing the Security and Partnerships Officer role found it difficult to articulate what they were doing and how. When interviewed by researchers, they clearly understood that they had been selected because of their skills in engaging with communities. Importantly however, as they told stories about their interactions with various individuals locally in the interviews, it became evident that their focus wasn't simply on accessing more and better 'intelligence', although this was important. Rather, they were also involved in trying to build alliances with a range of local community groups, to help to mobilize these, so that Islamist extremists in the community could no longer operate unopposed.

A recurring theme in the interview accounts of the Security and Partnerships Officers was a recognition that the community, who had repeatedly raised concerns about the local presence of overtly extremist individuals and groups to police, had largely been left to deal with the issues themselves. Police interventions had been fairly traditional counter-terrorism actions, rather than engaged in preventing processes of violent radicalization.

The attempt to re-orient the organization's counter-terrorism focus to a more 'upstream' preventative posture, of which the Security and Partnerships Officers were a physical embodiment, generated considerable internal resistance amongst some sections of West Midlands Police. Although variants of this kind of work have become more commonplace in UK policing and internationally now, in 2007 this was new. As such, the individuals were 'path-finding'—there was no real 'playbook' or training for this kind of activity. As a consequence, mistakes were made, bolstering the internal critics. But equally, a number of innovative and important successes occurred also.

For the first six months of their deployment, the Security and Partnerships Officers were tasked with engaging in their neighbourhoods. Initially local community groups were sceptical of the officers. But similar to the descriptions of Neighbourhood Policing officers 'breaking ground' and forging new relationships threaded through the preceding chapters, the Security and Partnerships Officers progressively gained acceptance and built a fragile and delicate form of trust. As one PCSO Security and Partnerships Officer described:

I faced lot of scepticism and hostility in the beginning, about being CT police in uniform, but slowly they came to trust *me* rather than the uniform and started to engage. Now they call me and talk to me all the time. (XO421CT)

A key insight provided by this officer, and something reiterated across the data, was how the trust that was constructed tended to be personalized, rather than institutional. That is, the key individuals in the community were building a relationship with her as an individual, as opposed to the police institution. Albeit this is a relatively 'thin' form of trust, as per O'Neill's (2017) interpretation, it is important in setting the foundations for more complex forms of social interaction and organization.

A steady process of building a social network of contacts within and across key communities over time stood in stark contrast to previous police approaches to managing counter-terrorism issues. Two separate instances, prior to the advent of Security and Partnerships Officers, were highlighted by multiple interview respondents as having impacted negatively upon their views. In both episodes, police, many armed and some with dogs, had descended en masse to conduct raids on residential houses in the early hours of the morning to affect arrests for terrorism offences. The overt police presence and the media attention it attracted was profoundly unsettling for residents, inducing animosity and anger towards the police, who they did not know, and who they could not engage with. At the time, the police retort to this was that they had received intelligence from other agencies and were working in co-operation with other police forces. They were in possession of intelligence suggesting the occupants were engaged in acts preparatory to terrorism, and it was thus necessary to move immediately and forcefully to protect the public. As a concrete example of how things changed, once established, the Security and Partnership Officers used their nuanced understanding of local community concerns and dynamics to engage with local people in order to organize and implement with them how to minimize the disruption and impact of such counter-terrorism 'Pursue' activities.

An important feature of these officers' early work was that they quite deliberately did not try and draw down any intelligence. Rather, their explicit focus was upon understanding the distribution of community influencers and building a network of meaningful contacts. In so doing, they were contingently building themselves into local power structures based on trust, not coercion. For instance, there was a group of community activists drawn from a number of local mosques who, without any police support, had been engaging in informal social control actions designed to disrupt and interfere with the activities of ALM members operating locally. This had included persuading the management committees of the local mosques to ban known extremists from mosque premises. As the Security and Partnerships Officers became increasingly 'literate' in terms of understanding community concerns, so they were able to tentatively make a 'bridge' to the activist group. This was accomplished by facilitating a meeting with senior police officers to discuss the group members' concerns and plan together. This meeting was a significant moment. The group members had never met face to face before with a senior officer, and had been previously referred to by officers as 'very anti'.

This police–community relationship developed so that when the group's members faced an external jihadist group and its national leadership repeatedly coming into their neighbourhood, overtly attempting to radicalize young people, they were willing and able to work with the police to try and problem-solve these issues to co-create a response. Describing this process, a police Inspector recalled how:

Another Mosque in ... rang up one of my sergeants and said we've got three guys coming here, and they were doing the proper radicalization thing. They were trying to draw kids in, they were trying to have little meetings, they were being quite radical. We'd appreciate your support if you could come and help us, and speak to these three individuals because we don't want them here but we're a little bit concerned. So [Name]'s gone down, confronted the three individuals, saying "The Mosque and the community don't want you here, what are you about? Do you want to talk to me about it? They didn't. They went. We know where they went.

Of note in this account is how the police intervention was relatively 'light touch' in a moment of potential conflict. However, the 'control signal' communicated was sufficient to persuade the extremist group to withdraw from the area. Recognizing that this kind of 'soft policing' is engaged in counter-terrorism work is an important corrective, given how much public attention surrounding this aspect of the police mission gravitates around dramatic 'shock and awe' occurrences.

Just as important and subtle was how the act of the community members phoning the Security and Partnership Officer, which triggered the above event, was the product of a long process of engagement and establishing 'fragile trust'. In interviews with members of the community concerned, they described how the decision to contact the police in this way was difficult. They had carefully discussed and considered the potential implications prior to them actually reaching out. They only did so because of the positive relationship formed with their Security and Partnerships Officer. This need for collective deliberation was understandable given the history of police–community relations rehearsed above.

Thus, what on the surface appears a relatively unremarkable act, was actually freighted with a much deeper significance, that could be easily missed. The community had a strong stimulus for action (Carr, 2005) but were unable to do anything meaningful without police support. Equally, police had their own stimulus for action and need to do something, which encouraged them to invest in developing a collaboration with the community group.

One respondent recounted how, as part of these interactions, detailed information about the group was shared by the police with the community. This was an act the police thought had some risk attached to it, but was necessary to demonstrate reciprocation for the trust the community were showing in them. The wider community reaction to this information-sharing was positive. From their perspective it signalled a 'tipping point' in police–community relations, where they began to jointly strengthen their opposition to the extremist group, creating a far more 'hostile environment' for them. Whilst past breakdowns were not forgotten and the relationship going forward was far from comfortable on occasion, it did support far more assertive informal social control actions being undertaken by members of the local community. The result was a sequence of locally generated disruptions performed both by police *and* community members, continually interfering with the ability of the extremists to organize activities and establish a 'footprint' in any new premises or on the streets. For example it empowered a member of the police–community group to confront the leader of the extremist group in the street:

[name redacted] said, 'we know who you are, we know what you're doing, we will not tolerate what you're doing, you'd better start thinking about it. Be clear, we are watching you'. Now that is an intervention … (2611-11)

In a subsequent conversation with this individual it was clear that he thought the police and the community had come together and now 'had his back' when he confronted the extremists. Through these processes, agreed and loosely coordinated formal and informal social control actions emerged whereby the extremist group came under active surveillance by both police and community. This recourse to 'disrupting' the activities of the extremists, rather than invoking a more traditional law enforcement intervention, reflects how the community were highlighting concerns about the group's anti-social activities rather than evidence of illegalities to the police. Moreover, interviews with police showed that whilst they saw practical utility in such disruptions, they were equally aware that acting in this way helped to build trust with the community by showing police were responsive and sensitive to their concerns. This was part of an investment strategy performed by both sides that built community capacity and capability so that together they would be able to co-produce problem-solving on an ongoing basis.

In the example above, co-producing social control involved the community acting as the 'eyes and ears' of the police, helping to identify and define the presence of problematic situations—'problem-finding'. The police, for their part, undertook to directly support implementation of resolutions to such matters. Extraordinarily, the fieldwork found occasions where this co-productive relationship was being reversed—with police defining the presence of a problem, and community action being applied to resolve it.[1] For instance, using covert intelligence sources, police identified several individuals assessed to pose a risk of engaging in violent extremism. These men were booking private meeting halls under false names. Police were concerned about what powers they had to intervene given that it was not clear they had yet committed any criminal offences, though clearly they were intent on recruiting new members. Moreover, the police were troubled that if they did confront the individuals concerned, then they would try and exploit this in the media and this might provide the 'oxygen of publicity' desired by the extremist group. So instead, they sought to engage through their Security and Partnerships Officers with the newly established community social network. It is worth reiterating at this juncture that somewhat counter-intuitively perhaps, this network was originally created within the neighbourhood as a result of community protests about the policing of the local Muslim community, and its members started as strong and vociferous opponents of the police.

However, as a result of the emergent trust created through the interactions outlined above, a series of meetings were convened. The police, building on the positive reaction to their earlier intelligence sharing, took the unusual step of disclosing in detail some of the intelligence they had, and the risks they perceived. In response, the intervention the community group devised was to

[1] This is evidence for the presence of 'Type 2' co-production in the model presented in the concluding passages of this chapter.

telephone all of the venues and to inform the proprietors about the 'real' identities of the people who they knew to be making the bookings for the venues under false identities. When informed in this way, all of the proprietors of the venues cancelled the bookings, thus invoking an informal social control intervention upon the extremist group. Ultimately then, in this case study we can see how the kinds of engagement processes embedded through Neighbourhood Policing subtly, but powerfully, changed the 'dynamics of the local social order'(see Hunter, 1985), enabling the successful confrontation of extremist groups, where previously this had proven high on impossible.

Violent street gangs in London

So, you know, it's funny. They actually started drawing attention to themselves because they can't help it, they started shouting at us, giving us abuse, 'bigging it up'. If they'd ignored us we would never have had an interest in them and they are now frustrated because we know who they are and we know where they live and we know what their street names are and so on, so they don't like it. So we always say 'hello so and so' to them and remember what their names are. They don't like it! (Cold-Pol3)

This is an extract from an officer serving in a Safer Neighbourhoods Team (SNT) in a South London Borough talking about his interactions with members of a local street gang. As he recalled, when the SNT officers were first introduced into the area, they were met with open hostility by some young men who saw the enhanced policing presence as representing an incursion into 'their territory'. It is worth clarifying that this inner-city ward had acquired a reputation for its high levels of armed gang activity and had the highest gang mortality rate in the country at the time of the study. Faced with such challenges, until the inception of the SNT as part of the nationwide roll-out of Neighbourhood Policing, policing presence had contracted. The majority of public contacts locally were being delivered by response teams, the Metropolitan Police's SO19 dedicated firearms unit, and Operation Trident, a unit dedicated at that time to 'black-on-black' gun and gang homicides.

This case study not only extends the exploration of Neighbourhood Policing into a different context, but expands our knowledge of other aspects of Neighbourhood Policing and its effect on complex spatial dimensions of local social order and agent-based interaction.

Similar to what was observed with the Security and Partnerships Officers in the West Midlands, when first deployed, the Metropolitan Police's officers, invested time and effort in building relationships in the neighbourhood:

When we first started we used to walk round and we would say 'hello, good morning' and they'd just blank us, but now we say 'hello' and they say 'hello' back and we stand chatting for five minutes, just like getting to know them. Even the people we stopped like the drug users are now talking to us. When you walk past an address and you think that's not Mr Smith and then you ask questions and you could be stopping a burglary in progress whereas if you are in a Police car and you see someone's light on you don't take notice of it. We get to know people, we get to know the Housing Officers, we get to know the residents and we build a relationship and I think what the police have been lacking for a long time, is the relationship aspect between the police and the community. Because if you are dealing with 999 calls you just go and deal with it and that's the last you probably have to do with it, stick a CRIS report on, but with us we do follow ups so we actually solve local problems. (Cold-Pol4)

As articulated by this officer, there are two key dimensions to this approach. First is constructing a contextual understanding of the neighbourhood and its rhythms and routines in order to be able to spot matters that are out of place. Second, is building up a network of relationships with local residents, but also, equally importantly, individuals working for other local agencies who deliver services in the same place. As a different police interviewee explained, this latter dimension can be extremely helpful:

In the last six months I've got to know lots of people … We deal with all the things the police should do, but don't have the time to do it, but people want. We get to know all the services and get things done for people who don't know how. (Pol-MS6)

This ability to know who to talk to across different local service providers to obtain 'cut-through' and to be able to help someone resolve a problem they were encountering was an important vehicle for building community trust and social capital for neighbourhood police. By doing relatively small things for local citizens, such as sign-posting services that people were grateful for and needed, the officers were creating conditions where small pieces of community intelligence started to be passed. An act of reciprocity perhaps—but an important commodity in an area where gang violence was prevalent. Prior to the introduction of the SNT, the gangs were far more visibly present in the area, exercising considerable control over local residents, creating territories for themselves, fear of reprisals, and a sense of being 'untouchable'.

Through the process of progressive police visibility and engagement, a gradual change in confidence in the police became evident. According to data derived from interviews conducted with local residents, members of the community began to see policing actions being taken directly in response to their information. It is also interesting to note how the first police officer above recognized the flaw in his previous emergency response approach, that he succinctly summarized as 'attend and forget'. He acknowledged that this modality of policing was disconnected from the experiences of residents and made few demands on officers to solve their local problems. Going further, he questioned whether what he did previously was actually policing at all as he now understood it, given how he was now having tangible and observable effects.

Flipping the lens, the interviews conducted with residents in this area also revealed a strong 'code of the street' with a normative rule of not talking to the police, not 'grassing', and not engaging. However, through regular, repeated, and familiar contact with PCSOs and Safer Neighbourhoods officers, that code began to be eroded. 'Normalizing' the act of communication meant that it was no longer out of place or a taboo for someone to talk to the local officers. This was not a smooth or easy process, however. Indeed, with the gangs, it immediately became a point of tension and conflict:

Q) What are they like?
   A) They're very, anti!
   Q) Can you talk to them or do they just give you a load of grief?
   A) No, we do sometimes talk to them but like they are not very nice. I find them quite stupid really. They don't talk to us properly. They are just very argumentative and they just spend time telling us that we are 'bastard police' and, you know, we can't do nothing, we've got no powers and all this. (POL-MS6)

Although these were difficult encounters, to re-appropriate a phrase highlighted earlier in this book, they were still 'conversations with a purpose'. Just as the less conflict-laden interactions with ordinary residents were sources of community intelligence, so too were these ones, albeit this was unbeknownst to the gang members involved. There was an art to 'getting in the faces of these characters' as another officer described it, in order to elicit useable intelligence on who they were, and what they were up to.

Looking across the interviews conducted with the SNT officers they described how they had built up a reservoir of knowledge, such that they were able to recognize by sight the identity of key gang members. They were also able to gather a range of other intelligence on their activities by observing them. By employing this newly acquired 'field craft' during all their interactions and exchanges with these individuals, officers were highly attuned to:

- Gang symbols, clothing, and jewellery that might be on display;
- The visual identification of known individuals and those persons with them;
- The absence of persons normally expected to be associated with the person;
- The geographic location of the contact and time of day;
- Mobile phones used and other objects in the possession of the subject;
- Vehicles present and registration numbers;
- What the person was doing;
- The direction the person came from and where they were going;
- Signs of agitation or annoyance;
- Language used and any stories told;
- Names used by one person to identify another within the gang.

Such data are highly significant when dealing with gangs and territoriality. For example, location data can be useful in identifying 'safe areas'—specific places that gang members felt to be safe that they retreat to if a crime had been committed elsewhere, particularly those involving confrontations with other gangs and the discharge of firearms. Importantly however, collection of this type of intelligence was only instigated at the behest of an experienced community sergeant who had long learnt its value. Officers arriving in the SNT were not trained in such methods and were unaware of its situational importance. But it was something they were quickly instructed in so that they could contribute to constructing a 'rich' intelligence picture.

Resonating with some of the analysis in the earlier chapters, this rich picture understanding was deployed tactically and intentionally to engineer a certain sense of interactional tension and conflict:

They [gang members] think they are really powerful, but when we have got that knowledge over them, it's like the old saying 'knowledge is power'. It makes them feel very vulnerable. They will be thinking, they know my name, what else do they know about me. It creates a tension ... they feel most vulnerable when they know we know their name and use it. It's interesting, when a cop calls them by their name, especially when they are in front of other gang members, they really don't like it at all. (Pol-MS5)

The latter comment is especially intriguing. Quite why gang members respond so negatively to the use of their names by police is not really clear. Different officers spoken to in the course of the research proffered different explanations for this. Some suggested it might be because the use of their name demonstrates that they are 'known' to police and thus their 'shield' of anonymity is punctured. Others were of the opinion that naming in this way might be 'read' by others that the gang member was a potential 'grass', because they were on personal terms with police.

Comparing these two case studies of the local policing of counter-terrorism and gang violence, there are clear parallels and affinities between them. For what they both display is how something bundled up and even dismissed by some as 'expensive community work', can have profound pro-social effects on the local social order in contested communities. Importantly, the work of the police in such settings and situations has to be seen and understood, not in isolation, but in terms of how it can interact with pro-social factions to enable informal control capacities and capabilities to come to the fore. Thus tipping the extant balance of power—growing pro-social capital while diminishing anti-social capital.

This is an important and under-appreciated aspect of how and why community policing works (when it does) and just how complex it is. The norm is for police officers to focus upon their actions and the consequences that flow from them. However, they are at their most effective when Neighbourhood Policing interventions are able to leverage informal community social control assets to co-produce a response.

Operation Michigan in Cardiff

Extending and elaborating these themes in a third and final empirical example in this chapter, we turn to Operation Michigan, a South Wales Police-led action targeting serious and organized drug offenders in the city of Cardiff. It is an especially insightful case study owing to how it connects and blends a number of the themes discussed across previous chapters to the particular focus of this one. For it demonstrates how Neighbourhood Policing processes can function as a platform for other policing interventions. Specifically, it evidences how Neighbourhood Policing-based engagement processes that systematically collect community intelligence can often detect new problems missed by more specialist covert policing methods. Moreover, these are matters necessitating a scale, type, and intensity of policing response above and beyond that available via neighbourhood-based problem-solving.

As part of the large-scale community engagement exercise in Cardiff in 2009, that was the focus of Chapter 6, there were three areas in the city where 'drugs' signals were noticeably prominent. In orthodox policing terms, drug crime is frequently dealt with in a focused manner by specialist drugs squads. But as the then Head of Specialist Operations described, having read the community intelligence report on the city generated via the research, approaching these issues from a Neighbourhood Policing point of view simply highlighted how a range of harms were gravitating around the drugs issues:

When you presented the i-NSI data we all had access to it and some of the things that came out of that data to me was around signal crimes. Around the community feeling, and I started to look at [three prominent areas in the city] where in every ward the feedback was drugs, drug use, drug related behaviour and you know that would link to the anti-social behaviour. Some of the areas, the park areas and the graffiti, and the rundown areas that were linked with the drugs, I just thought perhaps we could do something that you can combine it all.

Significantly though, the three areas highlighted as being impacted by drugs problems according to the community intelligence were not aligned to the existing police intelligence picture concerning those areas. According to the police's view, informed principally by recorded crime data and criminal intelligence feeds, the three areas identified were not especially problematic in respect of drugs problems.

Consequently, the Detective Chief Inspector decided to 'test' the validity and reliability of the analysis. To do this he deployed 'Test Purchase Officers' (TPOs) into the areas, starting with one area, which coincidentally had the highest recorded crime rate in the city. The role of a TPO involves working undercover purchasing drugs from local dealers, in the process seeking to identify them and their associates. Covert technologies deployed by TPOs include covert image capture and the use of hidden microphones to record conversations for evidential purposes.

Reflecting the particular impetus for their deployment, an innovative aspect of their tasking in Cardiff was that they were encouraged to also gather intelligence on the impact on quality of life for residents of the drugs market crime:

So, we gave them an open mandate that their objectives were to engage only class A users/dealers. They were to gather intelligence and information around anti-social behaviour, so environmental scanning if you want to call it something better. I wanted to know the areas where drug dealers were active which might be having an impact on the quality of life issues for the community when we were working there.

Having collected lots of material on who was active locally, the police operation then moved on to the next stage:

It was a great success the first 4 months, what they found in [area 1] which is not a surprise really was a totally open market, street dealing going on all over the place in the communities. They were able to buy drugs within days of being there. It was like a sweetie shop really!

Having verified that the community intelligence was quite accurate, a second innovation to standard practice was then introduced:

I used NPT (Neighbourhood Policing Team) Officers on the operation in the back room. Now of course you know the Chief Super took a lot of persuading on this, because you are taking community officers away from their community work on a covert operation for four months, but I think we would never change that now because it was fantastic. They knew the people on the streets. They knew them by sight, they knew them by name and they could say, that's so and so, so and so. And it was great, that community intelligence, that knowledge!

Validating and reiterating several of the key conceptual points highlighted across the preceding chapters, in this quotation he accented the value of the 'field craft' of community policing work and the power of the knowledge built up by officers engaging in street-level interactions.

As described above, when the covertly obtained surveillance images were made available to the Neighbourhood Policing officers, they could identify many of those pictured on the basis of the contextual and highly situated knowledge they had built up about street life in the area. The results were striking:

The first phase resulted in 42 dealers being arrested, but around the arrest phase ... we did a two-week arrest phase we fronted it up by our Neighbourhood Policing Teams. Now, that to me hadn't been done before because historically specialist operations like this have always been fronted by the suits, or the investigators or the detectives. What I wanted to do was show to the public in [area 1] was that their Neighbourhood Management Teams had done this. Were on it, 'you said we did' sort of thing. 'You asked, we've done.'

Furthermore, what is also conveyed by this exemplar is a recognition of the importance of policing delivering visible control interventions, within the context of neighbourhood social order. By utilizing uniformed Neighbourhood Policing officers to deliver the control interventions, they were involved in sending a control signal to the community.

The perceived success of this approach and the key innovations embedded into it meant that it was reused a short time later when a modified form of the drugs problem started presenting in a different area of the city. This second instance was connected with London street gangs trying to establish a footprint for themselves in Cardiff. One cell in particular was actively building its powerbase in one of the target areas, and was later joined by members of a London-based crew. Although the Neighbourhood Policing Team officers were receiving a community intelligence feed via their engagement structures about a range of incidents connected to the gang, it was equally apparent they lacked sufficient capacity and capability to tackle them:

They were basically doing street robberies, they were intimidating the youths of [an area] and trying to 'mark their territory'. They were trying to make it a no-go area for the Police. And the community, they were effectively telling us that they were a problem, we knew they were a problem!

Consequently, once again, TPOs and specialist surveillance assets were deployed to gather intelligence, with Neighbourhood Policing Team officers tasked to identify the suspects. As previously, the Neighbourhood Policing Team conducted the arrests, building their credibility further within the community:

The arrest phase for the second phase I think we arrested some 30 odd dealers, hugely successful. We had young kids, I say young kids, teenagers on the streets coming up to the arrest teams on the arrest phase and saying, 'I can't believe you took them out, they thought they were untouchable' and for me that sort of feedback is just fantastic. (NPT-262)

Documenting these kinds of successes is important in building the knowledge base about what Neighbourhood Policing is and can be. Ultimately however, despite these successes, the timing of them is important in terms of the overarching story that is being told. For these innovations were taking place just on the cusp of the onset of the reductions to police funding being imposed by central government as part of their public sector austerity programme. As a consequence, the ability of specialist Neighbourhood Policing officers to support these kinds of working rapidly atrophied. This was because, in absolute terms, the number of officers assigned to these roles rapidly declined, but also those who were left on Neighbourhood Policing Teams were not securing the kinds of long-term assignment to areas that enabled them to build up their situational intelligence. It serves as a salutary lesson about just how delicate some key operating mechanisms of Neighbourhood Policing are.

What this case study speaks to then is something important about the focus of Neighbourhood Policing and how it works when applied to organized crime problems. In intelligence-led policing, the focus is upon intelligence gathering; in problem-oriented policing the focus is the multi-dimensional 'problem' that can be defined. Neighbourhood Policing, in contrast, takes the neighbourhood as its base delivery unit. When operationalized properly, it has the potential to draw out the inter-connections between a range of people, incidents, and issues, which might include recognizing 'presenting symptoms' of deeper, more organized pathologies. In turn, this keys us into a more sophisticated and nuanced understanding of the role of policing. For what can be observed is how Neighbourhood Policing is about more than targeted interventions against crime and disorder incidents.

Where it is successful, it is engaged in trying to influence and incrementally shape the structuring conditions of local social order over an extended time.

Co-producing social control

The three case studies providing the 'spine' of this chapter were selected because of how they involve problems that are typically understood as the preserve of 'high policing', rather than the stuff of local, community policing-based operations. For what has been foregrounded by the empirical data available in respect of each of them is how the locally embedded officers were in possession of locally situated and textured understandings that it would have been very difficult for officers more remotely engaged in national security functions to acquire. Equally important was how a common ingredient spanning the individual cases was police working directly with members of the public afflicted by an issue to devise meaningful responses to some complex and deeply ingrained problems.

In Chapter 2 of this book, reflecting upon the position and contribution of co-production to the formulation of Reassurance Policing and Neighbourhood Policing, it was recalled how many police officers and teams struggled with co-producing solutions. That said, as evidenced by the instances above, when it was harnessed properly it could prove powerful.

In his analysis of 'new parochialism' in Chicago, Carr (2003; 2005) attends to the processes of mutual adjustment between police and community that underpin the co-production of the social control he observed. Arguably, the most interesting aspect of his analysis surrounds what motivated the parties to enter into this process in the first place. For his account charts how the development of 'new parochial' ways of working did not miraculously appear. Rather, they were presaged by several false starts and failures. It was only when the groups involved were confronted by a 'stimulus for action' that was perceived as sufficiently threatening and serious, that both police and community accepted that their more orthodox responses were insufficient to manage the situation and 'barriers to action' were overcome. As a consequence, they were motivated to innovate and co-operate.

In an effort to try and conceptualize how and why co-production engaged between police and communities matters to the conduct

Table 8.1 A Framework for Positioning Types of Co-produced Social Control

	Police Defined	Community Defined
Police Delivered	Protective	Type 1 Co-production
Community Delivered	Type 2 Co-production	Mobilization

of social control, Table 8.1 differentiates between who assumes responsibility for defining the presence of a problem that requires social control, and ownership of the delivery of interventions intended to effect it. Cast in this way, four principal configurations of interactive social control can be distilled.

'Protective social control' is where the police 'own' both identifying a problem and the intervention. The tactics they engage can vary from disruption to law enforcement, but the crucial aspect is that the nature of the problem is determined and responded to by police. The converse mode to this is 'mobilization' where community members harness their informal social control resources to construct a self-help response. Critically, police and their local authority partners are reduced to bystanders, or indeed may be wholly unaware of the activity.

Of more direct interest though are what have been labelled 'Type 1' and 'Type 2' co-production. The former concerns how, in some situations, the police act to deal with issues brought to their attention by the community. For example, when involved in preventing violent extremisms, police may enter into 'Type 1' style collaborations with community and civil society organizations either because a problem is sufficiently troubling that it is beyond the scope of purely community-led interventions to impact upon it, or to build community trust and confidence. 'Type 2 co-production' is an 'ideal-type' used where police identify a problematic issue, but enable or encourage community-based actors to deal with it. This can either be through material/practical support, or more tacit forms of backing. Engaging this style of collaboration reflects how some problems encountered are complex and cannot be effectively treated through application of the criminal law. To the best of our knowledge, this style of working has not been previously identified by researchers.

Potentially profound theoretical implications can be derived from introducing the concept of co-production to the conduct of social control in this way. For in one of the pre-eminent and most influential accounts of social control, Donald Black (1976) set out the proposition that at an aggregate level there was an inversely proportionate relationship between the quantum of informal and formal social control in any given social order. In effect, he was suggesting some form of loosely coupled interaction, so that if there is an expansion in the amount of formal social control this will be matched by a contraction in the volume of informal control, and vice versa. What Black's social geometry does not engage with is the possibility that formal and informal social control may, in some circumstances, be interpolated and generative of each other. Nor does it account for how there may be 'pulses' of control—that is temporary increases in activity that then subside once a threat or risk (stimulus for action) is mitigated.

More generally though, grounded empirical studies of social control 'in action' tend to focus either upon the conduct of formal social control institutions (e.g. Reiss, 1992; Young 1991), or the operations of informal social control (Pattillo, 1998; Suttles, 1968). Only a limited number of works have sought to consider interactions between formal and informal social control and the conditions under which they might be mutually generative (Silver and Miller, 2004).

For instance, whilst there are now many studies of partnership working in the manufacture of social control (Crawford, 1997; Thatcher, 1998), these tend to focus upon collaborative arrangements between similarly positioned agents and agencies. Developing a concept of co-productive social control accents something slightly different. A defining quality shared by Type 1 and Type 2 co-production is that they involve work across the formal and informal divide. Indeed, it is this bridging between institution and non-institution that is essential to their ontology and makes them of particular analytic interest to students of Neighbourhood Policing.

Conclusion

One of the seminal insights of early studies of police crime investigation work was that the principal determinant of police success, in terms of identifying suspects and undertaking prosecutions, was the quality and quantity of information passed to them by members of the public (Greenwood et al., 1977). On those occasions where victims and witnesses passed useable information to detectives about what had happened and/or who was responsible, then there was a far greater likelihood of a prosecution resulting or some form of legal sanction being applied than where such input was lacking.

Analogous to which, a key theme pursued in this chapter has been how Neighbourhood Policing provides an 'engagement platform' that can be harnessed by aspects of policing focused upon non-local issues. Importantly, this ability to access and acquire 'community intelligence' is not envisaged as a replacement for more traditional mechanisms, such as covert human sources and electronic intercepts, through which intelligence on terrorism and organized crimes threats is traditionally obtained. But what Neighbourhood Policing mechanisms do afford, almost uniquely, is channels of communication, often based on trust relationships, through which people can convey information about suspicions they have, or where something just doesn't feel quite right.

Critically, this is not predicated upon an understanding that police–public engagement is 'always on'. Rather, it sets up communication channels that can be utilized as and when needed, so that citizens can pass on 'soft facts' with uncertain provenance, but that may prove important for police to know about. This is a rather different conceptualization of police–community engagement from that which predominates in many discussions in the literature or in policing.

The second principal conceptual theme brought through in this chapter has been the workings of the co-production of social control. Returning to the early formulation set out in Chapter 2, working with communities and other public service partners was always understood to be a key element of this approach to policing. The three case studies introduced all showcase different ways in which this can happen across a range of substantive problems.

Whilst these are important themes, the ultimate intent behind this chapter has been to illustrate how the conduct of Neighbourhood Policing can integrate with and function as a platform for the delivery of wider policing services. There has been a tendency to understand the work of managing neighbourhood security and national security as largely distinct. After all, they are functions that historically have tended to be undertaken by distinctive organizations, units, and officers. In the academic world, formulations such as Brodeur's (2010) conceptual division between 'high' and 'low policing' have worked to reproduce such notions. What the evidence presented herein suggests is that on occasions and in certain situations, there is more of a 'blended policing' approach than hitherto supposed. Aspects of the Neighbourhood Policing operating model lend themselves to supporting interventions directed towards these broader risks and threats.

Of course, it is important not to over-state the frequency with which these blended policing interventions occur. Looking across the data collated by the ten-year research programme that undergirds this book as a whole, it is salient that these three case studies stood out as exceptional exemplars of what Neighbourhood Policing can accomplish, rather than what is the norm.

9

Conclusions

Neighbourhood Policing has been one of the most significant and high-profile innovations in UK policing of recent times. It has also been one of the most successful in garnering widespread political and public support, both in terms of its objectives and the processes that it has sought to embed to achieve these. Indeed, in several recent reports by Her Majesty's Inspectorate of Constabulary and the Independent Commission on Policing, it has been described as the 'cornerstone' of the British policing model (HMIC, 2017: 4). The nomenclature and underpinning premises have also been adopted by the New York Police Department, albeit the British roots of this instance of policy transfer appear to have gone unacknowledged.

It is salient to this discussion however, that Neighbourhood Policing was not always so lauded. In its development phases it encountered considerable opposition and scepticism from both within and outside of the police. Some because the commentators concerned felt police should retain a far greater focus upon crime control. Others were of the view that community policing methods were passé. This book has sought to tell the story of how and why Neighbourhood Policing was able to overcome these objections, at least for a time, and then what induced its subsequent relative decline in status and prominence. The precise picture is more nuanced of course; whilst a number of police forces abandoned their commitment to Neighbourhood Policing, others sought to preserve some semblance of a defined local presence. At the time of writing, challenged by an up-turn in violent crime, there are indicators of a potential partial revival in Neighbourhood Policing's fortunes, propelled by a political intent to re-invest in the police both economically and normatively.[1]

---

[1] For example, in July 2019 Prime Minister Boris Johnson signalled a sharp policy shift to recruit 20,000 police officers across England and Wales, in a move

Neighbourhood Policing. Martin Innes, Colin Roberts, Trudy Lowe, and Helen Innes, Oxford University Press (2020). © Martin Innes, Colin Roberts, Trudy Lowe, and Helen Innes.
DOI: 10.1093/oso/9780198783213.003.0001

Neighbourhood Policing was designed as a flexible and adaptable model, defined by its use of a geographic footprint to organize the delivery of policing services and interventions intended to support neighbourhood security. The latter is an important construct in terms of acknowledging that, unlike some other policing models, Neighbourhood Policing is interested in both the objective and subjective dimensions of public safety. In its earlier iterations, a lot of emphasis was placed upon the value of ensuring officers in neighbourhoods were visible, accessible, and familiar. Under pressure from the consequences of public sector austerity and changing community dynamics associated with new communication technologies, this notion of physical presence lessened. Nevertheless, a sense has been retained that all variations of Neighbourhood Policing retain a fundamental commitment that there are specific officers identified with particular neighbourhoods who are responsible for what happens in that locality and are accountable to the people therein in some sense.

A key dimension of the analysis has been capturing how the processes and systems associated with the delivery of Neighbourhood Policing, whilst 'platformed' by the principles and ideas associated with the community policing tradition, also integrated elements drawn from problem-solving and intelligence-led models of policing. Especially in the chapters that discussed the work in Sutton and Cardiff, it was observed how a systematic and structured approach to generating community intelligence through specific proactive engagement mechanisms was utilized to target police attention and interventions towards local public priorities. Inflected by the principles of the Signal Crimes Perspective, the key point was not whether the problems identified were defined as crime or disorder, nor whether they were grounded in actual experiences or perceptions, but that they were having a discernible impact upon local people's thoughts, feelings, and behaviour as they relate to neighbourhood security management.

Significantly then, this methodology was performing a kind of 'demand management' function. A long-standing critique of community policing-based approaches is that they have failed to

that would replace the number of officers lost under the previous Conservative government's austerity programme described below. See https://www.bbc.co.uk/news/uk-49123319 (accessed 21 October 19).

define precisely what their key points of intervention are and are not. As a consequence, they can be a bit inchoate and sprawling in terms of where policing engages locally. By converting community engagement into a proactive and systematic task, and using the findings from this process to target interventions with a greater degree of precision than is commonplace in policing, a more concerted sense of direction and purpose is achievable. In addition, the data presented as part of these discussions are insightful in helping us to understand, in fine-grained detail, how the contours of local problems flex and evolve, and how these movements can be influenced by what police do.

A vital aspect of the research evidence presented is how it derives from a ten-year programme of research. So many accounts of innovations in police theory and practice are based upon short-term evaluations. It remains rare to be able to track and trace the evolution of an insurgent idea through initial implementation and then to see how it develops and matures over time. Allied to which, it has been equally important that the evidence reported herein has been collated from a range of police forces. This further enables an understanding of how local conditions and social climactics induce changes in what is actually delivered on the ground and what an initiative actually becomes. Neighbourhood Policing may have been a national programme, but it shape-shifted according to the local conditions into which it was introduced.

Reprise

The origin story of Neighbourhood Policing can be understood as an attempt to resolve several deeply ingrained and overlapping issues and tensions in respect of the police role in society. Specifically, it sought to clarify that the proper focus of police interventions should not just be restricted to crime, and it sought to improve how officers relate to and interact with citizens and communities. Layered on top, there was a need to try and overcome some of the limitations that had been identified with previous iterations of community policing. This required developing a policing model with sufficient flex that it could be moulded to different community contexts and circumstances, whilst at the same time being more structured and systematic in terms of its organization and processes than had hitherto been typical of community policing approaches. This is the narrative thrust of Chapters 1 and 2.

The quasi-experimental approach that underpinned the National Reassurance Policing Programme (NRPP) did a lot of the design work that was threaded through Neighbourhood Policing's principal processes and systems when it was subsequently rolled out across the country. In seeking to further our understanding and insight about the conduct of Neighbourhood Policing, the analysis blended into the empirical material concepts drawn from Erving Goffman's dramaturgical analyses of the micro-politics of social interaction. Particular attention was directed to how police conduct face-to-face interactions with members of the public cast in different roles, and to the social organization of police–community meetings. As such, this covers both one-to-one and one-to-many interactions. In addition to shining a light on the nature of the conduct of Neighbourhood Policing, the aspiration is that this conceptual framing will be of wider interest to students of police work. 'Close readings' of police–citizen behaviours when they are co-present in encounters with each other remains a relative rarity.

This theoretical impetus was developed through a focus upon the work and role of Police Community Support Officers (PCSOs), key members of all Neighbourhood Policing Teams. The direction of the discussion was oriented towards drawing out some of the tensions about what role Neighbourhood Policing type processes are intended to perform within a policing system. This is accomplished by considering whether, positioned within Neighbourhood Policing Teams, PCSOs are conceived as performing 'police support' or 'community support' functions. Different police forces have adopted alternative solutions to the dilemmas associated with these different orientations. Those that have defined a more 'police support' role for their officers have aligned them more explicitly with a crime control mission: more of their focus is invested in conducting tasks that in some way contribute to the management of de facto criminal offending. In contrast, a privileging of 'community support' conceives the key tasks and functions as engaging with and understanding community needs. Often this involves building their resilience and cohesion.

That these different configurations of the work of officers engaged in the delivery of Neighbourhood Policing services to the public exist signals something deeper about the contemporary construction of the police mission. These have been accentuated by some of the social forces associated with public sector austerity, the onset of the information age, and shifts in the aggregate profile of crime, rehearsed previously. Some political and police leaders have advocated that the response to this situation should be a 'narrowing' of the focus of policing to focus explicitly upon crime. This has been contested by other thought leaders on the grounds that this narrower form will ultimately prove detrimental to policing's ability to prevent crime over the longer term.

Engaging with these dilemmas, Chapters 6 and 7 focused upon a community intelligence methodology designed and deployed in support of the delivery of Neighbourhood Policing. In the terms outlined previously, the key affordance was keying police into 'what matters' from the perspective of local communities. Informed by some of the precepts of the Signal Crimes Perspective, by engaging in a proactive, systematic, and structured manner, the idea was to derive a form of locally oriented evidence-base about which crime and disorder incidents were influencing communities' perceptions and experiences of neighbourhood security. Practically, this performed a demand management function, inasmuch as it indicated that police do not need to try and tackle all the problems presenting in a local area. Rather, by working to understand which issues were especially harmful in the eyes of local residents, and intervening in respect of these, they can more effectively and efficiently impact upon neighbourhood security.

In addition to the interesting insights associated with the practical utility of this method being integrated within the delivery processes of Neighbourhood Policing, the data deriving from it provide some intriguing aperçus into the condition of different neighbourhoods. For example, data presented from Cardiff clearly highlighted how, even within one city, there were marked variations between different areas in terms of the prevalence and distribution of crime and disorder issues. Such data are important in clarifying that the security needs of communities and what they are looking for local policing to do varies. Accordingly, Neighbourhood Policing has always had to be able to adapt and adjust to local requirements. Scaling up from which means that, in terms of the detail of its processes and systems, what Neighbourhood Policing is and how it is experienced in some parts of the country differs substantially. Indeed, in some cases such differences are to be found in coterminous neighbourhood areas.

Important questions are also posed about precisely what a neighbourhood is. For although the concept was adopted and integrated readily by police leaders, insufficient thought was given in the early days as to precisely what this might involve. This is relevant inasmuch as the 'administrative neighbourhoods' that police adopted were defined in very different ways across different forces. As a consequence, although in all forces there was a Neighbourhood Policing Team assigned to each neighbourhood, the scale of the territory covered differed markedly. Moreover, where citizens' definitions of what constitutes their neighbourhood do not align with those being operationalized by police, then this can function as a source of friction. But potentially the most intriguing finding of the analysis of neighbourhoods as a delivery unit related to how public constructions of neighbourhood could be influenced and shaped by the occurrence of crime. This is important because of how it reverses the 'neighbourhood effects' logic. As a well-established perspective in social science, this holds that the socio-economic conditions pertaining to neighbourhood units effectively determines the prevalence and distribution of crime and other social problems within them. Instead, the data reported herein pulls through how the occurrence of crimes alters how members of the public think about and perceive the construction of neighbourhood boundaries and frontiers.

The material drawn from Sutton was used to show how similar kinds of data can leverage very different insights. Specifically, how over time Neighbourhood Policing interventions can shape and influence citizens' perceptions of crime and disorder. A key finding from this analysis is not that all community concerns disappear and are managed out by the active presence of Neighbourhood Policing assets, but they can be moulded into less harmful forms.

The systematic and structured collection and use of community intelligence has considerable value to the conduct of Neighbourhood Policing. As set out in the first chapter, in this sense it has integrated some of the ideas and logics familiar from intelligence-led and problem-oriented models into a community policing frame. Bringing this full circle, by the penultimate chapter, the focus was upon how the core systems and processes associated with Neighbourhood Policing afford ways of working that have value to counter-terrorism policing and responses to serious organized crime. In terms of these issues that by their intrinsic nature stretch beyond the frontiers of any neighbourhood, the kinds of rich picture that can be developed through Neighbourhood Policing-led engagement often detects the 'presenting symptoms' of deeper and more profound problems. As such, it frequently requires police knowledge and expertise to interpret the meaning of the kinds of concerns that community members might be picking up on, in order to diagnose their underlying causes.

A story of rise and fall

In a series of reports published since 2015, HMIC have articulated, increasingly forcefully, concerns about the fragile state of Neighbourhood Policing. This reached an apex in the 2016 PEEL national overview report where it was stated:

we have seen further evidence of the erosion of preventative policing in our neighbourhoods. Today, the police service is not as well equipped to stop crime happening in the first place as it has been in the past. (HMIC, 2017: 4)

This was elaborated in more detail as follows:

HMIC is increasingly concerned that local policing is being eroded … In our assessment, local policing is the area of operational policing that shows the greatest decline in performance … Where dedicated local policing teams exist, too often the warranted police officers on them are routinely taken away from their local policing duties to handle immediate tasks elsewhere … The work of local policing teams can thus be inconsistent, unstructured and ineffectively supported by other parts of the force. (HMIC, 2017: 10–11).

According to their analysis, subject to a range of pressures, preeminent amongst which has been reductions in police funding resulting in insufficient officers to service delivery in the ways originally envisaged, many forces have drifted away from the key precepts of the established Neighbourhood Policing model. This is clearly symbolized by how a number of police forces have replaced the terminology of Neighbourhood Policing with that of 'Local Policing'. Accompanying this rhetorical shift, where Neighbourhood Policing officers were largely protected from having to engage in response policing tasks, such as answering 999 calls, this is a core function for those engaged in 'Local Policing'. As a consequence, there is far less focus upon community engagement and proactive preventative tasks. Relatedly, the degree of rhetorical fealty expressed by some senior police towards Neighbourhood Policing has been noticeably less consistent and comprehensive than perhaps it was five years ago.

Similar conclusions were reached by Higgins and Hale (2017) in their comparative analysis of Slough and Luton, which they cast as akin to a 'natural experiment' in policing. They captured how the number of officers formally engaged in Neighbourhood Policing diminished over the four-year period where data was being collected, and that those remaining in such roles were increasingly engaged in general policing tasks. In particular, they highlight the increasing importance of responding to forms of 'hidden harm' and vulnerability, as well as the aggregate profile of crime restructured. Ultimately however, the 'solutions' they proffer to the predicaments they identify in Thames Valley and Bedfordshire Police with regards to their delivery of Neighbourhood Policing are restatements of the base principles of this approach, rather than any radical re-imagining of them. As such, it suggests that the problems being illuminated were more to do with local force implementation failures than the fundamental theoretical precepts.

In terms of the overarching pattern then and taking 'the long view' of police reform, what can be observed is how, in its early days, Neighbourhood Policing drew together and synthesized findings and learning from earlier policing models, blending these together in a community policing frame. In the process, Neighbourhood Policing supplanted its predecessors, establishing itself as akin to a common platform for the delivery of key policing services. In turn, as the world moved on, Neighbourhood Policing itself looked vulnerable to being replaced. Several causal factors account for how and why this degrading of its fortunes came about: public sector austerity; the decline in recorded crime; the information age; and the 'fashionability' of ideas. However, at the time of writing, there are some indications of attempts to revive and sustain at least some of the essential ingredients of Neighbourhood Policing, albeit these may not be quite the same as when it was at its peak of implementation.

Austerity bites

Following the onset of the global financial crisis of the late 2000s, there were significant and well-documented cuts to policing budgets, which in turn have induced reductions in the number of police officers across England and Wales. This matters particularly for Neighbourhood Policing, given how its design and delivery was relatively resource hungry. For although in the previous chapters much attention has been directed to utilizing community intelligence for targeting police interventions and thereby managing aggregate demand, not all forces integrated such mechanisms into their processes.

A sense of how these reductions to police budgets impacted Neighbourhood Policing can be gleaned from BBC analysis looking at changes to the police workforce between 2012 and 2017.[2] This reported that around 14 per cent (n= 1,500 out of 11,000) of the officer posts that have gone nationally were Neighbourhood Policing roles. On top of this, the number of PCSOs reduced from 14,393 to 10,205. Reflecting the complexities of the Police Funding Formula, these reductions have not fallen uniformly and equally across all forces. Moreover, different forces have sought to absorb or adapt to the reductions in different ways, with some trying to sequester neighbourhood-facing services more than others.

This explains why, in their national overview of the state of Neighbourhood Policing, HMIC (2017) were careful to delineate that different forces have responded in different ways to the financial challenges they have encountered. Interacting with the increasing accent on local subsidiarity in police policy making, most obviously embodied in the figure of the Police and Crime Commissioner, the reductions in police funding have led Neighbourhood Policing to be edited and adapted in a variety of ways. More generally, these trajectories of development serve to justify the approach to assessing Neighbourhood Policing adopted herein. That is, drawing upon evidence from across a number of police forces, rather than conducting detailed case studies of one or two and extrapolating from these.

'Restructuring' recorded crime

A second key theme in accounting for the weakening of Neighbourhood Policing that was alluded to in the preceding sections is the restructuring of recorded crime. By invoking the notion that crime is 'restructuring', rather than just that it is increasing or decreasing, we seek to draw attention to how its

---

[2] http://www.bbc.co.uk/news/uk-42403590 (accessed 15 February 2018).

aggregate profile is altering. Specifically, managing forms of crime and antisocial behaviour associated with interpersonal relations, and various forms of vulnerability, are responsible for consuming increasing amounts of police attention.

As was described in Chapter 2, one of the initial impetuses for the policy development of Neighbourhood Policing, via its reassurance-oriented forebear, was the fact that reductions in recorded crime did not appear to be being tracked in more subjective public perception measures, such as fear of crime and confidence in the police. More recently, whilst the headline rates of recorded crime declined, driven by ongoing reductions in volume property crimes and relatively minor public order offences committed by young people, more subtly other crimes have assumed increasing relative importance. Domestic and sexual abuse and violence committed against women and children, as well as handling incidents involving those with mental health distress, are an increasing amount of demand on police. In police parlance these kinds of issues tend to be referred to under the soubriquet of 'public protection' and vulnerability, and it has tended to be assumed that they constitute a different policing 'discipline' from that of Neighbourhood Policing.

Consequently, subject to the kinds of financial pressures rehearsed in the preceding section, most forces have tended to blend their Neighbourhood Policing assets with response policing tasks. However, most have preserved the distinction between Neighbourhood Policing and public protection. This needs to be questioned as it does seem possible to conceive of a form of Neighbourhood Policing that is equipped to engage with vulnerable people and places. After all, one of the advantages of the precepts of the Neighbourhood Policing model was the importance that it placed upon proactivity and precision prevention and intervention.

Such an approach would likely possess compatibilities with the kinds of 'therapeutic policing' that Stuart (2016) identifies as increasingly prominent in California. In configuring this concept, his point is that we need more complex and sophisticated understandings of how policing is being enlisted in the governance of the poor and marginalized; one that moves beyond a faulty dichotomy of care or control. There has, he posits, been an erosion of the boundaries between punitiveness and rehabilitation in the practice of policing. The resulting 'coercive benevolence' has:

... explicitly called on the police—as the maintenance men par excellence of the local spatial order ... As a result, the police now maintain a close and symbiotic relationship with the local welfare organizations they opposed for most of the twentieth century. (Stuart, 2016: 255–6)

One implication of these developments according to Stuart's analysis, is that:

As society's premier guardians of the social order, the police possess a great deal of symbolic power to diagnose, classify and authorize particular ideas about neighbourhoods, their residents and their problems. (Stuart, 2016: 259)

This is clearly coherent with many of the concepts and themes that have been brought to the fore across the chapters of this book. A point of departure however, would be in seeing this as constituting a 'new' development in the orientations of police work, as is implied by Stuart. This may be an inflection of the American context, where the crime control components of the police mission to understandings of what the police do has been far more pivotal. The British policing tradition and the scholarship surrounding it has in general always placed more accent upon the importance of what the public thinks about policing as a legitimate and appropriate issue. More than this, the notion that police work routinely stretches beyond crime control was one of the principal findings of the seminal police ethnographies of the 1970s that were so important in setting out the field of police studies. That this is so was gestured to in the titles of these works, for example Maurice Punch's (1979) construction of police as the 'secret social service'.

Digital policing and online crime

There is widespread consensus about, and much commentary upon, how social media and big data are combining to generate a new information ecology that is having a transformative impact across the institutional and interactional ordering of social, political, and economic life. These shifts are manifestly being detected within the investigative, intelligence, and engagement functions of policing. Several recent studies attest to how the conduct of police intelligence and investigation work is being reconfigured by the availability of new data processing algorithms that enable increasingly large volumes of data to be 'mined' and analysed (Brayne,

2017). Likewise, the panoply of social media platforms afford new ways for police to engage with different communities, at greater scale, faster, and at lower cost than their more traditional methods allow, notwithstanding the doubts that have been expressed about the efficacy of police strategies in this domain (Marx, 2016).

The development of the increasing interest in digital policing is itself partly a corollary of how increasing amounts of crime have acquired a digital component or shifted online entirely. In the wake of such profound changes and shifts, the focus of Neighbourhood Policing can appear distinctly 'analogue' and slightly outmoded. There is certainly a feeling that the centre of gravity for interest and attention in policing circles has shifted away from the neighbourhood towards the digital.

This notwithstanding, there is a wider and deeper point to be made here. The police as a formal social institution was formulated as a response to the crucible of the industrial revolution and the entwined processes of urbanization that it induced. Its precepts were designed to mitigate the conflicts and social tensions unleashed by new patterns of working and living (Reiner, 1992). However, what is perhaps under-appreciated in many histories of the police, is the extent to which the inception of the police was just one of a number of institutions established during this period for the purposes of regulating social harms (Neoclus, 2000).

Recognition of this dimension to police history is especially germane to the contemporary moment, given how so many commentators are suggesting that the 'information revolution' is liable to be just as profound and influential in terms of its social impacts and effects as was its industrially driven forerunner. Inevitably, this brings to the fore complex and challenging questions both about the crime and disorder problems that police are required to be able to manage, but also the principles underpinning the organization of policing. Importantly, just as the response to the social forces unleashed by the Industrial Revolution necessitated multiple kinds of innovations in the societal regulatory apparatus, so a similar multi-channel response might be required for the disruptions associated with the information age revolution.

Undoubtedly, policing will have a key role to play in any such arrangements. But equally, the nature and scale of some of the challenges involved will require new and innovative forms of regulation and social control, the focus of which lies outside of the police's purview. As such, it will be vital that the police do not neglect their responsibilities for more 'analogue' kinds of problem; precisely the kinds of local conflicts and disputes that are centred by Neighbourhood Policing

Given the scale and intensity of the social forces that the digital information revolution is unleashing, it is perhaps unsurprising that a considerable amount of policy and practice development over the past couple of years has attended to digital policing issues. Indeed, having been at the centre of debates about policing for several years, more recently Neighbourhood Policing has been eclipsed by concerns about 'the digital'. However, an element of policing will always be focused upon 'analogue' conflicts and disorders.

Intellectual fashions in policing

So far, this account of the causes shaping the relative decline in the status of Neighbourhood Policing has highlighted and accented a series of external 'drivers' of change. However, we should not ignore the fact that, in addition to these external social-structural forces, there are also more 'endogenous' explanatory factors that have played a part in this trajectory of development. These are associated with the internal politics of police innovation and reform.

According to Tim Godwin, former Acting Commissioner of the Metropolitan Police Service, who played a pivotal role in the early development of reassurance and Neighbourhood Policing, the history of UK policing can be understood through a 'reinvention cycle' process. That is, there is a tendency for it to oscillate between periods when senior police leaders and those involved in steering its policy development define a clear focus upon crime reduction, and other periods where the principal mandate is oriented to more nebulous community support functions. This will hold for a while, before it cycles around to become a more crime-centric mission again.

That these kinds of dynamics can be observed reflects something about the politics of police reform and improvement. Individual reputations and careers are made by re-orienting the direction and focus of organizations. To a certain degree, successful senior police leaders are those who can divine when mission focus needs to be adjusted to keep in step with political and public sensibilities. But there are deeper and more profound forces in play also. Policing by its nature spans a diverse range of functions and tasks, and so reform efforts typically seem to centre and privilege certain elements. Over time issues build up amongst those aspects of police responsibilities that are being relatively neglected, until such time as pressure grows and some adaptation and recalibration needs to be made.

Framed by this amalgam of endogenous and exogenous influences, it is notable that although Neighbourhood Policing capacity and capability has undoubtedly been degraded, recently there has been something of a 'recovery' action mounted to preserve and sustain it. For example, in 2017, the College of Policing convened a national expert committee to determine a new and updated set of national Neighbourhood Policing 'guidelines', reflecting how the context for policing had changed in the ways elaborated above. Reporting in October 2018, seven signature attributes of a rebooted Neighbourhood Policing were distilled as: engaging communities; solving problems; targeting activities; promoting the right culture; building analytical capacity; developing officers, staff, and volunteers; and developing and sharing learning.[3] Although the Guidelines are less prescriptive about how these components are to be aligned for service delivery, the very fact of their production perhaps signals something about how the essentials of Neighbourhood Policing cohere with the ways the UK police service reflexively conceives of itself and its social functions.

A police science

The narrative about Neighbourhood Policing's rise and fall (and partial recovery) that has been told across the chapters of this book has wider relevance and resonance in terms of understanding how and why policing as an institution evolves and adapts its methods and values. By tracking the development of this particular approach to policing over an extended period of fifteen years, it has been possible to observe how the processes and systems associated with Neighbourhood Policing have encountered and responded to some fairly profound challenges. These include: fundamental changes to the governance of policing brought about through the introduction of Police and Crime Commissioners;

---

[3] https://www.college.police.uk/What-we-do/Standards/Guidelines/ Neighbourhood-Policing/Documents/Neighbourhood_policing_guidelines.pdf (accessed 21 October 2019).

the rise of terrorism as a prominent political and social problem; public sector austerity and the consequent reductions to the police workforce; changes to the information environment and media ecology wrought by the penetration achieved by mobile and digital communication technologies; and profound changes to the demand profile of police organizations as traditional forms of volume crime have reduced, replaced by the increased prominence of public protection and working with vulnerable victims and citizens.

All of these changes have occurred during the time period that Neighbourhood Policing has been in existence. It is unsurprising therefore that it has been adapted and reconfigured. The deeper message to be drawn from this pattern of development is just how much context matters to policing. It is all too easy to adopt a reductive stance and cast policing as a series of standardized activities: foot patrol; arrests; interviews; community meetings; and so forth. However, the meanings of these policing behaviours and how they are interpreted and understood is situated. High levels of police presence in some towns and neighbourhoods will be the cause of very different social reactions to those elicited in other areas. Indeed, one of the key thrusts of the preceding chapters has been to try and illuminate how and why it is important, if we want to ascertain the impacts and outcomes of Neighbourhood Policing style interventions, that any account retains a sense of the local texture and dynamics of police–community relations.

In the annals of Criminology and Sociology of Policing this is an unusual study because of how it has sought to empirically track and trace an approach to policing in a sustained manner across an extended period of time. Such longitudinal approaches are familiar in the study of criminal careers, but they have rarely been applied to the institutional responses that are designed and delivered in an effort to curtail these career paths.

In this regard, the contents of this book hopefully offer much to contemporary students of policing, especially since it is being written in a moment where the concept of evidence-based policing is being promoted as having a vital role to play in the improvement of police work. As such, it is worth spending a little time disaggregating how the evidence and insights, set out previously herein, cohere with the predicates of this evidence-based policing movement that has acquired such traction.

One of its principal advocates has defined evidence-based policing as:

... the use of the best available research on the outcomes of police work to implement guidelines and evaluate agencies, units and officers. Evidence based policing is about two very different kinds of research: basic research on what works best ... and ongoing outcomes research. (Sherman, 1998: 3–4)

That said, consistent with the wider debates about the public value of so-called 'evidence-based policy making' more generally, evidence-based policing is a contested construct. In effect, there are supporters of what might be termed a 'strong programme' of evidence-based policing, lined up against which is a second more 'catholic' interpretation.

The 'strong' programme is particularly associated with the work of Sherman (1998), Weisburd and Neyroud (2011) and Weisburd et al. (2010). In this formulation, particular value is accorded to findings derived from randomized control trial designs and systematic reviews, frequently justified by analogous references to the ways in which medicine and healthcare provision tends to generate and validate new knowledge about 'what works'. Resonating with these intellectual influences, proponents espouse a hierarchy of evidence, with instruments such as the Maryland Scale deployed to ascertain the relative strength and credibility of studies.

As an approach, this 'strong' formulation of evidence-based policing can mount powerful claims about the need for, and approach to, reform in respect of the policing of particular social issues and problems. Indeed, the clarity of expression in terms of suggesting what police leaders need to do renders it alluring for those tasked to intervene in respect of frequently challenging and pressing public concerns. Consequently, the strong programme of evidence-based policing has proven highly influential politically.

There are, however, multiple concerns that can be identified with such an approach, many of which are long-standing. For example, Sir Leon Radzinowicz, the founding Director of the Cambridge Institute of Criminology, although a strong supporter of using empirical research to inform policy and practice development, pragmatically cautioned criminologists that factual evidence alone will never determine what results in policy terms (see Hood, 1974; Radzinowicz, 1961). Consistent with this view, those of a more 'catholic' persuasion tend to prefer notions that practice or policy is 'evidence informed'.

This more pluralistic and open approach to what should count as 'evidence' is exemplified in the title of Moore's (2006) chapter where he refers to 'experience, expertise and experiments' as a basis for police improvement. It is an approach that attributes a greater range of research methodologies and materials possess the legitimate capacity to influence policing policy and practice development. This more pluralistic approach was certainly present in the NRPP where much of the design work for Neighbourhood Policing took place. The extensive research conducted as part of the NRPP was avowedly multi-method in its orientations, blending: a quasi-experimental evaluation design; extensive public attitude and perception surveying using structured instruments; harnessing of co-production methodologies; systematic social observations of local neighbourhoods; in-depth interviews with residents and police; and ethnographic field observation. Arguably the key proponent of this more flexible and adaptable approach is Malcolm Sparrow (2016).

A key point of tension between these two positions is whether a 'scientific' approach can only be predicated upon findings from formal experiments or might encompass evidence derived from more 'naturalistic' observation. In support of the latter notion, Sampson (2012) notes the theory of evolution, which has a claim to be arguably the most important and influential scientific theory of all time, was derived from extensive systematic observation of the natural world, as opposed to the experimental manipulation of defined variables.

We would certainly locate the present study in this more 'catholic' tradition. The form of science we have tried to practise has been based upon extensive observation of Neighbourhood Policing over an extended period of time. Moreover, we have ensured that these observations have occurred across a range of different conditions and circumstances, allowing for us to compare and contrast variants of Neighbourhood Policing in practice across a number of dimensions. To aid this, a number of methodological innovations have been developed and deployed in support of the research effort. It is of note that, allegedly for almost a decade, the evidence of programme effectiveness derived from the NRPP was the only such material that the UK Treasury would accept as being of a sufficiently robust quality to support their funding decisions. In this regard, the research conducted then and reported on herein played a vital role in undergirding the national roll-out of Neighbourhood Policing.

More recently, Sherman (2013) has distilled three defining principles that he labels 'the Triple T', for evidence-based policing. 'Targeting' references the importance of ensuring that the application of any intervention is focused upon the presenting condition requiring treatment. 'Testing' emphasizes the need to rigorously and robustly determine the efficacy of any policing response that is to be applied. Finally, 'tracking' involves close monitoring of the effects on those exposed to the treatment condition.

Although the design work that established many of the key operating systems and processes associated with Neighbourhood Policing's delivery predated Sherman's 'Triple T', it clearly conforms with it as a framework. Targeting was achieved by the kinds of community intelligence work described in Chapters 6 and 7. Systematic and structured engagement with local communities was used to define the signal crime and signal disorders having a disproportionate impact on neighbourhood security and focusing policing interventions towards these. The potential of these approaches to policing were practically tested by adopting an evaluation design that spanned a range of community conditions and contexts. This was important in ensuring that the approach translated across different types of communities and their respective crime and disorder problems. Finally, as rehearsed above, considerable energy has been expended in tracking the results of Neighbourhood Policing's implementation by multiple police forces, and at different moments in time. Taken together, the aggregated empirical materials reported in this book suggest that Neighbourhood Policing didn't always produce a discernible and measurable effect, but on other occasions it did.

Importantly, the effects of having Neighbourhood Policing operating in a locality were sometimes quite subtle and difficult to quantify. A prime example was an event observed a few years back. In and around the South Wales town of Bridgend, there had been a cluster of suicides involving a number of young people. Because of the unusual pattern of seeing multiple individuals with a similar demographic profile taking their own life, from a relatively compact geographic area, and in a condensed period of time, it had become a national and international media story, with press and broadcast journalists running high profile features. Although such events are tragic, such clustering is not unheard of it transpires. Given their involvement in safeguarding work, the local police were working closely with their partners in public health to try and manage the situation and its community impacts. In one case in particular, where a young person from a village in the valleys had taken their own life, officers from the local Neighbourhood Policing Team, were used to police the funeral. Because this incident had been preceded by several similar ones, and given the media interest, the funerals held during this period became significant public events with large attendances. As the local police commander at the time described it, the decision to use the local neighbourhood officers was a deliberate one on the grounds that, given the circumstances, they had been working closely with many of the young people. As a consequence, they were well placed to spot any individuals showing signs of mental distress on what was a very difficult and emotionally charged day for the friends and family of the deceased.

The validity of claims such as these are hard to evaluate and thus derive evidence of support for. It is important therefore, that when discussing the evidence-base for something like Neighbourhood Policing, we are clear that not everything it delivers will be measurable. Harnessing the community connectivity of Neighbourhood Policing officers, in the way described above, certainly represents a creative and innovative approach to managing a potentially difficult situation.

In accord with the accent Sherman places upon time and 'tracking', it is worth reiterating the importance of the temporal dimension of the research design to the value of the findings and insights that have been reported. For the vast majority of studies that tend to be celebrated as paragons of 'strong' evidence-based policing, are based upon cross-sectional designs comparing how an intervention performs at a particular point in time, possibly across different contextual settings, the results of which are used to conclude whether or not the intervention in question 'works' or not. What such approaches are not able to do however is discern what happens over time, as an approach matures, or is changed in terms of its tenor and tone, by wider social, political, and economic forces.

In the case of Neighbourhood Policing for instance, the style and focus of policing practised under this banner in 2017 was very different to what it was in 2007. It adapted as social life changed around it. As such, if one was to try and read off evidence from 2007 of 'what worked' and assume that it would be equally relevant in 2017, this should be done very cautiously indeed. The scientific value of adopting a systematic and structured approach to observing 'the career' of an initiative like Neighbourhood Policing is that, alongside illuminating the intricacies and nuances that attend its formulation and delivery as it moves from being an insurgent 'innovation' to an integral part of the policing system, it also brings through more profound insights concerning the structuring influences of wider social and political relations on police behaviour.

There is more than a hint of irony that these discussions about the value of different kinds of evidence in leveraging improvements in policing have come to the fore in a moment that a number of commentators have defined as 'post-factual' or 'post-truth' (Kakutani, 2018; Pomerantsev, 2019). So that whilst accounts of 'being evidenced based' are increasingly important elements of the stories a number of police organizations are 'telling themselves about themselves', these are in tension with a set of societal atmospherics that suggest 'hard', objective, factual information is an increasingly less compelling determinant of how publics think, feel, and behave. Associated with which is a general waning of trust in key social institutions and the legitimacy of traditional authorities.

Framed in this way, the particular affinities and operating logics of Neighbourhood Policing illuminate some deeper and more profound insights about the conduct of social control and the social ordering of reality. First, because unlike most other policing models Neighbourhood Policing takes seriously the task of 'perception management', and the public value accruable from influencing people's subjective experiences of neighbourhood insecurity, it might actually be well suited to counteracting some of the negative institutional effects associated with a 'post-factual' age. But we should not overstate any such potential. For concomitantly, there is a recognition that many of the 'problems' that are the standard fare of the work of Neighbourhood Policing Teams are archetypal 'wicked problems'. The signal crimes and signal disorders that tend to trigger individual and neighbourhood insecurity, fear, and anxiety are typically products of deeper, more structural societal challenges and fissures. Whilst carefully formulated policing may prevent some of these 'presenting symptoms' from manifesting, and mitigate some of their harmful effects, 'solving' the deep causal problems that are generative of crime and disorder lies beyond the purview of police power.

Coda

Ultimately then, understanding Neighbourhood Policing necessitates thinking about the role of policing in society in multiple conceptual registers and forms. Perhaps more than most other models of policing, it is predicated upon a relatively sophisticated and subtle depiction of the role of the police in the production of social order. In terms of its design and predicates, it is conceived as involving interventions that seek to influence and shape the prevalence of crime, disorder, and insecurity indirectly, as well as more direct forms of impact. When properly implemented, it should be directly and democratically responsive to community needs and concerns, engaging with issues in ways that support community cohesion, resilience, and collective efficacy. To put it another way, formal social control performed by police should leverage enhanced informal social control.

This all points to the power of 'soft policing'. Police as an institution of the state are effectively defined by the wide-ranging capacity they are afforded to introduce legally justified coercive power to restrict the liberty of their fellow citizens across a range of social situations. Fifty years of research on their work has documented how they often do social good, but sometimes have more malign effects. It is perhaps unsurprising that, for some authors and policy developers, this capacity and capability to invoke legal force has exercised a gravitational pull upon their thinking about the fundamentals of what policing is and what it does.

There is, however, a tradition of scholarship that has developed a rather more nuanced depiction of what 'good' democratic policing looks like. For example, arguably the defining finding of the seminal early studies of police work conducted in the late 1960s and 1970s was that, in contrast to mass media discourses that largely celebrated the police as action-oriented 'crime-fighters', most police, most of the time, were engaged in managing relatively mundane individual and collective harms induced by a diverse range of social problems and pathologies. It was a dispensation appositely captured by Keith Hawkins (2003) as involving the use of 'law as a last resort'. A recurrent finding of empirical studies of police work has emphasized variants of this tendency, evidencing that a key feature of the art and craft of police work is utilizing a range of interactional strategies and behaviours to diffuse potential social tensions and conflicts. As such, whilst the police's ability to induce and impose order may be buttressed by their legally endowed coercive powers, these are foregrounded relatively sparingly.

Similar understandings permeate the more sophisticated accounts of police work that have been developed from within the police service. For example, Sir Robert Mark, whose writings give him a claim to be the most incisive of police leaders, talked of the importance of police 'winning by appearing to lose'. By this phrase he meant to articulate how repeated, 'naked', and unbridled displays of overwhelming police power may actually defray levels of social support and public confidence over time. Instead, he advocated police foregoing too much 'hard power' and instead engaging forms of soft power to negotiate the conditions and state of social order with citizens and communities.

This is clearly consistent with the grounding dispositions of Neighbourhood Policing. Intriguingly however, what the evidence compiled and reported across the chapters of this book documents is that police organizations frequently find this kind of 'soft policing' hard to deliver consistently and at 'scale'. Pretty much every police force could point to isolated examples of innovative and impactive interventions being conducted under the auspices of their Neighbourhood Policing arrangements, but the challenge is for this to be consistently and repeatedly programmed.

Appendix
Methodologies

As noted in the opening chapter, this book draws upon a fifteen-year long research programme that incorporated a number of diverse studies examining different aspects of Neighbourhood Policing. Different research designs and methodologies were employed along the way, including ethnographic field observation, in-depth qualitative interviews[1] and focus groups, secondary analysis of large-scale public attitude surveys, and documentary analysis. This appendix describes the approach taken in each of the key studies within this collection.

The National Reassurance Policing Programme

The National Reassurance Policing Programme (NRPP) was funded by the Home Office and Association of Chief Police Officers in sixteen sites, distributed across eight police forces throughout England. It was established to develop and test what precisely could be delivered through a reassurance approach to policing, and ran between April 2003 and 2005.

The sites were selected to provide sufficient contextual variation to explore how the strategies and tactics associated with these reforms induced change (or not) in different types of neighbourhood. Several sites were characterized by concentrated urban deprivation and high crime rates. There were also sites that were comparatively more affluent and semi-rural. Some of the police forces involved had been working within the community policing and problem-solving tradition, but for several the NRPP represented a more radical refocusing of their approach.

The research effort associated with the programme was divided into two principal strands. The first of these involved the authors, and was focused upon building up a detailed and granular evidence-informed picture of each of the community contexts and the crime, disorder, and social control issues that were impacting upon local people's sense of safety and security. As has been noted at several points throughout this book, equal

---

[1] Throughout this volume, we draw upon raw qualitative data extracts from respondents involved in a number of studies conducted over fifteen years. Each study employed different conventions for identifying individual respondents, so where verbatim quotations are utilized, the respondent identifier cited directly after the quotation is that used for the original study and no attempt has been made to standardize.

importance was attributed to perceptions and experiences. A range of methods were used to understand the situation of the areas and their inhabitants including local crime and disorder surveys, which explored residents' exposure to different forms of antisocial behaviour and criminality, the prevalence and distribution of fear of crime, and their views about the provision of policing and community safety services. These surveys were used by both the research and evaluation teams (see below).

For the research team, these survey data provided a comparator against which the evidence and insights distilled from the more in-depth qualitative research which was the principal focus could be triangulated. In the first year of the programme, across the sixteen trial sites a total of 218 in-depth, semi-structured interviews with local people (the average time of interview was around one and a half hours), sixteen focus groups, and fifteen on-site interviews (where the respondent accompanied the researcher to a location to discuss the issues therein) were completed. These were augmented by at least one week's field observation in each area, where researchers accompanied officers on patrol, attended police–community engagement meetings, and visited locations identified through the interview process. The resulting data were analysed and assembled into reports providing a very detailed account of the key places, problems, and people responsible for increasing public concern in each ward. These were made available to the local policing teams to inform their responses.

The intent underpinning this work was to operationalize the theoretical precepts of the signal crimes perspective to engage in precision 'problem-finding'. Fundamentally, the signal crimes approach holds that some events elicit a particular impact that influences public understandings of neighbourhood security. Therefore, by focusing upon managing the causes and consequences of these signal events in a systematic and structured way, it should be possible to shape how local safety is perceived and experienced. The value of qualitative method to this effort is that it provides the level of contextual detail that police find operationally useful. Being able to say that it is a particular group of youths hanging around outside a specific parade of shops, where they are drinking alcohol and being abusive to passers-by, is the kind of material police can utilize (as opposed to saying x per cent of people in the ward are concerned by youth-related antisocial behaviour). It was precisely this level of granular insight that the research process was designed to deliver. By drawing together the different data streams at a ward level, it was possible to construct a robust understanding of what were the priority issues for policing interventions that could impact upon levels of neighbourhood security.

In the second year of the programme, a number of follow-up interviews with the same respondents and several additional focus groups were conducted. Albeit on a smaller scale than the work conducted the previous year, similar checks were made to ensure that those participating in the research were representative of the ward resident population according to key socio-economic indicators. These second wave of interviews and focus groups were more focused upon tracking whether local people were detecting any change in terms of police being more focused upon the kinds of neighbourhood issues that concerned them than had occurred previously.

The evaluation for the trial of reassurance policing was conducted by members of the Research, Development and Statistics Department of the Home Office. Across the sixteen trial sites, they collected data on police interventions, police recorded crime data, and public perceptions. The latter were gathered through a two-wave telephone survey of approximately 300 residents in each ward, where respondents were asked a range of questions designed to measure their perceptions of crime, disorder, risk, social capital, and changes in these. Six of the trial sites were matched with 'control sites' in other locations, where an undertaking was provided by the local police commander that no reassurance-oriented policing interventions would be undertaken for the trial period. The purpose of this was to try and establish a robust measure of what difference the reassurance policing interventions might have over and above any wider regional or national trends that might be occurring. The other ten research sites were not matched with control sites. For the purposes of this chapter though, we do not draw upon this evaluative data. Our focus is instead upon a second strand of more 'basic research'. As detailed below, this extensive largely qualitative work was conducted in order to develop a knowledge base for reassurance activities. In what follows we want to explore and explain the significance of this work for understanding the conduct of reassurance policing.

Neighbourhood Security Interviews

As indicated above, during the initial NRPP work a key research instrument developed was an innovative semi-structured interview approach. Although it has been developed and refined over the years, it has underpinned a number of the main studies that have been drawn upon for this book. As such, it is useful to just highlight its key components.

Broadly, the unique feature of the Neighbourhood Security Interview schedule was the combination of academic qualitative social research methodology with a geo-spatial element, allowing for a visual representation of the data collected in a map format. In their original form the interviews were paper-based, utilizing printed maps of local wards and asking interviewees to draw some of their responses to questions on these, which were then subsequently digitized for the purposes of analysis. Given the interest in the approach, following on from the NRPP, a decision was taken to develop it into an 'app' that could run on laptops and tablet-PCs. This rendered the whole process significantly more user-friendly and interactive, making it far more efficient also. The principal iterations of the interview methodology are described in more depth below.

For the NRPP research, the opening segment of the interview structure utilized open, semi-structured questions to encourage respondents to talk freely and at length about their experiences of crime, disorder, and policing in the areas where they lived. The interview instrument comprised a standard set of questions, but interviewers were also encouraged to use follow-up questions to probe any particularly interesting aspects of respondents' answers in more depth.

In addition, several more structured questions were included, with the user oriented to a variety of issues by the use of a series of 'shuffle cards' and 'show cards' listing different crime and disorder problems. The intent being to help them think about issues that might not be in the front of their mind, thus helping them break out of any standard crime and antisocial behaviour narrative tropes that may be familiar to them. This part of the interview was only commenced once respondents had provided as much spontaneous information as they could to the open questions.

The final segment of the interviews focused upon the use of mapping processes. During the interviews respondents were shown a large paper map of the local area and were asked a series of questions about the problems near to where they lived and further afield. Following various prompts from the interviewer, respondents plotted on the maps the locations of any problems they identified. The geo-spatial data produced by this section of the interview provided a sense of where problems were located and how they clustered.

The design of the interview schedule, and the integration of the specific techniques listed above, was intended to encourage respondents to focus upon their actual experiences and knowledge of crime and disorder. This reflects a key conceptual difference between fear of crime studies, which tend to be interested in general attitudinal data about crime and disorder, and the signal crimes perspective, where the focus is upon how knowledge about specific incidents informs attitudes and behaviour. Despite this explicit focus within the interview schedules, it was nevertheless apparent that in many instances respondents' answers were hypothetical. That is, they had little knowledge or experience of a number of crime and disorder types, but would still offer an answer to the question posed. In effect, trying to be helpful, they readily supplied 'pseudo-opinions' that drew upon what appeared to be culturally validated 'scripts'. By this we mean that the replies to the question did not necessarily reflect an individual's actual, previously deliberated opinion on a subject, but rather, what the person thought a 'normal' individual in such circumstances would say. For example, they would preface their answers with phrases such as 'it must be awful if that happens to you and if it was me I think it would …' or 'If that happened to me, I would …' and so forth. Given that the interviews were qualitative, it was often possible to identify those occasions when these kinds of answers were being given and these were excluded from analysis.

One particular methodological challenge identified during the data collection and analysis phases concerned the meaning of people's crime talk. In narrating their experiences of crime and disorder, people draw upon a 'natural discourse' that often frames problems in a different way from the more technical and precise definitions to be found in 'legal discourse'. For example, they will talk about 'mugging' rather than 'robbery', 'telephone boxes being smashed up' or 'people being beaten up', rather than in terms of the formal offence types in law.

For the researchers, the translation of the varieties of indigenous phraseology into defined crime and disorder types proved problematic. In an effort to overcome this difficulty, a variety of phrases were used by the researchers during the interviews to give people an array of options in discussing their concerns. These were then 'collapsed' back together at the analysis stage. So, for example, in relation to drugs, different people would variously talk about drug houses, drug transactions in public, signs of drug use in public, and physical signs such as used syringes. Similarly, criminal damage and vandalism were used to describe the destruction of physical property. These issues are important in terms of reading and understanding the ways in which aspects of the data analysis has been presented.

Neighbourhood sentinels

Respondents for involvement in the Neighbourhood Security Interview process were selected on the basis of a purposive sampling strategy. Rather than recruiting a random sample of neighbourhood residents, the methodology deliberately set out to recruit 'high knowledge' individuals, likely to be aware of problems in the area, dubbed 'neighbourhood sentinels'. Interviewers were advised to identify and select individuals based upon two key factors:

- Those who were embedded within local social networks, with an investment in a neighbourhood, such that they took a greater interest in its fortunes and have a high degree of situational awareness of what is happening, where, when, and to whom;
- Those who spent significant time out and about within the public spaces of the area and utilized its facilities, meaning that they were more attuned to long-standing problems and singular events that may be troublesome or concerning. For example, mothers with children, those involved in voluntary community activities, together with people working in local service functions, such as health and leisure,

delivery services, and taxi drivers all seem to have a particular awareness of local problems;

Precedent for thinking in these terms and seeking to harness the unique
knowledge and insights that such individuals possess can be traced back
to Sykes (1951) and Campbell (1955). Sykes' (1951) analysis identified
that if one is interested in the information about an area possessed by
its residents, rather than the attitudes that they hold towards it, then
there are socially structured patterns detectable between those groups
who hold 'more' and 'less' neighbourhood information. Developing this
line of thinking, Campbell (1955) systematically examined this 'asymmetry of knowledge'. He differentiated between a randomly selected
group of respondents who were surveyed and a smaller group of deliberately selected 'high knowledge' informants who were questioned using
a semi-structured interview, concluding the latter group was marginally
more accurate than the far larger sample of randomly selected survey
respondents.

Applied to the task of police engaging community members, this
might lead to trying to develop relationships with people in roles such as
mothers with children, those involved in voluntary community activities,
together with people working in local service functions such as health
and leisure, delivery services, and taxi drivers. This is on the grounds
that they spend significant time out and about within the public spaces
of the area and utilize its facilities. The result being that they are more
attuned to long-standing problems and events that may be troublesome
or concerning.

The size, geographic distribution, and representativeness of the respondent sample selected for interviewing was determined by a combination of Census unit structure and data. Each of the NRPP trial
sites was sub-divided by overlaying a grid of the Office for National
Statistics smallest unit of Census, the Output Area (OA; Office for
National Statistics, 2020). Each OA contains a relatively consistent
head of population of around 250–300 and interviewers were tasked
to recruit at least one respondent from each. As such, total sample
size was determined by the number of OAs within the area of interest
whilst a consistent proportion of the population of around 1:300 was
maintained across all sites. Additionally, interviewers were required
to keep broadly within a demographic profile in terms of age, gender,
and ethnicity, based upon the most recent recorded Census data for
the area. Applying this geographic distribution dimension to the sampling strategy helped to prevent researchers (and police) from engaging
solely with people who were easy to recruit, requiring them to 'widen
the radar' to develop neighbourhood sentinels in other localities they
might not know so well.

Data analysis

Analysis of Neighbourhood Security Interviews took both established and novel paths. The interviews were audio recorded, transcribed, and coded by researchers using a coding frame to identify the component parts of signal crimes, disorders, and control signals (Innes, 2014). The signals identified by each respondent were then compared and contrasted in order to identify any common patterns. This work was assisted by the use of the computer assisted qualitative data analysis software package N-Vivo. The software enabled the manipulation of the large amounts of discursive data and complex searches to be conducted once the material had been coded.

In addition to which, three other analytical approaches were employed. Data collected during the mapping exercises within the interviews were digitally coded and subject to a form of geo-spatial analysis. The geo-coded data were analysed through Hotspot Detective 1.2, a program often used by police for the purposes of identifying crime hotspots. For the purposes of this research, the computer algorithm was employed to identify 'risk perception hotspots'. These are defined as locations that groups of people all perceive as risky due to a belief that crime and disorder problems cluster there. In a small number of forces where it was available, geo-coded crime data was also collected and processed using the same program to identify crime hotspots. The location of crime and perception hotspots was then compared. In addition, a database was built in Excel relating to the problems identified by respondents during the mapping exercises.

Data from the more structured questions asked during the course of the interviews were analysed through quantitative techniques using SPSS. Finally, content analysis was conducted of the interview data to locate instances in the interviews where people mentioned crime and disorder problems (expressions), but they did not relate contents and effects to them, and thus the incident did not constitute a full signal.

Community intelligence programmes in Cardiff and London Borough of Sutton

Following the NRPP, the research team set about simplifying the original Neighbourhood Security Interview methodology in such a way as to ensure it retained the ability to elicit information from residents about which local problems are generative of insecurity, whilst simultaneously making it able to be administered by front-line Neighbourhood Policing officers as part of their engagement role. Both personally and at an organizational level, the police were not equipped to take on an elaborate, and quite involved, social research methodology.

The solution arrived at was converting the original interview instrument into a form of Computer-assisted Personal Interviewing (CAPI) programme. Reflecting its purpose to generate structured and systematic community intelligence, it was named the 'intelligence oriented Neighbourhood Security Interview', or 'I-NSI' for short. It was this approach, and its refresh SENSOR, that underpinned the work in the London Borough of Sutton from 2007 onwards and Cardiff in 2008/9 that is reported in Chapters 6 and 7.

The core of the programme was a commercially available Geographic Information Systems (GIS) software. Loaded on to a laptop computer, the programme enabled the locations of problems identified by interviewees to be directly plotted digitally onto a map of the local area, and the accompanying qualitative data to be captured quantitatively using a series of 'tick box' data entry screens integrated into each plotted location.

A second software was developed along with the 'data-capture' module, designed to enable the collected data to be automatically analysed and output as a series of geographic and thematic maps with accompanying data tables. Thereby providing a form of 'community intelligence' on significant locations and crime and disorder problems respectively. Community intelligence can be defined here as information elicited from the community that, when analysed, provides foresight into the risks posed to or by a particular person or group of people. Similar to both crime and criminal intelligence it has a prospective dimension, but what gives it its unique value is that it has a 'collective' imprimatur.

Designed to be *integrated* into the day-to-day role of neighbourhood officers and Community Support Officers (CSO), rather than being the exclusive preserve of internal and external 'research' departments, the data capture software module was installed on a laptop computer taken to the interview by the officer. Integrated into the programme was an electronic map of the specific neighbourhood and surrounding area which, following some general, structured questions about levels of community cohesion and shifts in crime and disorder prevalence in the neighbourhood, was shown to the respondent. The interviewer first asked the respondent to trace out the boundaries of what they considered to be their 'neighbourhood' on the map. In effect, this part of the interview was obtaining data on residents' self-defined natural neighbourhoods (see Chapter 3).

Interviewers were then prompted to ask the respondents about 'any problems' they were aware of in the neighbourhood they had defined, and indeed further afield, indicating where on the map each of the identified problems occurred. One at a time, each problem was plotted as either a 'point' (specific location), 'line' (between two or more points, for example a road) or 'area' (for a park or shopping centre, for example). Each plot triggered the appearance of a data entry screen containing a combination of questions, pre-defined tick boxes, and free text fields designed to capture a detailed description of the issue at hand. Through probing and prompting, the interviewee was encouraged to provide details of when the problem occurred, how it manifested itself, and, importantly to reflect the signal crimes concept, if it had directly influenced how they think, feel, or behave in relation to their personal or collective security. Additionally, the software guided interviewers to ask other questions providing useful supplementary information, including an assessment of police and council services in relation to the specific problems they had identified and, if appropriate, 'who they believed to be responsible?' Once completed, the data entry screen 'attached' this information to the geo-coded data. The average respondent, in an average neighbourhood, typically plotted between three and four signal crimes or disorders.

Before finishing the interview, the respondent was asked if there are any specific locations where they felt afraid and/or that they avoided, describing the particular issues there that led them to feel this way. This frequently resulted in interviewees identifying additional concerns and 'neighbourhood areas' with which these problems were associated. The interview process then was something of a hybrid methodology combining a semi-structured qualitative interviewing technique with more structured data recording and coding in a fashion more akin to quantitative surveys.

The data generated through the interviews were initially analysed by a second piece of bespoke software which used predefined algorithms to output maps and data tables based on geography, individual crime or disorder type, and themed groupings or signal effect. The purpose here was to ensure that officers were being provided with rapid feedback from their work that they could deploy operationally. Different maps provided at-a-glance visual representations of the distribution of problems identified by respondents and accompanying quantitative data to determine their strength and coherence among the sample as a whole. Problematic locations could be output as large-scale maps to fully explore the impact of co-existing problems with free-text descriptive data linked to provide the 'richer picture'. By aggregating the data in this way, the analysis sought to develop an insight into what signal crimes and disorders were impacting most within different communities, and the significant locations where they occurred. Further interpretation by human analysts helped to gain an even deeper insight, but the particular advantage of the automated analysis was that it allowed large amounts of data to be processed quickly with little resource implications, ensuring findings were available in a timeframe that gives them practical relevance to police and community safety partners.

One of the practical limitations of the early versions of the i-NSI data capture software was the need for it to run on a laptop computer.

Front-line officers found carrying a laptop around prohibitive and meant they were unable to act spontaneously with regard to interviewing members of the public. The increasing use of smartphones and tablets by forces gave the research team the opportunity to develop a solution to this problem by rewriting the data collection module as an application for Apple OS and Android devices that we dubbed SENSOR. Aside from a few minor adaptations and improvements to the structured interview questions, the methodology remained identical to the earlier I-NSI iteration described above and the same automated analysis algorithms were employed to output the data collected. One further significant improvement of this tablet-based application was that it also enabled data to be automatically sent, in an encrypted format, to a secure server at the end of each interview, negating a need for data to be retained on the hardware and allowing even faster analysis.

Police officer interviewer training

As was outlined earlier, the prime reason for the development of a simplified version of the Neighbourhood Security Interview was to render it accessible and easy to use by operational neighbourhood police officers and other community safety practitioners as part of their engagement activities with members of the public in the areas they serve. Reflecting the 'action learning' spirit of the NRPP, in doing so, the methodology has moved from being a research activity to a tool with the demonstrated capacity and capability to deliver useful tactical and strategic intelligence. Crucial in this transition, however, was the development of a training programme for officers which captured both the background constructs and practical skills they would need to successfully capture the knowledge and perceptions shared by those they interviewed. And given the competing demands upon their time, this had to be delivered succinctly over a short as possible timescale. After experimenting with a number of different approaches in the early stages of the methodology's development, the most successful training programme involved a three-stage process:

1. Officers and PCSOs from the Neighbourhood Policing Teams in each of areas to be surveyed were provided with a one-to-two-hour pre-briefing by members of the academic team, approximately two weeks prior to commencing their data collection period. At this meeting, the purpose of the exercise was explained in operational terms, followed by a brief outline of the process and detailed instruction on how to pre-identify neighbourhood sentinels to approach for interview.

2. This was followed by a one-day training session in the classroom at the beginning of the first week of the data collection period. This input commenced by giving trainees a more in-depth explanation

of the signal crimes perspective followed by some exercise-based interviewing skills training in relation to identifying key concerns in people's crime-speak and probing for more relevant detail. Finally, delegates were familiarized with the interview software application and the technology used to deliver it.

3. Having completed the classroom training, each officer's first 'live' interview was also attended by the trainer in order to consolidate the learning and coach the newly trained interviewer on a one-to-one basis.

Although considerable effort went into the design and delivery of the training programme, it is fair to say that the majority of officers were resistant to the process, perceiving it as dragging them away from 'their real police work'. For some, this resistance softened as the results started to be returned, but this was not the case for all. Potentially, this tells us something about the value ascribed to community engagement within police culture and organizations. That is as a good thing to do, but only deserving of a circumscribed effort.

The role of (Police) Community Support Officers

The contents of Chapter 5 are derived from a project evaluating the role of the CSO, which was commissioned by the Welsh Government following their funding of an additional 500 officers across Wales in 2014. The research was conducted in all four Welsh police forces, focused on six selected case study areas. The work employed secondary analysis of quantitative data from a number of existing sources, including:

Crime Survey for England and Wales (CSEW), formerly the British Crime Survey. This is a large-scale public victimization survey with interviews conducted on a continuous basis each year, on behalf of the Office for National Statistics (ONS). It provides a robust sample of public perceptions about policing in England and in Wales.

Police Recorded Crime and Incident Data, from each of the four Welsh police forces showing the volume of offences and non-crime incidents, call grade, and information about whether or not a CSO attended that incident. These data were used to show monthly trends over time.

Police force public perception surveys. Each Welsh police force supplied their surveys of the general public, or victims of crime and anti-social behaviour, covering the period before and after Welsh Government investment. These data are used where possible to compare public attitudes in the two time periods.

Beaufort Omnibus Survey. The Welsh Government funded questions about CSOs in this survey over a three-year period—it was based upon a representative quota sample, consisting of a minimum of 1,000 adults aged 16+, resident in Wales. It was used in our research to investigate any change in public perceptions of CSO visibility, the CSO role, and safety at police force area level between 2012 and 2013.

In addition, the study also utilized the following qualitative methods:

Qualitative Interviews. In-depth interviews with senior police officers at force and local level to understand strategic approaches to the deployment and utilization of the new CSO resource. These data are supplemented with some exploration of the tactical impact of the intervention, obtained from interviews with Neighbourhood Policing Team sergeants or inspectors in each locality.

Focus Groups. Further data relating to the tactical impact of the intervention were obtained via focus groups with CSOs themselves. At least one focus group was conducted in each of the six case study areas and involved both Welsh Government CSOs and other CSOs within the Neighbourhood Policing Team s.

Documentary and Media Analysis. Analysis of key documents relating to the policy as provided by the Welsh Government and individual forces, including strategy documents, monitoring reports, and human resources documents, together with local news media and online information by way of force websites.

Observational Research. Observation of CSOs on patrol and PACT meetings by researchers.

Linking neighbourhoods to national security

The third tranche of our work drawn upon in the course of this book involved investigations of the role of Neighbourhood Policing assets in tackling serious and organized crime and preventing violent extremism. This is the substance of Chapter 8. During both 2007 and 2010 the research team undertook multi-method research for the Association of Chief Police Officers (ACPO) and Home Office designed to evaluate the implementation of the Prevent strand of the UK Government's CONTEST counter terrorism strategy.

Work was conducted across four areas of England and Wales: South London and Surrey; West Midlands; Greater Manchester; and Cardiff. Observational field-research and in-depth interviews were conducted with both police officers working in the Prevent sphere and community representatives. A total of forty-one semi-structured interviews were conducted with police practitioners engaged in prevent delivery. These were supplemented by fifty-three interviews with community members who had engaged with Prevent interventions in some fashion. The latter group in the sample were involved in co-producing disruptions with the police, or had participated in informal social control disruptions, rather than being the subjects of such measures.

The police respondents were typically police constables and sergeants, with one or two more senior officers also interviewed across each of the four forces participating in the study. In addition, two of the police interviewees were senior officers seconded to the Home Office Prevent Delivery Unit. The community respondents were drawn from several communities within the four police force areas. The majority of the interviewees were male and over twenty-five, many of them having been engaged with the police and Prevent in a range of capacities for several years. All interviewees were assured their anonymity as a condition of their involvement with the research.

Typically, interviews were about an hour in length, although some were longer. The interview accounts were tape recorded and fully transcribed. The respondents were located in four police force areas across England and Wales. The interview schedules utilized for both police and non-police respondents covered perceptions and attitudes towards Prevent as a strategy, but accented local experiences of implementation. These interview data were augmented with observational material from fieldwork at meetings where a range of Prevent related problems and issues were discussed, and a variety of tactical and strategic interventions considered and reported on.

Summary

As has been noted at several points in this book, it is unusual to be able to report on the evolution of a policing innovation from its origins well into maturity. To do this, and provide this longer perspective, has required drawing upon and integrating data and materials from a number of different studies. These have involved multiple funders with very different imperatives propelling their interests in Neighbourhood Policing. As a result it has perhaps not been possible to achieve the kinds of empirical cohesiveness that can be found in large-scale research commissions that are supported by one set of over-arching interests. More positively however, the more 'catholic' perspective adopted has enabled Neighbourhood Policing to be viewed from a variety of angles. Maybe even, because of the methodological diversity, the whole is stronger than the sum of its parts.

References

Ackerman, S. (2015) 'Homan Square Revealed: How Chicago Police 'Disappeared' 7,000 People'. *The Guardian* [online] 19 October. Available at: <https://www.theguardian.com/us-news/2015/oct/19/homan-square-chicago-police-disappeared-thousands> [Accessed 20 December 2017].

Ackerman, S. and Stafford, Z. (2015) 'Chicago Police Detained Thousands of Black Americans at Interrogation Facility'. *The Guardian* [online] 5 August. Available at: <https://www.theguardian.com/us-news/2015/aug/05/homan-square-chicago-thousands-detained> [Accessed 20 December 2017].Alderson, J. (1979) *Policing Freedom*. Plymouth: Macdonald and Evans.

Aneshensel, C. S. and Sucoff, C. A. (1996) 'The Neighbourhood Context of Adolescent Mental Health'. *Journal of Health and Social Behaviour*, 37(4), 293–310.

The Argus (2016) 'PCSO Changes Could Harm Policing, Union Warns'. *The Argus* [online] 25 March. Available at: <http://www.theargus.co.uk/news/14384026.PCSO_changes_could_harm_policing__union_warns/> [Accessed 14 December 2017].

Association of Chief Police Officers (2006) *Practice Advise on Professionalising the Business of Neighbourhood Policing*. Wyboston: Centrex.

Association of Chief Police Officers (2007) *Guidance on Police Community Support Officers*. London: ACPO.

Audit Commission (1993) *Helping with Enquiries: Tackling Crime Effectively*. London: HMSO.

Awan, I. (2012) 'I Am a Muslim Not An Extremist: How the Prevent Strategy Has Created a "Suspect" Community'. *Politics & Policy*, 40(6), 1158–1185.

Bahn, C. (1974) 'The Reassurance Factor in Police Patrol'. *Criminology*, (12), 338–345.

Beake, N. (2015) 'Met Police Considers Scrapping 1,000 Neighbourhood PCSOs'. *BBC News* [online] 9 September. Available at: <http://www.bbc.co.uk/news/uk-england-london-34200384> [Accessed 19 December 2017].

Black, D. (1976) *The Behavior of Law*. New York: Academic Press.

Blokland, T. (2003) *Urban Bonds: Social Relationships in an Inner City Neighbourhood*. Cambridge: Polity.

Boden, N. and Slack, J. (2008) 'Rank-and-File Uproar at Plan to Hand 90% of Police Work to Civilian Staff'. *Daily Mail* 7 February.

Available at: https://www.dailymail.co.uk/news/article-512781/Rank-file-uproar-plan-hand-90-police-work-civilian-staff.html [Accessed 21 November 2019].

Bottoms, A. and Tankebe, J. (2012) 'Beyond Procedural Justice: A Dialogic Approach to Legitimacy in Criminal Justice'. *Journal of Criminal Law and Criminology*, 102(1), 120–170.

Bowers, K. J., Johnson, S. D., Guerette, R. T., Summers, L., and Poynton, S. (2011) 'Spatial Displacement and Diffusion of Benefits among Geographically Focused Policing Initiatives: A Meta-analytical Review'. *Journal of Experimental Criminology*, 7(4), 347–374.

Bowling, B. (1999) 'The Rise and Fall of New York Murder'. *British Journal of Criminology*, 39(4), 531–554.

Boyle, D. and Harris, M. (2009) *The Challenge of Coproduction. How Equal Partnerships between Professionals and the Public Are Crucial to Improving Public Services*. London: Nesta.

Bradford, B. and Myhill, A. (2015) 'Triggers of Change to Public Confidence in the Police and Criminal Justice System: Findings from the Crime Survey for England and Wales Panel Experiment'. *Criminology and Criminal Justice*, 15(1), 23–43.

Braga, A. and Weisburd, D. (2006) 'Problem-oriented Policing: The Disconnect between Principles and Practice', in D. Weisburd and A. Braga (eds.), *Police Innovation: Contrasting Perspectives*. Cambridge: Cambridge University Press.

Brantingham, P. J., Brantingham, P. L., and Molumby, T. (1977) 'Perceptions of Crime in a Dreadful Enclosure'. *Ohio Journal of Science*, 77(6), 256–261.

Brayne, S. (2017) 'Big Data Surveillance: The Case of Policing'. *American Sociological Review*, 82(5), 977–1008.

Brodeur, J. P. (1983) 'High Policing and Low Policing: Remarks about the Policing of Political Activities'. *Social Problems*, 30(5), 507–520.

Brodeur, J. P. (2010) 'High and Low Policing', in J. P. Brodeur (ed.) *The Policing Web*. Oxford: Oxford University Press.

Brower, S. (1996) *Good Neighbourhoods: A Study of In-town and Suburban Residential Environments*. Westport, CT: Praeger.

Bullock, K. and Sindall, K. (2014) 'Examining the Nature and Extent of Public Participation in Community Policing'. *Policing and Society*, 24(4), 385–404.

Burgess, E. (1925) 'The Growth of the City: An Introduction to a Research Project', in *The Trend of Population* Chicago: Publications of the American Sociological Society.

Burney, E. (2005) *Making People Behave: Anti-Social Behaviour, Politics and Policy*. Cullompton: Willian Publishing.

Caless, B. (2007) 'Numties in Yellow Jackets: The Nature of Hostility towards the Police Community Support Officer in Neighbourhood Policing Teams'. *Policing*, 1(2), 187–195.

Campbell, D. (1955) 'The Informant in Quantitative Research'. *American Journal of Sociology*, 60(4), 339–342.

Carr, P. J. (2003) The New Parochialism: The Implications of the Beltway Case for Arguments Concerning Informal Social Control'. *American Journal of Sociology*, 108(6), 1249–1291.

Carr, P. J. (2005) *Clean Streets: Controlling Crime, Maintaining Order and Building Community Activism*. New York: New York University Press.

Casey, L. (2008) *Engaging Communities in Fighting Crime*. Cabinet Office: London.

Cherney, A. and Chui, W. H. (2010) 'Police Auxiliaries in Australia: Police Liaison Officers and the Dilemmas of Being Part of the Extended Police Family'. *Policing and Society*, 20(3), 280–297.

Choongh, S. (1997) *Policing as Social Discipline*. Oxford: Clarendon Press.

College of Policing (2015a) *Police and Community Support Officer: Operational Handbook*. [online] College of Policing. <http://recruit.college.police.uk/pcso/Documents/National_Policing_PCSO_Operational_Handbook.pdf> [Accessed 18 December 2017].

College of Policing (2015b) *Estimating Demand on the Police Service*. [online] College of Policing. <http://www.college.police.uk/News/Collegenews/Documents/Demand%20Report%2023_1_15_noBleed.pdf> [Accessed 17 December 2017].

Cordner, G. (1988) 'A Problem-oriented Approach to Community-oriented Policing', in J. Greene and S. Mastrofski (eds.), *Community Policing: Rhetoric or Reality*. Westport, Conn.: Greenwood Press.

Cordner, G. and Biebel, E. (2005) 'Problem-oriented Policing in Practice'. *Criminology & Public Policy*, 4(2), 155–180.

Cosgrove, F. and Ramshore, P. (2013) 'It Is What You Do as Well as the Way You Do It: The Value and Deployment of PCSOs in Achieving Public Engagement'. *Policing and Society*, 25(1), 77–96.

Cox, S. M. and Fitzgerald, J. D. (1992) *Police in Community Relations: Critical Issues*. Iowa: Wm. C. Brown.

Crawford, A. (1997) *The Local Governance of Crime*. Oxford: Polity Press.

Crawford, A. (1998) *Crime Prevention and Community Safety*. Harlow: Longman.

Crawford, A., Lister, S., and Wall, D. (2003) *Great Expectations: Contracted Community Policing in New Earswick*. London: Joseph Rowntree Foundation.

Daily Express (2010) 'Plastic Police' Were Fooled by a Rubber Snake. *Express* [online] 20 October. Available at: <https://www.express.co.uk/news/uk/206449/Plastic-police-were-fooled-by-a-rubber-snake> [Accessed 15 December 2017].

Daily Mail (2009) 'Plastic Police' Sent to Pick Up Litter ... While Crime Continues to Rise'. *Mail Online* [online] 27 August. Available at: <http://www.dailymail.

co.uk/news/article-1209385/Plastic-police-sent-pick-litter--crime-continues-rise. html> [Accessed 15 December 2017].

Dalgleish, D. and Myhill, A. (2004) *Reassuring the Public: A Review of International Policing Interventions*. London: Home Office.

Damschroder, L., Aron, D., Keith, R., Kirsh, S., Alexander, J., and Lowery, J. (2009) 'Fostering Implementation of Health Services Research Findings into Practice: A Consolidated Framework for Advancing Implementation Science'. *Implementation Science*, 4, 50.

De Camargo, C. (2019) 'They Wanna Be Us'; PCSO Performances, Uniforms, and Struggles for Acceptance'. *Policing and Society* DOI: 10.1080/ 10439463.2019.1598998.

Ditton, J. (1979) *Contrology: Beyond the New Criminology*. London: Macmillan.

Downs, R. M. and Stea, D. (1977) *Maps in Minds*. London: Harper & Row.

Eck, J. (2006). 'Science, Values and Problem-oriented Policing: Why Problem-oriented Policing', in D. Weisburd and A. Braga (eds.), *Police Innovation: Contrasting Perspectives*. Cambridge: Cambridge University Press.

Ericson, R. V. and Haggerty, K. D. (1997) *Policing the Risk Society*. Oxford: Oxford University Press.

Ferreira, B. (1996) *The Use and Effectiveness of Community Policing in a Democracy*. Washington, DC: National Institute of Justice.

Fielding, N. (1995) *Community Policing*. London: Clarendon.

Flanagan, R. (2008) *The Review of Policing: Final Report*. London: Home Office.

Foster, J. and Jones, C. (2010) ' "Nice To Do" and Essential: Improving Neighbourhood Policing in an English Police Force'. *Policing*, 4(4), 395–402.

Gilbertson, D. (2003) 'Plastic Policemen'. *Police Review*, 111(5712), 28–29.

Glaster, G. (2001) 'On the Nature of Neighbourhood'. *Urban Studies*, 38(12), 2111–2124.

Goffman, E. (1952) 'On Cooling the Mark out: Some Aspects of Adaptation to Failure'. *Psychiatry*, 15(4), 451–663.

Goffman, E. (1959) *The Presentation of Self in Everyday Life*. New York: Doubleday.

Goffman, E. (1967) *Interaction Ritual: Essays on Face-to-Face Behaviour*. New York: Doubleday.

Goffman, E. (1972) *Relations in Public: Microstudies of the Public Order*. New York: Harper Colophon.

Goffman, E. (1983) 'The Interaction Order'. *American Sociological Association*, 48(1), 1–17.

Goldstein, H. (1979) 'Improving Policing: A Problem-Oriented Approach'. *Crime & Delinquency*, 25, 236–258.

Goldstein, H. (1990) *Problem-Oriented Policing*. New York: McGraw-Hill.

Golledge, R. G. (1987) 'Environmental cognition', in D. Stokols and I. Altman (eds.), *Handbook of Environmental Psychology*. New York: Wiley.

Goss, S. (2005) *National Evaluation of Local Strategic Partnerships*. Issues Paper: Leadership in Local Strategic Partnerships. London: ODPM.

Greenwood, P., Chaiken, J., and Petersilia, J. (1977) *The Criminal Investigation Process*. Lexington: D.C. Heath.

Greig-Midlane, J. (2014) *Changing the Beat? The Impact of Austerity on the Neighbourhood Policing Workforce*. Cardiff: Universities Police Science Institute.

Guest, A. M. and Lee, B. A. (1983) 'The Social Organisation of Local Areas'. *Urban Affairs Review*, 19(2), 217–240.

Hargreaves, J., Cooper, J., Woods, E., and McKee, C. (2016) *Police Workforce, England and Wales*. London: Home Office.

Hawkins, K. (2003) *Law as Last Resort: Prosecution Decision-Making in a Regulatory Agency*. Oxford: Oxford University Press.

Hereford Times (2016) 'PCSOs to Be Trained as Retained Firefighters'. *Hereford Times* [online] 8 January. Available at: <http://www.herefordtimes.com/news/14191657.PCSOs_to_be_trained_as_retained_firefighters/> [Accessed 14 December 2017].

Her Majesty's Inspectorate of Constabulary (2001) *Open All Hours: A Thematic Inspection Report on the Role of Police Visibility and Accessibility in Public Reassurance*. London: HMSO.

Her Majesty's Inspectorate of Constabulary (HMIC) (2013) *Policing in Austerity: Rising to the Challenge*. London: HMSO.

Her Majesty's Inspectorate of Constabulary (HMIC) (2014) *Policing in Austerity: Meeting the Challenge*. London: HMSO.

Her Majesty's Inspectorate of Constabulary (HMIC) (2015) *PEEL: Police Effectiveness 2015 (Vulnerability) A National Overview*. London: Home Office. Available at: <https://www.justiceinspectorates.gov.uk/hmic/wp-content/uploads/police-effectiveness-vulnerability-2015.pdf> [Accessed 16 December 2017].

Her Majesty's Inspectorate of Constabulary (2017) *PEEL: Police Effectiveness 2016. A National Overview*. London: HMIC.

Herbert, S. (2006) *Citizens, Cops and Power: Recognizing the Limits of Community*. Chicago: University of Chicago Press.

Higgins, A. and Hale, G. (2017) *A Natural Experiment in Neighbourhood Policing*. London: The Police Foundation. <http://www.police-foundation.org.uk/publication/a-natural-experiment-in-neighbourhood-policing/> [Accessed 11 March 2020].

Home Office (2001) *Policing a New Century: A Blueprint for Reform*. CM 5326. Presented to Parliament December 2001. London: HMSO.

Home Office (2002) *The National Policing Plan 2003–2006*. London: Home Office.

Home Office (2004) *Building Communities, Beating Crime: A Better Police Service for the 21st Century*. CM 6360. Presented to Parliament November 2004. London: HMSO.

Home Office (2007) *Standard Powers and Duties of Police Community Support Officers (PCSOs)*. Home Office circular 033/2007. Available at: <https://www.gov.uk/government/publications/standard-powers-and-duties-of-police-community-support-officers-pcsos> [Accessed 21 November 2019].

Home Office (2008) *From the Neighbourhood to the National: Policing our Communities Together*. CM 7448. Presented to Parliament July 2008. London: HMSO.

Home Office (2014) *Anti-social Behaviour, Crime and Policing Act 2014: Anti-social Behaviour Powers. Statutory Guidance for Frontline Professionals*. Published July 2014, updated August 2019. London: HMSO.

Home Office (2015) *Police Workforce England and Wales: 31 March 2015*. Published 16 July. London: HMSO.

Hood, R. (1974) *Crime, Criminology and Public Policy: Essays in Honour of Sir Leon Radzinowicz*. London: Heinemann.

Humby, P. (2013) *A profile of Deprivation in Larger English Seaside Destinations, 2007 and 2010*. Published 21 August 2013. London: Office for National Statistics.

Hunter, A. (1979) 'The Urban Neighbourhood Its Analytical and Social Contexts'. *Urban Affairs Review*, 14(3), 267–288.

Hunter, A. (1985) 'Private, Parochial and Public Social Orders: The Problem of Crime and Incivility in Urban Communities', in G. D. Suttles and M. Zald (eds.), *The Challenge of Social Control*. Norwood, NJ: Ablex.

Independent Commission on Mental Health and Policing (2013) *Independent Commission on Mental Health and Policing Report, May 2013*. London: Independent Commission on Mental Health and Policing.

Innes, M. (2001) 'Control Creep'. *Sociological Research Online*, 6(3), 1–6.

Innes, M. (2003) *Understanding Social Control: Deviance, Crime and Social Order*. Maidenhead: Open University Press.

Innes, M. (2014) *Signal Crimes: Social Reactions to Crime, Disorder and Control*. Oxford: Oxford University Press.

Innes, M. and Fielding, N. (2002) 'From Community to Communicative Policing: "Signal Crimes"'. *Sociological Research Online*, 7(2): 56–67

Innes, M., Hayden, S., Lowe, T., MacKenzie, H., Roberts, C., and Twyman, L. (2004) *Signal Crimes Volume 1*. Guildford: University of Surrey.

Innes, M., Abbott, L., Lowe, T., Roberts, C., and Weston, N. (2009) *Signal Events, Neighbourhood Security, Order and Reassurance in Cardiff*. Cardiff: Cardiff University.

Innes, M., Roberts, C., and Lowe, T. (2017) 'A Disruptive Influence: Preventing Problems and Countering Violent Extremism Policy in Practice'. *Law and Society Review*, 51(2), 252–281.

Irving, B., Bird, C., Hibberd, M., and Willmore, J. (1989) *Neighbourhood Policing: The Natural History of a Policing Experiment*. London: Police Foundation.

Jackson, J., Bradford, B., Stanko, E. A., and Hohl, K. (2012a). *Just Authority? Trust in the Police in England and Wales*. Oxon: Routledge.

Jackson, J., Bradford, B., Hough, M., Myhill, A., Quinton, P., and Tyler, T. R. (2012b) 'Why Do People Comply with the Law? Legitimacy and the Influence of Legal Institutions'. *British Journal of Criminology*, 52, 1051–1071.

Jacobs, R. (1996) 'Civil Society and Crisis: Culture, Discourse, and the Rodney King Beating'. *American Journal of Sociology*, 101(5), 1238–1272.

Jansson, K. (2006) *The British Crime Survey—Measuring Crime for 25 Years*. London: HMSO.

Judge, K., Barnes, M., Bauld, L., Benzeval, M., Killoran, A., Robinson, R., Wigglesworth, R., and Zeilig, H. (1999) *Health Action Zones: Learning to Make a Difference*. London: Department of Health (DH).

Kakutani, M. (2018) *The Death of Truth*. London: Harper Collins.

Kaplan, S. and Kaplan, R (1982) *Cognition and Environment: Functioning in an Uncertain World*. New York: Praeger.

Kearns, A. and Parkinson, M. (2001) 'The Significance of Neighbourhood'. *Urban Studies*, 38(12), 2103–2110.

Keizer, K., Lindenberg, S., and Steg L. (2008) 'The Spreading of Disorder'. *Science*, 322(5908), 1681–1685).

Kelling, G., Pate, T., Dieckman, D., and Braun, C. (1974) *The Kansas City Preventive Patrol Experiment*. Washington, DC: Police Foundation.

Kretzmann, J. P. and McKnight, J. L. (1993) *Building Communities from the Inside out*. Evanston, IL: Asset-Based Community Development Institute, Northwestern University.

Ladd, F. (1970) 'Black Youths View Their Environment: Neighborhood Maps'. *Environment and Behavior*, 2(1), 74–99.

Lee, T. R. (1964) 'Psychology and Living Space'. *Transactions of the Bartlett Society*, 2(1), 1–36.

Leigh, A., Read, T., and Tilley, N. (1998) *Brit Pop II: Problem-Oriented Policing in Practice* (Police Research Series Paper 93). London: Home Office.

Leo, R. (2009) *Police Interrogation and American Justice*. Cambridge, MA: Harvard University Press.

Loader, I. (1997) 'Policing and the Social: Questions of Symbolic Power'. *British Journal of Sociology*, 48(1), 1–18.

Loader, I. and Mulcahy, A. (2003) *Policing and the Condition of England: Memory, Politics and Culture*. Oxford: Clarendon Press.

Loftus, B. (2009) *Police Culture in a Changing World*. Oxford: Oxford University Press.

Longstaff, A., Willer, J., Chapman, J., Czarnomski, S., and Graham, G. (2015) *Neighbourhood Policing: Past, Present and Future—A Review of the Literature*. London: The Police Foundation.

Lowe, T., Innes, H., Innes, M., and Grinnell, D. (2015) *The Work of Welsh Government Funded Community Support Officers*. Welsh Government.

Lowndes, V. and Sullivan, H. (2008) 'How Low Can You Go? Rationales and Challenges for Neighbourhood Governance'. *Public Administration*, 86(1), 53–74.

Lupton, R., Fenton, A., and Fitzgerald, A. (2013) *Labour's Record on Neighbourhood Renewal in England: Policy, Spending and Outcomes 1997–2010*. London: CASE.

Maccoby, E. (ed.) (1996) *The Development of Sex Differences*. Stanford: Stanford University Press.

MacPherson, W. (1999). *The Stephen Lawrence Inquiry*. Cm 4262-1. London: HMSO

Maguire, M. (2000) 'Policing by Risks and Targets: Some Dimensions and Implications of Intelligence-led Crime Control'. *Policing and Society*, 9, 315–336.

Manning, P. (1977) *Police Work—the Social Organisation of Policing*. Cambridge, MA: MIT Press.

Manning, P. (2003) *Policing Contingencies*. Chicago: University of Chicago Press.

Manning, P. (2010) *Democratic Policing in a Changing World*. Boulder, Co.: Paradigm.

Marx, G. (1981) 'Ironies of Social Control: Authorities as Contributors to Deviance through Escalation, Nonenforcement and Covert Facilitation'. *Social Problems*, 28(3), 221–246.

Marx, G. (2016) *Windows into the Soul: Surveillance and Society in an Age of High Technology*. Chicago: University of Chicago Press.

McCarthy, D. J. (2013) 'Gendering "Soft" Policing: Multi-agency Working, Female Cops, and the Fluidity of Police Culture/s'. *Policing and Society*, 23(2), 261–278.

Moore, M. (2006) 'Improving Police through Expertise, Experience and Experiments', in D. Weisburd and A. Braga (eds.), *Police Innovation: Contrasting Perspectives*. Cambridge: Cambridge University Press.

Morris, J. (2006) *The National Reassurance Policing Programme: A Ten-Site Evaluation* (Findings 273). London: Home Office.

National Assembly for Wales (2017) *Community First Lessons Learnt*. Cardiff: National Assembly for Wales.

Neocleous, M. (2000) *The Fabrication of Social Order: A Critical Theory of Police Power*. London: Pluto.

Nesser, P. (2016) *Islamist Terrorism in Europe: A History*. London: C. Hurst & Co.

Newburn, T. (2008) 'Policing since 1945', in T. Newburn (ed.), *Handbook of Policing*. Cullompton: Willan.

Newman, O. (1972) *Defensible Space: Crime Prevention through Urban Design*. New York: Macmillan.

OECD (2011) *Social Cohesion and Development in Perspectives on Global Development 2012: Social Cohesion in a Shifting World*. OECD Publishing. DOI:https://dx.doi.org/10.1787/persp_glob_dev-2012-6-en

Office for National Statistics (ONS) (2012) 2011 Census: Population and Household Estimates for Wards and Output Areas in England and Wales. Available at: <https://www.ons.gov.uk/peoplepopulationandcommunity/populationandmigration/populationestimates/datasets/2011censuspopulationandhouseholdestimatesforwardsandoutputareasinenglandandwales> [Accessed 11 March 2020].

Office for National Statistics (ONS) (2016) *Towns and Cities Analysis, England and Wales, March 2016*. ONS.

Office for National Statistics (ONS) (2017) Crime in England and Wales: Police Force Data Tables. Available at: https://www.ons.gov.uk/peoplepopulationandcommunity/crimeandjustice/datasets/policeforceareadatatables [Accessed 21 November 2019].

Office for National Statistics (ONS) (2020) Census Geography. Available at: <https://www.ons.gov.uk/methodology/geography/ukgeographies/censusgeography> [Accessed 4 March 2020].

Omand, S. D. (2012) 'The Terrorist Threat to the UK in the Post–9/11 Decade'. *Journal of Terrorism Research*, 3(1), 6–12.

O'Neill, M. (2017) 'Police Community Support Officers in England: A Dramaturgical Analysis'. *Policing and Society*, 27(1), 21–39.

O'Neill, M (2019) *Community Support Officers*. Oxford: Clarendon Press.

Orford, S. and Lee, C. (2014) 'The Relationship between Self-reported Definitions of Urban Neighbourhood and Respondent Characteristics: A Study of Cardiff, UK'. *Urban Studies*, 51(9), 1891–1908.

Ostrom, E. (1996) Crossing the Great Divide: Coproduction, Synergy, and Development'. *World Development*, 24(6), 1073–1087.

Park, R. E. and Burgess, E. W. (1925) *The City: Suggestions for Investigation of Human Behavior in the Urban Environment*. Chicago: University of Chicago Press.

Pattillo, M. (1998) 'Sweet Mothers and Gangbangers: Managing Crime in a Black Middle-class Neighborhood'. *Social Forces*, 76(3), 747–774.

Pelfrey, Sr., W. V. and Pelfrey, Jr., W. V. (1995). 'Fear of Crime and Victimization: Changes Over Time in Age and Gender Relationships'. Paper presented to the Academy of Criminal Justice Sciences, Boston, March.

Peterson, R. D. and Krivo, L. J. (2010) *National Neighborhood Crime Study (NNCS), 2000*. Ann Arbor, MI: Inter-university Consortium for Political and Social Research [distributor], 2010-05-05. https://doi.org/10.3886/ICPSR27501.v1.

Police Act 1996 (c. 16) London: HMSO.

Police Review (2004) United Kingdom: IHS Global Limited.

Pomerantsev, P. (2019) *This is NOT Propaganda: Adventures in the War Against Reality*. London: PublicAffairs.

Poortinga, W. (2012) 'Community Resilience and Health: The Role of Binding, Bridging, and Linking Aspects of Social Capital'. *Health Place*, 18(2), 286–295.

Punch, M. (1979) 'Secret Social Service', in. S. Holdaway (ed.), *The British Police*. London: Edward Arnold.

Putnam, R. D. (2000) *Bowling Alone: The Collapse and Revival of American Community*. New York: Simon and Schuster Paperbacks.

Pye, K. (2007) *Geological and Soil Evidence; Forensic Applications*. Boca Raton, FL.: CRC Press.

Quinton, P. and Morris, J. (2008) *Neighbourhood Policing: The Impact of Piloting and Early National Implementation*. London: Home Office.

Radzinowicz, L. (1961) 'The Study of Criminology in Cambridge'. *Medico-Legal Journal*, 29(3), 122–133.

Ratcliffe, J. H. (2016) *Intelligence-led Policing*. Abingdon, Oxon: Routledge.

Reiner, R. (1978) *The Blue-Coated Worker*. Cambridge: Cambridge University Press.

Reiner, R. (1992) *The Politics of the Police*, 2nd ed. Basingstoke: Harvester Wheatsheaf.

Reiner, R. (1994) 'The Dialectics of Dixon: The Changing Image of the TV Cop', in M. Stephens and S. Becker (eds.), Police Force, Police Service. London: Palgrave.

Reiner, R. (2000) *The Politics of the Police*, 3rd ed. Oxford: Oxford University Press.

Reiner, R. (2010) *The Politics of the Police*, 4th ed. Oxford: Oxford University Press.

Reiner, R. (2012) *In Praise of Fire Brigade Policing: Contra Common Sense Conceptions of the Police Role*. What if ... ? series of challenging pamphlets. London: The Howard League for Penal Reform.

Reiss, A. J. (1992) 'Police Organization in the Twentieth Century'. *Crime and Justice*, 15, 51–97.

Rengert, G. F. and Pelfrey, Jr., W. V. (1998) 'Cognitive Mapping of the City Center: Comparative Perceptions of Dangerous Places'. *Crime Prevention Studies*, 8, 193–217.

Rogers, C. (2014) *A Study of Activities Undertaken by Police Community Support Officers in Northern Basic Command Unit within South Wales Police*. University of South Wales.

Rubinstein, J. (1973) *City Police*. Philadelphia: Farrar, Straus and Giroux.

Russell, J. A. and Ward, L. M. (1982) 'Environmental Psychology'. *Annual Review of Psychology*, 33, 651–682.

Sampson, R. J. (2012) 'Moving and the Neighbourhood Glass Ceiling'. *Science*, 337, 1464–1465.

Sampson, R. and Raudenbush, S. (1999) 'Systematic Social Observation of Public Spaces: A New Look at Disorder in Urban Neighborhoods'. *American Journal of Sociology*, 105(3), 603–651.

Savage, S. (2007) *Police Reform*. Oxford: Oxford University Press.

Scarman, Lord J. (1982) *The Brixton Disorders, 10–12th April (1981)*. London: HMSO.

Scribbens, M., Flatley, J., Parfrement-Hopkins, J., and Hall, P. (2010) *Public Perceptions of Engaging with the Policing, Engagement with the Police and Victimisation: Findings from the 2009/10 British Crime Survey*. London: Home Office.

Sennett, R. (2008) *The Craftsman*. London: Penguin.

SEU (2001) *A New Commitment to Neighbourhood Renewal: National Strategy Action Plan*. London: Social Exclusion Unit.

Sherman, L. W. (1992) *Policing Domestic Violence: Experiments and Dilemmas*. New York: Free Press.

Sherman, L. W. (1998) *Evidence-Based Policing. Ideas in American Policing Series*. Washington, DC: Police Foundation.

Sherman, L. (2013) 'The Rise of Evidence-based Policing: Targeting, Testing and Tracking'. *Crime and Justice*, 42(1), 377–451.

Silver, E, and Miller, L. (2004) 'Sources of Informal Social Control in Chicago Neighborhoods'. *Criminology*, 42(3), 551–584.

Silverman, E. (1999) *NYPD Battles Crime: Innovative Strategies in Policing*. Boston, MA: Northeastern University Press.

Skogan, W. (1990) *Disorder and Decline: Crime and the Spiral of Decay in American Cities*. New York: Free Press.

Skogan, W. (1996) 'Evaluating Problem-solving Policing: The Chicago Experience'. Available at: www.northwestern.edu/ipr/publications/policing_papers/caps17 [Accessed 26 July 2004].

Skogan, W. (2006) *Police and Community in Chicago; A Tale of Three Cities*. New York: Oxford University Press.

Skogan, W. and Hartnett, K. (1997) *Community Policing, Chicago Style*. New York, NY: Oxford University Press.

Skogan, W. and Steiner, L. (2004) *CAPS at 10*. Evanston, IL: Northwestern University, Institute for Policy Research.

Soja, E. W. (1996) *Thirdspace: Journeys to Los Angeles and other Real-and-Imagined Places*. Cambridge, MA: Blackwell.

Sparrow, M. K. (2016) *Handcuffed: What Holds Policing Back, and the Keys to Reform*. Washington DC: Brookings Institution Press.

Sparrow, M. K., Moore, M. H., and Kennedy, D. M. (1990) *Beyond 911: A New Era for Policing*. New York: Basic Books.

Stapleford, R. J. (2017) *Digital and Social Media: The Panacea of Transformative Engagement with Young People; Rhetoric or Reality? Qualitative based research exploring police led digital and social media engagement with young people in Nottinghamshire*. A thesis submitted for the award of Professional Doctorate in Policing, Security and Community Safety, London Metropolitan University. Available at: http://repository.londonmet.ac.uk/1252/1/Richard%20Stapleford%20-DProf%20-full%20thesis.pdf [Accessed 21 November 2019].

Stoker, G. (2004) *How Are Mayors Measuring Up?*. London: ODPM/HMSO.

Stuart, F. (2016) *Down, Out, and Under Arrest: Policing and Everyday Life in Skid Row*. Chicago: University of Chicago Press.

Sturgis, P., Sindall, K., and Jennings, W. (2012) 'Public Confidence in the Police: A Time Series Analysis'. *British Journal of Criminology*, 52(4), 744–764.

Sullivan, H. and Skelcher, C. (2002) *Working across Boundaries: Collaboration in Public Services*. Basingstoke: Palgrave Macmillan.

Suttles, G. (1968) *The Social Order of the Slum*. Chicago: University of Chicago Press.

Sykes, G. (1951) 'The Differential Distribution of Community Knowledge'. *Social Forces*, 29(4), 376–382.

Szreter, S. and Woolcock, M. (2004) 'Health by Association? Social Capital, Social Theory, and the Political Economy of Public Health'. *International Journal of Epidemiology*, 33(4), 650–667.

Taylor, R. B. (2001) *Breaking Away from Broken Windows*. Boulder, Colo.: Westview Press.

Taylor, R. B. (2015). *Community Criminology*. New York: NYU Press.

Tetteh, E. (2009) *Electoral Performance of the British National Party in the UK*. London: House of Commons Library.

Thatcher, D. (1998) *Developing Community Partnerships: Value Conflicts in 11 Cities*. Cambridge, Ma.: John F. Kennedy School of Government Working Paper 98-05-15, Harvard University.

Tilley, N. (2008) 'Modern Approaches to Policing: Community, Problem-oriented and Intelligence-led', in T. Newburn (ed.), *Handbook of Policing*. Cullompton: Willan.

Trojanowicz, R. and Bucqueroux, B. (1990) *Community Policing: A Contemporary Perspective*. Cincinnati, OH: Anderson.

Trojanowicz, R. and Bucqueroux, B. (1992) 'The Basics of Community Policing'. *Footprints*. National Center for Community Policing: Michigan State University.

Tuffin, R., Morris, J., and Poole, A. (2006) *An Evaluation of the Impact of the National Reassurance Policing Programme* (Home Office Research Study 296). London: Home Office.

Turley, C., Ranns, H., Callanan, M., Blackwell, A., and Newburn, T. (2012) *Delivering Neighbourhood Policing in Partnership*. London: Home Office.

Tyler, T. (2006) *Why People Obey the Law*. Princeton, NJ: Princeton University Press.

Vasagar, J., Ward, D., Ethim, A., and Keating, M. (2001) ' "No go for whites" in race hotspot' *The Guardian* Special Report: race issues in the UK, 20 April.

Waddington, P. (1991) *The Strong Arm of the Law*. Oxford: Clarendon.

Wake, R., Simpson, C., Homes, A., and Ballantyne, J. (2007) *Public Perceptions of the Police Complaints System*. IPCC Research and Statistics Series: Paper 6. London: IPCC.

Weatheritt, M. (1988) 'Community Policing: Rhetoric or Reality?', in J. R. Greene and S. Mastrofski (eds.), *Community Policing: Rhetoric or Reality*. New York: Praeger.

Weisburd, D. (2015) 'The Law of Crime Concentration and the Criminology of Place'. *Criminology*, 53(2), 133–157.

Weisburd, D. and Eck, J. (2004) 'What Can Police Do to Reduce Crime Disorder and Fear?', in W. Skogan (ed.), 'To Better Serve and Protect: Improving Police Practices'. The Annals of the American Academy of Political and Social Science, 593, 42–65.

Weisburd, D. and Neyroud, P. (2011) *Police Science: Towards a New Paradigm. New Perspectives in Policing*. Washington, DC: Department of Justice, National Institute of Justice.

Weisburd, D., Telep, C., Hinkle, J., and Eck, J (2010) 'Is Problem-orientated Policing Effective in Reducing Crime And Disorder? Findings from a Campbell Systematic Review'. *Criminology & Public Policy*, 9(1), 139–172.

Welsh, B., Braga, A., and Bruinsma, G. (2015) 'Reimagining Broken Windows'. *Journal of Research in Crime and Delinquency*, 52(4), 447–463.

Welsh Government (2014) *Welsh Index of Multiple Deprivation 2014: Revised*. Cardiff: Welsh Government.

Werlen, B. (1993) 'On Regional and Cultural Identity: Outline of a Regional Culture Analysis', in D. Steiner and M. Nauser (eds.), *Human Ecology*. London: Routledge.

Wiktorowicz, Q. (2005) *Radical Islam Rising: Muslim Extremism in the West*. Oxford: Rowman & Littlefield Publishers, Inc.

Wilson, J. and Kelling, G. (1982) 'Broken Windows: The Police and Neighborhood Safety'. *Atlantic Monthly*, 211, 29–38.

Wood, M. (2004) *Perceptions and Experience of Antisocial Behaviour: Findings From the 2003/2004 British Crime Survey*. Home Office Online Report 49/04.

Wycoff, M. A. (1988) 'The Benefits of Community Policing: Evidence and Conjecture', in J. R. Greene and S. Mastrofski (eds.), *Community Policing: Rhetoric or Reality*. New York: Praeger.

Young, M. (1991) *An Inside Job: Policing and Police Culture in Britain*. Oxford: Oxford University Press.

Zhao, J., Scheider, M., and Thurman, Q. (2002) 'The Effect of Police Presence on Public Fear Reduction and Satisfaction: A Review of the Literature'. *The Justice Professional*, 15, 273–299.

Zimring, F. E. (2011) *The City that Became Safe: New York's Lessons for Urban Crime and Its Control*. Oxford: Oxford University Press.

Index

Note: *For the benefit of digital users, indexed terms that span two pages (e.g., 52–53) may, on occasion, appear on only one of those pages.*
Tables and figures are indicated by *t* and *f* following the page number